God's Promises ARE FOR YOU

Richard L. Gill

GOD'S PROMISES ARE FOR YOU
Copyright © 2015 by Richard L. Gill

All rights reserved. Neither this publication nor any part of this publication may be reproduced or transmitted in any form or by any means, electronic or mechanical, including photocopying, recording or any information storage and retrieval system, without permission in writing from the author.

Scripture quotations marked (ESV) are from the ESV® Bible (The Holy Bible, English Standard Version®), copyright © 2001 by Crossway, a publishing ministry of Good News Publishers. Used by permission. All rights reserved. Scripture quotations marked (KJV) taken from the Holy Bible, King James Version, which is in the public domain. Scripture quotations marked (MKJV) taken from the Modern King James Version of the Holy Bible. Copyright © 1962–1998 by J.P. Green Sr. Used by permission of the copyright holder. Scripture quotations marked (NASB) taken from the New American Standard Bible®, Copyright © 1960, 1962, 1963, 1968, 1971, 1972, 1973, 1975, 1977, 1995 by The Lockman Foundation. Used by permission. Scripture quotations marked (NIV) taken from the Holy Bible, NEW INTERNATIONAL VERSION®, NIV® Copyright © 1973, 1978, 1984, 2011 by Biblica, Inc.® Used by permission. All rights reserved worldwide. Scripture quotations marked (NIrV) taken from the Holy Bible, New International Reader's Version®. NIrV® Copyright © 1995, 1996, 1998 by Biblica, Inc.™ Used by permission of Zondervan. The "NIV," "NIrV," and "New International Version" are trademarks registered in the United States Patent and Trademark Office by Biblica, Inc.™ Scripture quotations marked (NKJV) taken from the New King James Version®. Copyright © 1982 by Thomas Nelson. Used by permission. All rights reserved. Scripture quotations marked (WNT) taken from Weymouth's New Testament, which is in the public domain. Richard F. Weymouth (1912), 3rd Edition. Words that are placed in square brackets within the Scriptures used throughout this book are the author's words of clarification or paraphrase, or are modernizations of antiquated forms of words, and are not intended to change the original text or its meaning.

ISBN: 978-1-4866-0934-5

Word Alive Press
131 Cordite Road, Winnipeg, MB R3W 1S1
www.wordalivepress.ca

Library and Archives Canada Cataloguing in Publication

Gill, Richard L., author
    God's promises are for you / Richard L. Gill.

Issued in print and electronic formats.
ISBN 978-1-4866-0934-5 (pbk.).--ISBN 978-1-4866-0935-2 (pdf).--ISBN 978-1-4866-0936-9 (html).--ISBN 978-1-4866-0937-6 (epub)

    1. Christian life. I. Title.

BV4501.3.G54 2015   248.4   C2015-902874-4
                                      C2015-902875-2

Dedication

This book and the words written here, which are based on God's Word, are dedicated to God, Jesus, His Son, and the Holy Spirit. Thank You, God, for all the wonderful revelation, understanding, and experience I have received from you.

Words cannot express the gratitude I feel towards God for His marvellous blessing in giving me the inspiration to complete this work, and in giving me the words to put pen to paper. May this book help to shed light on the wonderful Word of God, and may it bring glory to God over and over again!

Contents

	Introduction	vii
1.	Why Hang Out with God?	1
2.	God's Conditions	12
3.	Who Lives in My Temple?	18
4.	How Do We Get Connected?	40
5.	Staying Connected	46
6.	Hearing from God	95
7.	God's Multiplied Abundance	114
8.	Triumphant Faith	130
9.	Walking in Love	178
10.	Watch Your Mouth	185
11.	The Fear of the Lord	193
12.	Banishing Strife and Discord	200
13.	Victory through God's Discipline	207
14.	Flex Your Muscles	213
15.	God's Gold Medals	229
16.	Are There Any Loose Ends?	233
	About the Author	235

Introduction

A number of years ago, one of my brothers-in-law, a pastor for many years, was diagnosed with terminal cancer. After a major struggle and much pain, he passed away at the age of fifty-nine. About two years later, another brother-in-law, a close friend and long-time Christian, was also diagnosed with terminal cancer. He also passed away, at seventy-three years of age. Much prayer had been sent heavenward for both of these dear brothers. I personally spent much time praying for both of them. I had believed God for their physical healing here on this earth—at least, I thought I did.

I became frustrated and concerned, because my prayers weren't being answered the way I thought they should be. I began to talk to God in earnest about this matter in an effort to hear from Him and find out what was wrong with this picture.

Two years later, one of my sisters-in-law, a very beautiful Christian woman, was also diagnosed with terminal cancer. Once again much prayer was sent heavenward by many people, including myself. She also passed from this life; she was only fifty-eight years old. Finally, one of my wife's nephews, fifty years old, died from cancer after being prayed for many times by many Christians, including me.

By this time, I was on a passionate and fervent mission to find out what was wrong with me, because my prayers didn't result in the sick being healed. I knew that if there was a problem, it certainly wasn't God; it had to be me, the people for whom I was praying, or both. Since it's not up to me to change other people, I needed to take a look at myself. I had to look at what I was doing, or not doing, and what I needed to change in order to see different results in my prayer life.

In the last twelve years, I have been studying and reading the Word of God like I never have before. I've been reading books written by godly men, devouring everything appropriate I could get my hands on with respect to my relationship with God. God means business when He says that if we're hungry

He'll fill us to overflowing, and if we're thirsty He'll give us of the living waters to drink in abundance. He has been pouring revelation and understanding of His Word into my life in an awesome and abundant way. He has also given me a marvellous understanding of who I am in Christ, and the true experience of what it is to live in relationship with Him, day by day.

The Lord has given me a desire to share the understanding of His Word, which He has revealed to me. For this reason, this book was born. Did I want to write this book? No, not really! I had been asking the Lord what was wrong with my life, especially with regard to praying for the sick, and He told me that I should write a book. I never liked writing and I knew it would be a lot of work, so I wasn't anxious to do it; however, every time I asked God what He wanted me to do, He always had the same answer: "I want you to write a book." Well, when God tells or asks you to do something, you had better do it.

Now, I don't like to give God conditions before I do something for Him, but I felt incapable of writing a book on God's promises. Therefore, I gave God the condition that I would write the book providing I didn't have to put any of my own opinions or words into it. I would just be His vessel, with pen in hand to write down what He gave me. However, this book still has some of my influence in it, such as my style of writing and my life experiences. But God will work with anyone who's willing.

This is not another run-of-the-mill book, and I trust that it will challenge you to go for all that God has for you. He has more for you then you can fathom. Our journey to experiencing God's promises will include how to live our lives in a way that will allow us to receive from God more then we can imagine. It will also include a lot of side trips in an effort to give you a well-rounded understanding of the subject.

I pray that the Holy Spirit will enlighten your spiritual mind as you read this book and the scriptures referred to in it. As you read it and apply it, God will bless you beyond your wildest dreams. I trust that through the words God has given me to share, and through the scriptures I have included, you will learn and understand how to live in God's promises. This is His desire for every area of your life.

Chapter One:
Why Hang Out with God?

I often ask the question, "Why not?" There are tremendous perks, gifts, blessings, and rewards available to those who enter into a relationship with God. One of those gifts is eternal, never-ending life, to be lived in God's presence here and in the hereafter when we leave this earth.

To hang out with someone implies friendship, so let's look at the words friendship, relationship, and acquaintance for a moment. Webster's Dictionary will help us to define each of them as follows:

1. Acquaintance: familiar knowledge; a person known slightly.[1]
2. Friendship: one attached to another by esteem and affection.[2]
3. Relationship: the state of being related or connected: connection by common ancestry or marriage.[3]

The purpose of defining these words is to lead us into a clear understanding of the different types of friendships and relationships we have in life. Let's look at the three levels:

1. Acquaintance—a neighbour, a mailman, a distant relative, or anyone you know only casually.
2. Friend—someone you connect with on a general level, such as at work, in sports, or with hobbies.
3. Close friend—someone with whom you share your innermost struggles and victories, your hurts, fears, dreams, and ambitions.

---

1 J.B. Foreman, MA, *The Webster Worldwide Dictionary* (Great Britain: William Collins Sons & Co. Ltd., 1960), 13.
2 Ibid., 210.
3 *Webster's Canadian Dictionary & Thesaurus* (Toronto, ON: Strathearn Books, 2011), 353.

> A friend loves at all times, and a brother is born for a time of adversity.
> —Proverbs 17:17, NIV

You see, a true, close friend isn't just an acquaintance but one who sticks with you whether you're going through a storm or through periods of sunshine. A true friend or brother is one who is there for you, when you're going through a time of misfortune, distress, or calamity.

Let's stop for a second and do an evaluation of our friendship and relationship with God. Then we need to ask the question: "Where does our relationship with Him fit in?" In order to receive from God in abundance, we need to know God as Father, and Jesus as Saviour, friend, and brother. This would put us at a Level Three relationship—a very close and intimate relationship.

Allow me to use a healthy marriage relationship to draw an analogy. We generally get into a marriage relationship because of all the benefits and advantages of the relationship. For instance, we're able to experience benefits in marriage such as love, joy, happiness, and care which bring fulfillment into our lives. In marriage, we also share in each other's physical, emotional, and spiritual attributes. We get to know each other closely and intimately.

The same applies when we develop a close relationship with God. We are able to share in God's love, joy, happiness, peace, provision, protection, and healing, to mention just a few of His gifts. These gifts bring tremendous fulfillment and satisfaction which are not attainable in this world without God. The more we get to know God, the more He does for us, and there really is no limit with God.

Let's imagine for a moment that God is our close, intimate friend. What kind of benefits do you think we might have?

- We are redeemed, righteous, and heirs of God.
- We experience love, joy, peace, and much more.
- God is our provider, healer, and protector.
- We have dominion, favour, and eternal life.

In addition, when we have a close relationship with God we also get to experience things such as "the believer's authority." We will look at this subject later in the book.

So if there are benefits and advantages to being in a good, positive relationship, what kind of benefits and blessings do we get in an intimate relationship with God? To answer this question, I would like to define the word "blessing," and then share some Scripture relating to God's blessings and rewards. I would also like to paraphrase some of the Scripture and make it relevant for today.

God's Blessings

The definition of blessing, as taken from the Illustrated Davis Dictionary of the Bible and found in Deuteronomy 28:8, goes like this: "Favors, advantages conferred by God, and bringing pleasure or happiness in their train."[4] The International Bible Standards Encyclopedia defines the word bless as "the bestowal of good, and in this particular place the pleasure and power of increase in kind."[5] To clarify these definitions, I would define a blessing as the bestowal of good upon someone, or the giving of good gifts to someone to produce happiness in their life.

Let's take a look at just a few of the many promises and blessings God has laid out for us in His Word. I want you to read each of the following scriptures slowly and let them sink in—in other words, meditate and think on them. Begin to apply them to your life and accept them as yours, since they are meant for you and me, those of us who have made Christ Jesus Lord over our lives. We will look at scriptures first from the Old Testament and then from the New Testament.

Old Testament

To begin 1with, let's take a look at the blessings God gave to Abraham and his children (I will deal with the way in which these same blessings were made available for the Gentiles later on):

> Now it shall come to pass, if you diligently obey the voice of the Lord your God, to observe carefully all His commandments which I command you today, that the Lord your God will set you high above all

---

[4] *Illustrated Davis Dictionary of the Bible* (Nashville, TN: Royal Publishers Inc., 1973), 103.

[5] *International Standard Bible Encyclopedia,* "Bless" (Grand Rapids, MI: Wm B Eerdmans Publishing Co., 1979).

nations of the earth. And all these blessings shall come upon you and overtake you, because you obey the voice of the Lord your God: Blessed shall you be in the city, and blessed shall you be in the country. Blessed shall be the fruit of your body, the produce of your ground and the increase of your herds, the increase of your cattle and the offspring of your flocks. Blessed shall be your basket and your kneading bowl. Blessed shall you be when you come in, and blessed shall you be when you go out. The Lord will cause your enemies who rise against you to be defeated before your face; they shall come out against you one way and flee before you seven ways. The Lord will command the blessing on you in your storehouses and in all to which you set your hand, and He will bless you in the land which the Lord your God is giving you. The Lord will establish you as a holy people to Himself, just as He has sworn to you, if you keep the commandments of the Lord your God and walk in His ways. Then all peoples of the earth shall see that you are called by the name of the Lord, and they shall be afraid of you. And the Lord will grant you plenty of goods, in the fruit of your body, in the increase of your livestock, and in the produce of your ground, in the land of which the Lord swore to your fathers to give you. The Lord will open to you His good treasure, the heavens, to give the rain to your land in its season, and to bless all the work of your hand. You shall lend to many nations, but you shall not borrow. And the Lord will make you the head and not the tail; you shall be above only, and not be beneath, if you heed the commandments of the Lord your God, which I command you today, and are careful to observe them. So you shall not turn aside from any of the words which I command you this day, to the right or the left, to go after other gods to serve them.

—Deuteronomy 28:1–14, NKJV

God will empower us to prosper and bestow good on our children, businesses, investments, and jobs. He will multiply our material goods. God will prosper the work of our hands and everything we undertake to do. The enemy will come at us with sickness, poverty, strife, and every evil device, but he will run from us seven ways, desperate to get away. God will bestow good on us wherever we go and make us a holy people like Himself. The Lord will give us rain when we need it, we shall have plenty of money to give or lend, and we shall not have to borrow. The Lord will make us leaders, and the people of the earth will respect us. God will give us plenty of work, plenty of children, and prosperity in our work, homes, and relationships. What an amazing God! Wow! What a plan! What remarkable provision!

Remember that in this chapter, I have chosen to look at only a few of God's gifts and blessings to us. Let's continue on in the Old Testament, looking at some of God's rich blessings.

> And I have given you a land for which you did not labor, and cities which you did not build, and you live in them. You now eat of the vineyards and olive-yards which you did not plant.
> —Joshua 24:13, MKJV

Here in the book of Joshua, we're told how God gave His children cities which they hadn't built nor worked for. He also gave them gardens and forests which they hadn't planted. God took these things from people who didn't believe in or acknowledge God and gave them to His children to enjoy.

> For You, O Lord, will bless the righteous; with favor You will surround him as with a shield.
> —Psalms 5:12, NKJV

Let's pause for a moment and look at the definition of the word "favour" from Webster's Dictionary. It means "an act of kindness; to prefer especially unfairly."[6] God wants to give good gifts to His children and show them generosity, kindness, advantage, and success both with Him and with man. God's favour gives us preferences and advantages from Him which others don't get.

> The Lord is my shepherd; I shall not want. He makes me lie down in green pastures. He leads me beside still waters. He restores my soul. He leads me in paths of righteousness for his name's sake. Even though I walk through the valley of the shadow of death, I will fear no evil, for you are with me; your rod and your staff, they comfort me. You prepare a table before me in the presence of my enemies; you anoint my head with

---

6 *Webster's Canadian Dictionary & Thesaurus* (Toronto, ON: Strathearn Books, 2011), 157.

oil; my cup overflows. Surely goodness and mercy shall follow me all the days of my life, and I shall dwell in the house of the Lord forever.

—Psalms 23:1–6, ESV

Many of us are familiar with the well-known twenty-third Psalm. Here, the psalmist uses the analogy of a shepherd to describe how the Lord looks after His children.

- He takes care of us like a shepherd and we won't lack for anything.
- He gives us peace and rest, and refreshes us in mind and body.
- He leads us in ways that produce right-living in our lives.
- He is with us in times of sorrow and grief and will comfort, strengthen, and care for us.
- He provides a feast for us while our enemies watch us eat.
- He provides His Holy Spirit to empower us, and He does it all with overflowing abundance.
- He is merciful and good, and wants us to dwell in His presence, both here on earth and in heaven.

Isn't God so good?

Delight yourself also in the Lord, and He shall give you the desires of your heart. Commit your way to the Lord, trust also in Him, and He shall bring it to pass.

—Psalms 37:4–5, NKJV

If we take pleasure in the ways of the Lord, and if we love him with all our heart, He will grant us the things we desire in our lives. As well, He will work on our behalf to fulfill our desires.

He who dwells in the secret place of the Most High shall abide under the shadow of the Almighty... Because you have made the Lord, who is my refuge, even the Most High, your dwelling place, no evil shall befall you, nor shall any plague come near your dwelling; for He shall give His angels charge over you, to keep you in all your ways. In their hands they shall bear you up, lest you dash your foot against a stone... He shall call upon Me, and I will answer him; I will be with him in trouble; I will

deliver him and honor him. With long life I will satisfy him, and show him My salvation.
—Psalms 91:1, 9–12, 15–16, NKJV

I like to refer to this as the protection psalm, because it really talks about the Lord's protection over our lives.

- God is like a warm, inviting home which we can go into and feel safe.
- No evil or sickness shall come near our home.
- His angels shall keep us from getting hurt, and He shall send them to protect us from harm.
- When we call on Him, God will answer us. He will be with us in trouble and deliver us. He will favour us.
- God will give us a long, satisfied life.

Wow! What a God of protection and provision!

Praise the Lord, my soul, and forget not all his benefits—who forgives all your sins and heals all your diseases,
—Psalms 103:2–3 NIV

Two of God's greatest blessings are that He forgives our sins when we repent of them, and heals any and all disease which would try to come upon our bodies and minds when we ask.

Bring all the tithes into the storehouse, that there may be food in My house, And try Me now in this," says the Lord of hosts, "If I will not open for you the windows of heaven and pour out for you such blessing that there will not be room enough to receive it.
And I will rebuke the devourer for your sakes, so that he will not destroy the fruit of your ground, nor shall the vine fail to bear fruit for you in the field," says the Lord of hosts; "and all nations will call you blessed, for you will be a delightful land," says the Lord of hosts.
—Malachi 3:10–12, NKJV

The above three verses tell us that if we give the Lord our tithes, which is ten percent of our financial increase,

- We will not be able to contain the financial abundance He will pour upon us.
- He will not let the devil or evil destroy our financial affairs.
- The world shall know that we are favoured by God.

New Testament

Now let's look at a few scriptures from the New Testament with respect to God's abundant blessings towards His children. Again, we will paraphrase the scriptures to make them more relevant for today.

> If you then, imperfect as you are, know how to give good gifts to your children, how much more will your Father in Heaven give good things to those who ask Him!
> —Matthew 7:11, WNT

We who are born with a sin nature, and are able to be influenced by the devil and evil, know how to give good gifts, but how much better will our God give good things to those who ask for them?

> The thief comes only to steal and kill and destroy: I have come that they may have Life, and may have it in abundance.
> —John 10:10, WNT

Jesus came to the earth that we might have an abundant life. According to Strong's Hebrew and Greek Dictionary, the word abundance, from the Greek word *perissos*, means "super abundant (in quantity) or superior (in quality); exceeding abundantly above."[7] The last part of this verse promises us lives of great abundance and provision beyond measure.

> That the blessing of Abraham might come on the Gentiles through Jesus Christ; that we might receive the promise of the Spirit through faith.
> —Galatians 3:14, KJV

---

7 James Strong. *Strong's Dictionaries of the Hebrew and Greek Words*, "Perissos" (Nashville, TN: Abingdon Press, 1890), 21.

Even the New Testament scriptures tell us that the blessing given to Abraham in the Old Testament is available to Gentile Christians, and that they have the promise of the Holy Spirit, which they have received through faith in Jesus Christ. Further on we will delve into this blessing which is available to all of God's children. We will also learn how to operate in faith to receive it.

> Instruct those who are rich in this present world not to be conceited or to fix their hope on the uncertainty of riches, but on God, who richly supplies us with all things to enjoy.
> —1 Timothy 6:17, NASB

God wants to give us an abundance of all that He has—spiritually, physically, and financially. Everything in this universe is His, and He wants us to enjoy it.

> Every good and perfect gift is from God. It comes down from the Father. He created the heavenly lights. He does not change like shadows that move.
> —James 1:17, NIrV

Father God, who created the sun, moon, and stars, gives all of His children good and perfect gifts beyond our wildest imaginations, if we will only let Him. And He never changes.

God's Rewards

Many Christians would live their lives differently if they were aware of God's rewards and how they are obtained. There isn't enough emphasis placed on this subject in the church today. Some of God's children will receive rewards in heaven, and others will not receive any rewards at all.

Let me share some scriptures regarding God's rewards:

> The statutes of the Lord are right, rejoicing the heart; the commandment of the Lord is pure, enlightening the eyes; the fear of the Lord is clean, enduring forever; the judgments of the Lord are true and righteous altogether… Moreover by them Your servant is warned, and in keeping them there is great reward.
> —Psalms 19:8–9, 11, NKJV

Here we see that if we live according with God's Word and allow it to bring light into our lives, and if we have a healthy respect and reverence for the Lord, we will receive a great reward.

> Blessed are those who have been persecuted for the sake of righteousness, for theirs is the kingdom of heaven. Blessed are you when people insult you and persecute you, and falsely say all kinds of evil against you because of Me. Rejoice and be glad, for your reward in heaven is great; for in the same way they persecuted the prophets who were before you.
> —Matthew 5:10–12, NASB

According to these verses and others like them, if we are persecuted, treated wrongfully, and verbally abused because of our relationship with Jesus Christ, we will have a great reward in heaven.

> So then neither he who plants is anything, nor he who waters, but God who gives the increase. Now he who plants and he who waters are one, and each one will receive his own reward according to his own labor.
> —1 Corinthians 3:7–8, NKJV

In this verse, we can see that we will receive heavenly rewards based on the things we do for the Lord. This means that the size of the rewards will vary from no reward to great rewards, based on how well we let our light shine for others to see.

> Look, I am coming soon! My reward is with me, and I will give to each person according to what they have done.
> —Revelation 22:12, NIV

Finally, when Jesus comes for His children, He will bring His rewards, giving them to us based on how we lived our lives in accordance with the Word of God.

To recap, we need to be aware of God's promises according to His Word. He promises that He's going to give out rewards on earth and in heaven. Our part is to live our lives in such a way that we will receive His rewards.

God's Highest Blessings

The blessing found in the following scripture is probably the most important blessing we can receive from God:

> Blessed be the God and Father of our Lord Jesus Christ, who [has] blessed us with all spiritual blessings in heavenly places in Christ...
> —Ephesians 1:3, KJV

What does it mean to be spiritually blessed of God? Here are a few of God's spiritual blessings for us to ponder:

- Salvation and the baptism of the Holy Spirit are free gifts to us.
- We can be in tune with the Spirit of God.
- We can receive revelation of His Word from Him.
- We can be used through God's gifts of ministry in our lives.
- The fruit of the Spirit can operate in our lives.
- We can be God's spokespeople.
- We can have authority in the name of Jesus.

Just these few spiritual blessings which I have referred to sound pretty good to me. We will discuss how we can operate in these blessings later in the book.

Conclusion

Have you begun to see even a little bit of God's love toward you through the Scriptures I have shared in this chapter? We can't even comprehend or fathom the height, depth, and width of God's love and all that He has for us. As you continue to read the pages of this book and refer to the scriptures, my prayer is that your vision and understanding of God will be dramatically increased!

Chapter Two
God's Conditions

In order to bring accountability and respect into our relationships, we put conditions on our relationships, especially in the area of our generosity and giving. For example, as parents we may have told our children, "If you lie down and have a little sleep, you can go outside and play afterwards." Another example might be, "Son, if you go out and weed the garden this afternoon, you can have the car tonight." Finally, "If you come to work with me, I'll pay you thirty dollars per hour." These are very simple examples of how we use conditions in our relationships.

God also has conditions for us to receive His goodness. A condition is something that must occur or be done before something else will happen. Conditions, with respect to God, are His directions as to how He wants us to live, with His help, if we're going to be recipients of His blessings. So let's take a look at a number of scriptures where God lays out His conditions in order for His blessings to be released.

In Deuteronomy 28, God lays out the following conditions for Abraham to meet in order for his seed, or children, to receive God's blessings:

> And it will be, if you shall listen carefully to the voice of the Lord your God, to observe and to do all His commandments which I command you today, the Lord your God will set you on high above all nations of the earth. And all these blessings shall come on you and overtake you, if you will listen to the voice of the Lord your God.
> —Deuteronomy 28:1–2, MKJV

God's conditions are laid out in verse one: we must diligently obey God's voice and take care to live according to His Word. By the way, we must be able to hear His voice in order to obey it. As a result of doing these two things, we will be entitled to God's promises.

God then lays out the abundance that's in store for His children in Deuteronomy 28:1–14. I've included these fourteen verses in Chapter One. In 28:15–68, God lays out the curses that are in store for His children if they fail to obey Him and choose not to live according to His Word. Of course, there are many other blessings and promises from God to His children detailed throughout the Bible.

Later in the book, I'll explain what a covenant blessing means. These blessings are readily available to all of God's children if they obey God's instructions, as seen in the above two verses. Let's carry on looking at God's conditions.

> Then the Lord said to me, "Arise, proceed on your journey ahead of the people, that they may go in and possess the land which I swore to their fathers to give them." Now, Israel, what does the Lord your God require from you, but to fear the Lord your God, to walk in all His ways and love Him, and to serve the Lord your God with all your heart and with all your soul…
> —Deuteronomy 10:11–12, NASB

We see here that God wants His people to go in and occupy the land which He promised to give to their father, Abraham. In Deuteronomy 10:12, God places the following conditions on the people in order for them to possess the Promised Land:

- They must fear the Lord their God, meaning to live with a healthy respect and reverence for God.
- They must walk in all His ways, meaning to live their lives according to God's Word.
- They must love Him, meaning to care deeply about God's ways.
- They must serve the Lord their God with everything in them, meaning to live and work for Him with true, deep commitment.

In Deuteronomy 29:10–15, God renews the covenant promises He made with the children of Israel through Abraham. God continues to renew His commitment to the children of Israel and pour out His abundance upon them in return for their obedience.

> A Psalm of David. Lord, who shall dwell in Your tabernacle? Who shall dwell on Your holy hill? He who walks uprightly, and works righteousness, and speaks the truth in his heart; he does not backbite with his tongue, nor do evil to his neighbor, nor take up a reproach against his neighbour.
>
> —Psalms 15:1–3, MKJV

Here the psalmist asks, "Who is fit to dwell in the presence of God and have a close relationship with God?" In Psalms 15:2–3, God gives us His conditions:

We who live a God-filled life.
We who do that which is right and speak the truth from our hearts.
We who do not speak evil of others.
We who do not do evil to others.
We who do not disgrace or shame others.

Wow! These look like major requirements. Does this mean we have to be perfect? I hope not, because that would count me out. Actually, I don't think God expects us to be perfect; rather, He expects us to make an honest and sincere effort to live with the right principles and conduct in our lives, such as those given to us in Psalms 15:2–3. We must ask for help from God and be quick to repent and ask forgiveness when we fail. This is what God expects from us!

> Delight yourself also in the Lord, and He shall give you the desires of your heart.
>
> —Psalms 37:4, NKJV

Here we discover that if we take pleasure in the things of the Lord, His Word, and His way of living, He will give us the things we desire and dream about in our hearts and minds.

> Because you have made the Lord, who is my refuge, even the Most High, your dwelling place, no evil shall befall you, nor shall any plague come near your dwelling; for He shall give His angels charge over you, to keep you in all your ways.
>
> —Psalms 91:9–11, NKJV

God's Conditions

All of the blessings and conditions we have read prior to these three verses are very good, but I find the blessings in Psalm 91 especially intriguing. They are intriguing because God's condition here is that we make the Lord our dwelling place—the place where we live. John 1:1 indicates that God is the Word (the Bible). We can dwell in God by dwelling or living in His Word. This means that we must read and meditate on His Word, and change our lives to line up with it. If we meet these conditions, we will receive the following marvellous blessings:

- No evil will happen to us.
- No plagues of sickness will come into our homes.
- Angels will keep us from harm and look after us.

Do I really believe this is possible? Absolutely!

> Do not be over-anxious, therefore, asking "What shall we eat?" or "What shall we drink?" or "What shall we wear?" For all these are questions that Gentiles are always asking; but your Heavenly Father knows that you need these things—all of them. But make His Kingdom and righteousness your chief aim, and then these things shall all be given you in addition.
> —Matthew 6:31–33, WNT

Upon looking at some of God's conditions for us in the New Testament, we find these three verses in Matthew 6. They are pretty self-explanatory, but let me briefly summarize the conditions. We don't have to worry about what we're going to eat, drink, or wear. God will provide those things for us if we take time for Him, and put Him and His Word first in our lives. When we do this, He will bless us with food, clothing, and the things of life.

> And whatever we ask we receive from Him, because we keep His commandments and do those things that are pleasing in His sight.
> —1 John 3:22, NKJV

My paraphrase of the above would go like this: "When we ask God for something, we will receive what we ask for, if we obey His Word and live in a way that is pleasing to Him." In 1 John 3:23, God defines for us what it is to obey His commandments:

> And this is His commandment: that we should believe on the name of His Son Jesus Christ and love one another, as He gave us commandment. (NKJV)

Let me expand on this verse as well. It means that we are to believe that Jesus is God's Son. Believing in God's Son is more than a function of the mind; it really means we must live our lives in such a way that we demonstrate our belief in Jesus Christ. It goes without saying that loving our neighbours requires more than words and head knowledge; it is again the way we live our lives that shows we love our friends, family, and neighbours, thus showing that we obey God's Word and His conditions. As a result, we will receive whatever we have asked for in prayer.

> If we confess our sins, He is faithful and just to forgive us our sins and to cleanse us from all unrighteousness.
> —1 John 1:9, NKJV

In this verse, God says that if we confess our wrongdoings and sins, He will forgive us for those sins no matter how many or how bad they are. As a result, we can live our lives in a way that exhibits God's presence in us.

A Biblical Example

We have looked at a considerable number of scriptures. Now let's look at an account in the Bible which illustrates more practically how God's conditions work for us. This account will demonstrate that God has conditions which must be met in order to receive His blessings.

In Exodus 3:10–4:12, Moses is arguing with God. Moses doesn't feel like he is qualified to lead the children of Israel out of Egypt. Further, Moses tells God that he's not a public speaker, because he has some speech problems. Moses is looking for a way out of what God wants him to do. In 4:14, the Lord tells Moses that he can have his brother Aaron do his public speaking. However, God has some instructions or conditions which must be met. The conditions are that God will speak to Moses, and then Moses will speak to Aaron. Finally, Aaron will speak to the people of Israel.

Let's move to Numbers 12 and see what happens when Aaron disobeys God's condition. In 12:1–2, Aaron and his sister Miriam are criticizing Moses, saying that they can hear from the Lord just as well as Moses. In other words, they can hear from God directly and be His spokespeople; they don't need Moses. It was not God's instruction or condition, however, for Aaron to be God's spokesperson directly. As long as Aaron followed God's conditions, he remained in God's blessing, but when he persisted in disobeying God, he moved outside of God's blessing. As a result, in 12:10, Miriam contracts leprosy. You see, when we disobey God and sin, eventually we open the door for Satan and the curse to wreak havoc in our lives. This is why it's so important for us to follow God's conditions and God's Word if we want to remain in His blessing.

Conclusion

By now I'm sure you can see that God has a way, and He has conditions which we need to meet before He will release His abundance into our lives. God always puts the onus on us to make choices. So we can either choose to receive His blessings or we can choose to be without His blessings. The choice is ours.

I would like to add that God isn't just sitting in heaven watching and waiting for us to make a mistake. The blessing is not removed from us immediately just because we sin or fail. He is merciful and gracious, and He looks on our hearts to see whether we're trying to live in the blessing. This means that we should continually submit our lives into His hands so He can work the blessing through our lives. When we fail, God is waiting to forgive us if we repent.

In the following chapters, we'll cover subjects such as:

- How do our body, soul, and spirit work together?
- How do we live the Christian life successfully?
- How do we tap into God's promises, which are available to all of God's children?

If we're willing to discipline ourselves and make the effort, just like we would in any endeavour we want to accomplish, we can be the recipients of God's promises in our lives. The other things we accomplish in this life are nothing compared to accomplishing a close relationship with God, because His blessings are far above anything we can imagine or think.

Chapter Three

Who Lives in My Temple?

In order for us to understand how to live the Christian life, we need to have an understanding of the body, soul, and spirit, and how they relate to each other, especially the soul and spirit. In addition, we need to come to an understanding of the difference between the soul and spirit. This chapter will be somewhat technical in nature, but there isn't any way around it.

First of all, let's take a look at the following diagram to develop a picture in our minds of our different parts.

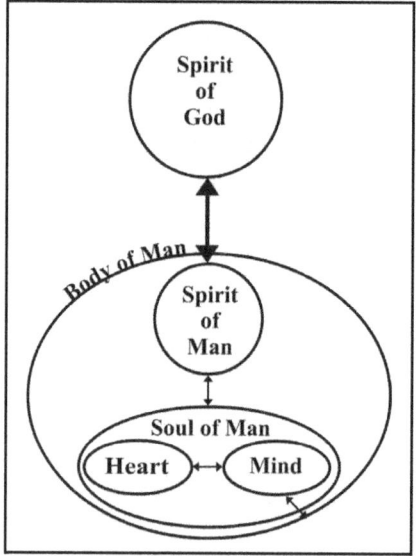

This diagram includes the Spirit of God in the top circle and the Body of Man in the larger circle below. The Body of Man circle includes the spirit, soul, heart, and mind of man. The arrows show the direction of communication between the different parts of the man and the Spirit of God.

As you read this chapter, the diagram should help you in putting together all the different parts of the human being and how they relate to God.

Our Body

First of all, let's look at the definition for the word body, as found in Strong's Hebrew and Greek Dictionary. It is found in the following verse:

> I Daniel was grieved in my spirit in the midst of my body, and the visions of my head troubled me.
> —Daniel 7:15, KJV

In the Greek, the word *nidneh* is used for the word "body" here. It is defined as "a *sheath*; figuratively the *body* (as the receptacle of the soul)."[8] This would indicate that the body is a house or temple. It is the place where you and I reside, the place where our soul and spirit live.

Let's start by taking a look at the body and its purpose. To put it in a nutshell, the body is the physical house, shell, or temple which houses our soul and spirit, as we shall see in the following references:

> And the Lord God formed man of the dust of the ground, and breathed into his nostrils the breath of life; and man became a living soul.
> —Genesis 2:7, KJV

> Thus says God the Lord, who created the heavens and stretched them out, who spread forth the earth and that which comes from it, who gives breath to the people on it, and spirit to those who walk on it ...
> —Isaiah 42:5, NKJV

Genesis 2:7 describes God making the body of man out of the dust of the ground and breathing life into him. In Isaiah 42:5, God gave people breath, natural life (a soul), and a spirit as well. From these two verses, it's evident that our body is the physical house where we, our soul and spirit, live.

Our body is made up mostly of water, approximately seventy percent of it. The balance is about twenty-five percent solid matter (flesh and bones). The body has been beautifully made by God to provide a house, or temple, where the spirit and soul actually live. The body provides the avenue for the

---

8 James Strong. *Strong's Dictionaries of the Hebrew and Greek Words*, "Nidneh" (Nashville, TN: Abingdon Press, 1890).

outward physical expression of who we are by way of the five senses: sight, hearing, touch, taste, and smell. Conversely, the five senses provide outside information to the brain for us to function in our surroundings.

Before we go further, let's define the brain, as taken from Webster's Dictionary. The brain is "the organ of thought and the central control point for the nervous system."[9] The brain is such a complex organ; it processes all of the information from and to the five senses, and performs all of the body's functions. The brain also contains our mind, memory, and heart. Our purpose in mentioning the brain here is to identify it in relation to the body, mind, memory, and heart.

Let's get back to our subject, which is the word "body." The word "flesh" is used in the Bible for the word "body." In fact, this word is used to refer to the body long before the word "body" is actually used. The first sighting of the word "flesh" is found in Genesis 9:4, from the Hebrew word *basar*, which Strong's Hebrew and Greek Dictionary defines as "flesh (from its freshness); by extension body; person."[10] In the following two verses, the body is described by the word "flesh."

> So the Lord God caused the man to fall into a deep sleep; and while he was sleeping, he took one of the man's ribs and then closed up the place with flesh.
>
> —Genesis 2:21, NIV

> For not all flesh is the same, but there is one kind for humans, another for animals, another for birds, and another for fish.
>
> —1 Corinthians 15:39, ESV

In the Bible, a number of different words are used interchangeably, and "flesh" is one of them. Let's look at the three common ways that the word "flesh" is used in the Bible:

1. It is used to describe the physical body, as we have discussed above.

---

9 *Webster's Canadian Dictionary & Thesaurus* (Toronto, ON: Strathearn Books, 2011), 50.

10 James Strong. *Strong's Dictionaries of the Hebrew and Greek Words*, "Basar" (Nashville, TN: Abingdon Press, 1890), 24.

2. It is used to describe a lifestyle we can live as human beings. The flesh-type of lifestyle is a life lived for ourselves, to fulfill our own desires. It's a life focused on living according to the ways of the world. On the other hand, a spirit-led life is one that is consecrated to the Lord. A spirit-led life focuses on God's ways, whereas a flesh-led life focuses on man's or the world's ways, which we see in Romans 8:5: *"For those who live according to the flesh set their minds on the things of the flesh, but those who live according to the Spirit, the things of the Spirit"* (Romans 8:5, NKJV). For clarification, consider Weymouth's translation of the same verse: *"For if men are controlled by their earthly natures, they give their minds to earthly things. If they are controlled by their spiritual natures, they give their minds to spiritual things"* (Romans 8:5, WNT).
3. It is used to refer to people in general, as we can see in the following references:

And it shall come to pass afterward that I will pour out My Spirit on all flesh; your sons and your daughters shall prophesy, your old men shall dream dreams, your young men shall see visions.
—Joel 2:28, NKJV

And all flesh shall see the salvation of God.
—Luke 3:6, KJV

In Weymouth's translation, the word "flesh" is actually changed to mankind:

…and then shall all mankind see God's salvation.
—Luke 3:6, WNT

When we're reading the scriptures, we must be mindful of the context the writer is using when we see the word "flesh."

Now, let's go back and summarize what we have covered so far regarding the body. The body is that house of flesh which God made for Adam, and of course for us. The body contains a brain and five senses, which work together to connect us to our surroundings. Also, our body is used to house our soul and spirit.

So where does the body get its life from? The body gets its life from the blood:

> But you shall not eat flesh with its life, that is, its blood.
> —Genesis 9:4, NKJV

> For the life of the flesh is in the blood. And I have given it to you on the altar to make an atonement for your souls. For it is the blood that makes an atonement for the soul.
> —Leviticus 17:11, MKJV

From the above scriptures, we see that the life of a person is in the blood, but how does that happen?

> And the Lord God formed man of the dust of the ground, and breathed into his nostrils the breath of life; and man became a living soul.
> —Genesis 2:7, KJV

God formed a physical flesh being (a body) and then breathed life into him. The life entered his blood and the blood began to flow in his body, making every part of his body alive. Man then became a living soul, a natural man, housed in a body. Man became a live human being with a soul, consisting of a mind, heart, and life, and a spirit, all housed in an enclosure called the body.

Let's continue by looking at the heart and mind as parts of our being.

Our Heart

> This is the covenant I will establish with the people of Israel after that time, declares the Lord. I will put my laws in their minds and write them on their hearts. I will be their God, and they will be my people.
> —Hebrews 8:10, NIV

In this verse, the Lord is making a covenant with His people in which He declares that He will put His Word into their minds. This means that He's giving them knowledge from His Word by placing it in their minds. However, He's also writing it on their hearts. This act of God refers to Him making His Word part of their minds and hearts. Hebrews 8:10 identifies the mind and heart as separate entities, since they have different purposes in the human being.

> And God saw that the wickedness of man was great in the earth, and that every imagination [intention] of the thoughts [plans] of his heart was only evil continually.
> —Genesis 6:5, KJV

Let's consider the heart first. God made us with a physical heart to pump the life which is in our blood through our body. However, there is another heart in man. Let's define this heart, as found in the above verse, using Strong's Dictionary. The word "heart" comes from the Hebrew word *labe*, which is "used (figuratively) very widely for the feelings, the will and even the intellect; likewise the center of anything."[11] The centre of anything is usually who or what it is. Some words we can use to describe the centre of a human being are emotions, feelings, desires, will, personality, and character. The word "character," as defined by Webster, means "the group of qualities that make a person, group, or thing different from others."[12] The word "personality" from the same dictionary means "the qualities (as moods or habits) that make one human being different from others."[13] Let's look at the following verse to expand on the heart's purpose and function:

> You brood of vipers, how can you who are evil say anything good? For the mouth speaks what the heart is full of.
> —Matthew 12:34, NIV

Let's focus on the last sentence of this verse. Your heart is full of your feelings, will, desires, character, and personality traits. Your heart is who you are. Whatever is in your heart will also come out of your mouth. It follows then that the character—or personality, will, desires, and qualities—which is

---

11 James Strong. *Strong's Dictionaries of the Hebrew and Greek Words*, "Labe." (Nashville, TN: Abingdon Press, 1890).
12 *Webster's Canadian Dictionary & Thesaurus* (Toronto, ON: Strathearn Books, 2011), 70.
13 Ibid., 313.

in your heart will match what comes out of your mouth, revealing who you really are. Consequently, your heart is who you really are. Let's continue to define the heart:

> A good man out of the good treasure of his heart brings forth good; and an evil man out of the evil treasure of his heart brings forth evil. For out of the abundance of the heart his mouth speaks.
> —Luke 6:45, NKJV

The words "good treasure" imply a store of wealth and abundance contained in the heart. Good treasures are good thoughts, attitudes, and motives. These are obtained from putting God's Word into our hearts. These treasures mould our desires, character, will, and emotions to make us who we are. Thus, we must conclude again that our hearts are our *feelings, emotions, conscience, desires, will, character,* and *personality.*

To further emphasize this, let me share some of the many KJV scriptures which describe the heart in the Word of God. Behind each verse I have placed one of the above words shown in italics. These words are used to characterize the heart, or to identify the heart's functions.

- ...the thoughts of his heart was only evil continually. (Genesis 6:5, KJV) *Emotions, will, character.*

- And Jacobs's heart fainted... (Genesis 45:26, KJV) *Feelings, emotions.*

- ...and serve him with all your heart... (Deuteronomy 11:13, KJV) *Character, desires.*

- My heart [rejoices] in the Lord... (1 Samuel 2:1, KJV) *Emotions.*

- ...and serve him with a perfect heart... (1 Chronicles 28:9, KJV) *Character.*

- ...and he shall give [you] the desires of [your] heart. (Psalms 37:4, KJV) *Desires, will.*

- Create in me at clean heart, O God. (Psalms 51:10, KJV) *Character.*

- ...an high look and a proud heart... (Psalms 101:5, KJV) *Personality.*

- ...for out of the abundance of the heart the mouth [speaks]. (Matthew 12:34, KJV) *Character, personality.*

- Let not your heart be troubled... (John 14:1, KJV) *Emotion.*

- ...they were [pricked] in their heart, and said unto Peter... (Acts 2:37, KJV) *Conscience.*

- ...and [shall] believe in [your] heart... (Romans 10:9, KJV) *Will.*

- ...I have found David the son of Jesse, a man after [my] own heart, [who] shall fulfil all my will. (Acts 13:22, KJV) *Character.*

I have used the words "character" and "personality" interchangeably since they are similar in meaning. However, from these verses and the definitions above, we can confirm that the character or personality of a person resides in the heart. Our hearts give evidence of who we are by what comes out of our mouths, and by our actions. The heart is used often in the Bible to refer to our character, which is who we are as a person.

So where is this other heart located in our bodies? Where else in the body would our character, will, desires, and emotions be stored? The brain, of course. The heart is located in the brain. Let me say here that I didn't get this understanding from a verse in the Bible; it was like a light came on in my mind as I meditated on it. The heart is that portion of the brain that formulates and contains our character. So even though the heart and mind are spoken of separately in the Bible, they are part of the same organ, called the "brain." The mind and heart each perform different functions as part of the brain. Once again, the heart is the area of the brain where the person's character resides. The heart communicates back and forth with the mind. The heart affects the mind's decision-making process, because it is the character of the individual.

Let's validate one further function of the heart by looking at something else which the heart performs:

> Now when they heard this, they were pierced to the heart, and said to Peter and the rest of the apostles, "Brethren, what shall we do?"
> —Acts 2:37, NASB

The heart of man is also his conscience, providing guidance for life in the area of good and evil, as depicted above.

Finally, let's look at the following verse:

> Keep your heart with all diligence, for out of it spring the issues of life.
> —Proverbs 4:23, NKJV

In the paragraphs above, we concluded that the heart is really who we are as a person. If we were to paraphrase Proverbs 4:23 with that understanding, it would go like this: "Above everything else, be careful of the type of person you could become or of who you are already, because everything you do and say is shaped by your heart; your heart is who you are and your mouth will reveal it."

To summarize, many of the things we experience in life which originate in us come out of the heart. The heart is the centre of who we are. It is the character, personality, conscience, will, desires, and emotions all in one package.

Next, let's look at the function of the mind.

Our Mind

Webster's Dictionary defines the word "mind" as "the part of the person that thinks, reasons, feels, understands, and remembers."[14]

> Thus says the Lord God, "It will come about on that day, that thoughts will come into your mind and you will devise an evil plan ..."
> —Ezekiel 38:10, NASB

---

14 Ibid., 268.

My definition of the mind associates it with a computer processor. The mind is the computer processor of the human being. It receives information from many sources, disseminates it, processes it, and then puts the human being into action according to the decisions it makes.

Where is the mind located? Of course we know that it is located in the brain. The brain is the physical organ of a human being which houses and facilitates the mind.

The mind has many different functions to perform, but to simplify things we will group them into categories:

- Processing information to and from the five senses.
- Memory.
- Decisions, thoughts, ideas, and actions.

Let's look at each of these functions of the mind from a practical standpoint.

The first function of the mind includes the five senses. The five senses are hearing, taste, touch, sight, and smell. The nervous system sends signals from our five senses to the brain, and the mind, in the brain, translates those signals into thoughts and actions.

The second function of the mind is the memory. It is the place where everything we take into our mind is stored for future reference.

Finally, the mind is the part of the brain where thoughts, ideas, decisions, and actions come from.

At this point, rather than just explain and illustrate the functions of the mind, let's tie the workings of the mind and heart together. This will provide a broader picture of how the mind works. The heart affects and influences the mind in its work, as our human computer processor. The heart has an influence on our subconscious activities, the five senses, and our memory, decisions, thoughts, ideas, will, and desires. For instance, if we are depressed, which is an emotion that comes out of the heart, the heart can affect the systems of the body. Depression tends to hinder the healthy functions of our bodies.

Next, let's illustrate how the heart works together with the mind and the five senses. For example, let's say we smell something in the house through our nose. Our mind decides that it's smoke. Our outward expression may be one of fear—fear that the house is on fire. The fear factor comes from our emotions, which come from our heart. So we see that our heart has an effect on our mind by sending information to it. In this case, it has the effect of presenting the emotion of fear; consequently, the mind has to take that emotion into account when making a decision about the smoke.

So far we have illustrated the heart's effect on our physical body functions and five senses. However, apart from the heart, there is also our memory, which stores information in the mind regarding past experiences. In this case, our sense of smell having detected smoke, our memory says that we've been taught to get everybody out of the house when there is smoke.

The electrical information generated in the mind from our senses, memory, and heart is translated into thoughts, pictures, or words in our mind. The result of incoming information ("There is a fire and I'm afraid") requires the mind to make some decisions as to what to do.

In conclusion, the mind is the thought processor and decision maker of the human being. The mind acts on the thoughts and decisions we make to give the brain the right signals to send to the right parts of the body to carry out our decisions. The mind, which is the intellectual faculty, and the heart, which is the emotional faculty of the brain, work together in many things to perform the functions of a human being. With the mind and heart, our intellectual and emotional functions are fulfilled and completed.

Our Soul

So far we've looked at the heart, the mind, and their functions. Now, let's look at the soul.

First of all, let's look at three Hebrew words and one Greek word, as found in Strong's Dictionary, to see how the word "soul" is defined.

- *Chay* (Hebrew), meaning "breathing creature, i.e. animal or (abstractly) vitality."[15]
- *Ruach* (Hebrew), meaning "*wind*; by resemblance *breath*, i.e. a sensible (or even violent) exhalation; figuratively *life*."[16]

---

15 James Strong. *Strong's Dictionaries of the Hebrew and Greek Words*, "Chay" (Nashville, TN: Abingdon Press, 1890).
16 Ibid., "Ruach."

- *Psuche* (Greek), meaning "to *breathe*."[17]
- *Nephesh* (Hebrew), meaning "a breathing creature, that is, animal or (abstractly) *vitality*."[18]

If we specifically look at these four words and their meanings, we come up with two words that are common to almost all the definitions. The words are "breath" and "life," since vitality also refers to life. Let's look at the following verse again:

And the Lord God formed man of the dust of the ground, and breathed into his nostrils the breath of life; and man became a living soul.
—Genesis 2:7, KJV

This indicates that the soul contained in the body is alive. It is God's breath of life which makes the soul alive. Without life, the soul wouldn't exist. We have discovered that the body contains a heart and a mind. Therefore, adding it all together, the soul consists of the heart, the mind, and the breath of life—natural, physical life contained in a body. The word "soul" is the name used to identify the human being as a natural man.

Now, let's tie the understanding of the body, heart, mind, and life together into a picture of what the soul looks like. First, I would like to summarize what we've just discussed regarding the body, mind, heart, and life. The mind, which is the computer processor of our being; the heart, which is our character and personality; along with the life God breathed into man—all contained in a body—make up the soul of a man. The soul, with all of its parts—the mind, heart, and life—relate to our surroundings (the world, and people) using the body's five senses.

Finally, let's take a look at how all the different parts of the soul work together. The thoughts made by the mind, part of the soul, sometimes affect the body directly. For instance, if I decided to climb a tree and jump off a branch, and I landed wrong and broke my leg, my body would suffer with the pain of the broken leg. Another example: if my heart's desire was to run a marathon and my mind went to work to make it happen, after the race my body would experience tiredness. From this we can see that the body, heart, and mind

---

17 Ibid., "Psuche."
18 Ibid., "Nephesh."

have an effect on each other. The body, mind, and heart of the soul were designed to work together in God's great plan and purpose for the human being.

It certainly is important for us to understand that we have much to learn about these parts of our being. As well, when we encounter these words—mind, heart, and soul—in the Bible, in order to get the meaning intended by the writer, it sometimes helps to delve into the Hebrew and Greek words, and to look at the context of what has been written. Ultimately, only by the revelation of the Holy Spirit are we able to understand the Word of God clearly and without confusion.

Let's look at the spirit next. But before we do, it's important to note that the soul operates in the realm of the physical, visible, and temporal, as opposed to the spirit, which operates in the unseen, permanent, and everlasting realm.

Our Spirit

I turn to Webster's Dictionary once again for a definition of the word "spirit." It's defined as "vital force; immortal part of man."[19] My own definition of this word goes like this: "an unseen force which God placed in man, and which enables us to communicate and relate to the Spirit of God." In light of this, let us now consider the spirit of a person.

God gave every human being a spirit separate from the soul, as we see in the following verse:

> For the word of God is living and active, sharper than any two-edged sword, piercing to the division of soul and of spirit, of joints and of marrow, and discerning the thoughts and intentions of the heart.
> —Hebrews 4:12, ESV

Let's look at the middle portion of this verse—*"piercing to the division of soul and of spirit..."* My paraphrase goes like this: "The Word of God penetrates the human being to the point of revealing the difference between the soul and the spirit." From this, we understand that this verse reveals that we have a soul and a spirit as separate entities.

---

19 J.B. Foreman, MA, *The Webster Worldwide Dictionary* (Great Britain: William Collins Sons & Co. Ltd., 1960), 469.

The spirit is that part of the human being that is physically unseen. The spirit can only be seen indirectly, by the influence it has on the soul and body of a person. Wind is a good example of something we can't see, but when the wind blows we see leaves moving past us and water forming waves; we feel the pressure of the wind against the outer part of our bodies.

In the same way, when the spirit which we can't see influences our lives, we see the outward evidence of its influence. For example, when an alcoholic accepts Jesus as their Saviour, their spirit connects to the Spirit of God. As a result of this connection, their addiction to alcohol stops. This is the outward, visible evidence of the Spirit of God at work changing their spirit and soul, even though the Spirit cannot be seen.

God is a Spirit, and it is our spirit that connects us to God, when the connection has been made by us and God. Let's draw an analogy using a laptop computer. The wall outlet is the source of power for the laptop, and the battery in the laptop is where the power is stored. If the cord that carries the power from the outlet to the battery is unplugged, there is no longer any power flowing into that battery, and after several hours of use the battery will die. When we connect our battery (our spirit) to God by confessing that Jesus is our Saviour, we plug our spirit into the wall outlet of spiritual life (God). When our spirit is in unison with God, or plugged in to the Spirit of God (the source of power), His Spirit provides power and life which influences our spirit, soul, and body. The influence of God's Spirit shows up in the actions of the soul and body. Even as we illustrated with the laptop, if we are to live godly lives we need to keep our spirit plugged into God. The following verse confirms this:

> Since you have purified your souls in obeying the truth through the Spirit in sincere love of the brethren, love one another fervently with a pure heart...
> —1 Peter 1:22, NKJV

This confirms the influence of the Spirit on the soul. It says that God's Spirit helps our soul to obey God's Word because His Spirit cleanses our soul.

To summarize our appreciation of the spirit, it is that unseen force which does not die and which God placed in every human being. Since God is a spirit, we need a spirit in order to communicate and relate to God. One of the reasons God made man was so that He could have a relationship with him, and that is accomplished through the spirit of man.

The Soul Man vs. the Spirit Man

In order to eliminate any confusion with respect to the soul and spirit, let's look at the following two verses:

> Thus [says] God the Lord ... he that [gives] breath unto the people upon [the earth], and spirit to them that walk therein ...
> —Isaiah 42:5, KJV

> ... and I pray God your whole spirit and soul and body be preserved blameless unto the coming of our Lord Jesus Christ.
> —1 Thessalonians 5:23, KJV

These indicate that we do have a soul and a spirit, and they are separate parts of the human being. From Isaiah 42:5, we can see that when God created man, He gave him breath (a soul) and He gave him a spirit. If God had only breathed a spirit into man, to give man life, man would have only been a spirit living in a body. Man wouldn't have been able to experience the physical realm of this earth, because the soul, through the five senses, is what connects us to this world. Thus, man would never have been able to experience the soul realm. God's plan for man was to experience the physical realm of this world, which required man to have a soul.

> Who knows the spirit of man that goes upward, and the spirit of the beast that goes downward?
> —Ecclesiastes 3:21, MKJV

Consider that animals only have a soul, which includes a mind, heart, body, and life. We are the only creatures which have a spirit and a soul. They do not have a spirit; consequently, when they die they do not go to heaven.

> Receiving the end [conclusion] of your faith, even the salvation of your souls.
> —1 Peter 1:9, KJV

On the other hand, our spirit is the part of us which leaves our dead body and soul, and arrives in eternity. In 1 Peter 1:7–8, the Apostle Peter speaks about the return of Jesus to the earth to receive the saints into heaven. In 1:9, we see the climax of our salvation. At the time of the resurrection, our bodies and souls will be made alive to be with God and His Son Jesus forever, and our salvation will be complete—body, soul, and spirit.

A belief needs to be clarified here. Some have said that the heart and spirit are one and the same thing. We have already established the functions of the heart and spirit as separate. The next verse puts that teaching to rest:

> They would not be like their ancestors—a stubborn and rebellious generation, whose hearts were not loyal to God, whose spirits were not faithful to him.
> —Psalms 78:8, NIV

It's pretty clear that the heart and spirit are two separate entities with different functions. The people referred to in this verse had hearts that weren't loyal to God; their characters lacked loyalty to God. In the same way, they were not faithful to Him in their spiritual lives.

Every body of every human being contains a soul man and a spirit man; in other words, a soul and a spirit, living in their body. The soul lives in an awareness of this world and the physical realm. The spirit is aware of and operates in the spirit realm. The spirit requires an awakening to God's Spirit realm in order to function in that realm. Once the spirit of a man becomes awake to God, it can influence the soul of the man and make him aware of God.

The words natural, carnal, flesh, and soul are used in the Bible to describe that part of us which connects and relates to the physical world. Natural, carnal, and flesh all refer to a human being with little or no divine influence. As well, carnal and flesh, as used in the Bible, are used to emphasize a human being who is mostly immersed in themselves and the ways of the world. Finally, soul is used to identify a human being in general, one with or without spiritual connection to God. From this we can conclude that the soul isn't able to be aware of spiritual things without the influence of the spirit.

The word "spirit" is used in the Bible, to describe our connection and relationship with the unseen spirit world. Of course, the ultimate spirit connection is that of our spirit connecting with God's Spirit.

> For if men are controlled by their earthly natures, they give their minds to earthly things. If they are controlled by their spiritual natures, they give their minds to spiritual things.
>
> —Romans 8:5, WNT

In this verse, we see that if we allow our soul, or natural man, to control us, we'll think about and dwell on earthly things. We must allow our soul to be controlled by our spirit, which is connected and intimate with God's Spirit, in order to understand God and experience His presence.

> But the natural man does not receive the things of the Spirit of God, for they are foolishness to him; nor can he know them, because they are spiritually discerned.
>
> —1 Corinthians 2:14, NKJV

Finally, the soul, or natural man, isn't able to receive truths and understanding from God. The soul cannot comprehend them without the spirit in tune with God. Without the Spirit of God being plugged in or connected to our spirit, our spiritual man doesn't have true life, causing our spirit to be dead to God's Spirit realm. In this condition, we're operating as a natural man in the realm of the soul.

Check out the following scriptures from the King James Version, and then in Weymouth's translation:

> For if [you] live after the flesh [natural, soul man], [you] shall die: but if [you] through the Spirit do mortify [put to death] the deeds [actions] of the body [the soul man], [you] shall live.
>
> —Romans 8:13, KJV

If we live our lives consumed by the things of this world, we will die spiritually. However, if we choose to have our spirit stay in communion with

God's Spirit regularly—or preferably daily—we will have true life here on earth and eternal life hereafter.

> Therefore, brethren, it is not to our lower natures that we are under obligation that we should live by their rule. For if you so live, death is near; but if, through being under the sway of the spirit, you are putting your old bodily habits to death, you will live.
> —Romans 8:12–13, WNT

We shouldn't choose to live by the dictates of the soul without God's influence. Rather, we should decide to put aside the things of this world and allow our spirits to be under the control of God's Spirit. Since the natural man, carnal man, fleshly man, and soul man are all similar, if we live as a natural man, our spirit is not actually dead; rather, it is asleep and not experiencing the higher life of God's Spirit to which we are called. The only true life that exists is God, because everything else leads to death. Any spiritual connection other than God ultimately leads to death. This is why the Word says we are dead spiritually if we aren't connected to God. This is the Word's way of saying that we aren't connected to the only true, everlasting life of God.

To illustrate this, let me use the example of a hibernating bear. Does a bear hunt for food when it's hibernating? No, it just sleeps and does nothing; it is not experiencing the world around it. Just think of a dormant spirit as a hibernating bear. As such, a person with a dormant spirit is not aware of the spirit realm of God. He or she isn't receiving the positive, abundant influence of that realm.

The realm where we live here in this world, apart from the influence of God's Spirit, is the natural or soul realm, and all it produces is darkness and death. So if our spirit isn't refreshed in the things of God regularly, our spirit can be connected to or influenced by the evil spirit realm, Satan, or the devil.

Even Christians can be used by the devil to do evil or sinful things when they haven't kept a close relationship with God, or when they've left themselves open to his influence. Wrongdoing (or sin) comes from either the soul or the devil. Christians cannot be possessed by the devil or evil spirits, possession being a state in which evil actually dwells in the body of the person. God will not share our body with evil, but the devil and his evil spirit world are able to afflict, oppress, or influence Christians externally.

For example, Satan could afflict a Christian with depression or sickness, or he could put an evil thought into the mind of a Christian. That does not constitute evil possession. As we see in the following verse, as believers we have been delivered from the devil's control into God's kingdom.

> He has delivered us from the power of darkness and conveyed us into the kingdom of the Son of His love ...
>
> —Colossians 1:13, NKJV

The realm of God's Spirit, on the other hand, is the heavenly realm that produces life and light. When we get our spirit connected to God's Spirit, we will begin to experience and live in the abundant, overflowing blessing of God in every area of our lives. We will then be able to understand God's Word, live in His authority and blessing, and imitate Christ in our lives.

So, to recap, if we live our lives mostly controlled by the soul, we're really living in what the Scriptures call the flesh or soul realm, as referenced in Romans 8:5. In this condition, we are subject to living our lives influenced by the world and the little it has to offer, and we are prone to the influence of the evil spirit realm (the devil). If we have our spirit awakened to the Spirit of God, we can be aware of and activate God's Spirit realm in our lives anytime we choose.

How does that work, you might ask? Well, we can choose God by asking Him to help us with something. We can ask Him to give us the words to say in situations we face, we can ask Him for wisdom anytime we need it, we can thank God for providing for us, and we can talk to Him about anything at any time. How amazing is that? We can connect with God in any situation at any time.

Let's begin to see remarkable things happen—wonderful things which God wants to do in our lives daily. The following diagram compares the soul and the spirit of a child of God, a person who has received salvation. It shows the distinct differences between the soul and the spirit:

Soul vs Spirit

Soul	**Bible Identity**	**Spirit**
Soul		God's Spirit
Carnal		Holy Spirit
Flesh		Jesus' Spirit
Natural		Man's Spirit

Characteristics

- Dies
- Connects to the physical realm
- Earthly life of the human being
- Soul and spirit can relate to each other

- Never dies
- Connects to the spirit realm
- Spiritual life of the human being
- Can relate to the soul if awakened

Abilities

1. Directs the physical life
2. Does not understand God's Word
3. Has no authority over evil
4. Can not imitate Christ
5. Misses God's blessings
6. Not redeemed without the spirit awakened
7. Not aware of God
8. Influenced by the spirit and body

1. Can influence the physical life
2. Understands God's Word
3. Has authority over evil
4. Can imitate Christ
5. Has God's blessings available
6. Is the channel for redemption
7. Aware of God
8. Receives influence from the soul

This Diagram is based on the individual receiving and living the salvation experience

God's Body, Soul, and Spirit

We read in Genesis 1:26: *"And God said, Let us make man in our image, after our likeness..."* (KJV) In this verse, God is saying that He has made us to look and act like Him; therefore, God has a body, soul, spirit, heart, and mind, just like we do. The parts of God that we're able to experience are His soul, mind, heart, and spirit. We're not able to experience or see God's body.

We are able to experience God's Spirit when our spirit is connected to His Spirit. Let's consider an example of spiritual influence. For instance, when a person who suffers from depression (suicidal tendencies and grief) receives salvation (their spirit connects with God's Spirit), their depression leaves; they become filled with the joy of the Lord. They are able to see and feel the outward visible evidence of God's Spirit connected to them, because of the joy.

> The Lord was sorry that He had made man on the earth, and He was grieved in His heart.
> —Genesis 6:6, NASB

In this verse, we are made aware of the fact that the Lord has emotions and character just like we do. God's character is to hate or dislike evil, and He was expressing His emotions in this regard.

We are able to experience God's heart (character) and mind in our lives when we believe God's Word and experience His blessings. Remember that the heart and mind are a part of the soul. For example, let's say that we have faith that God, according to His Word, has healed our body from diabetes, and consequently we receive the healing from God. This event enables us to experience God's heart (character) and mind, since God's Word expresses His mind and heart's desire to heal our bodies. Of course, all of these attributes of God come to us via God's invisible Spirit, and God's heart and mind are actually permeated by His Spirit, just like our hearts and minds should be.

Finally, we aren't able to see God's body because He has a glorified or spiritual body, and the glory of it is so great that we would fall over dead in His presence if we were to see Him. However, we can look forward to the day when we will also have a glorified body, and our soul will be totally and completely under the direction of our spirit, submitted to God's Spirit. At that time, the salvation of our body, soul, and spirit will be complete. Praise God! What amazing things we have to look forward to as believers in Jesus Christ.

Conclusion

So what does all this stuff about the body, soul, and spirit have to do with believers in Christ Jesus? In this chapter, we have defined the parts of a human being: the body, soul, and spirit.

- The body is the house where the spirit and soul actually live and it contains a brain and five senses, which work together to connect us to our surroundings.
- We have discovered that the soul is made up of a mind, a heart, and life, contained in a body.
- We concluded our heart is full of our feelings, will, desires, character, and personality traits. Our heart is who we are.
- The mind is the thought processor and the decision maker of the human being.
- Our spirit is an unseen force which God placed in us, and which enables us to communicate and relate to the Spirit of God.
- We have found that the heart and the spirit are not the same; rather, they each have their own function.
- We have also found that the soul and spirit of a person are separate and specific in their functions.
- The soul is our connection to the world and the spirit is our connection to God or the spirit realm.
- Most of all, we have determined that Christians can live in the soul realm or the realm of God's Spirit; we are given the choice.

By now we should have a better understanding of why we do the things we do. Secondly, we should have a better understanding of how to live a victorious Christian life.

Chapter Four

How Do We Get Connected?

How do we connect our spirits to the Spirit of God? The initial and ongoing experience which we need to make that happen is called salvation.

> For with the heart one believes unto righteousness, and with the mouth one confesses unto salvation.
>
> —Romans 10:10, MKJV

Strong's Hebrew and Greek Dictionary uses the Greek word *soteria* for the word "salvation." It is defined as "rescue or safety (physically or morally)... deliver, health, salvation, save, saving."[20] It seems to me that salvation is more than just an escape from hell. God gave all of mankind the free gift of salvation through His Son Jesus Christ that we might be delivered from sin, sickness, darkness, poverty, and every curse. We are not only delivered from death and the curse, but delivered into the marvellous life which God has to offer us, a victorious life in the blessing of God (God's abundant provision for every area of our lives, daily). Most importantly, the gift of salvation enables us to receive eternal, everlasting life.

Oftentimes pastors and/or Christians will ask, "Have you invited Jesus into your heart?" This can be rather confusing, because many of us aren't sure how to explain that properly. To clarify this statement, we need to go back to the previous chapter on the body, soul, and spirit. When we invite Jesus to come into our hearts, we're initiating the connection of our spirit with the Spirit of God or Jesus' Spirit. To come to an understanding of how this works, let's look at the following three verses:

---

20 James Strong. *Strong's Dictionaries of the Hebrew and Greek Words*, "Soteria" (Nashville, TN: Abingdon Press, 1890).

> It is the spirit which gives Life. The flesh confers no benefit whatever. The words I have spoken to you are spirit and are Life.
> —John 6:63, WNT

> But we have not received the spirit of the world, but the Spirit which comes forth from God, that we may know the blessings that have been so freely given to us by God.
> —1 Corinthians 2:12, WNT

> But he who is joined to the Lord is one spirit with Him.
> —1 Corinthians 6:17, NKJV

To begin with, John 6:63 says that the Spirit of God gives us life, which means that God's Spirit makes our spirit alive to Him. You see, our spirit is alive and never dies, but it's not alive to true life until we connect with God's Spirit. 1 Corinthians 2:12 indicates that we receive God's Spirit when we make Jesus our Saviour. Finally, 1 Corinthians 6:17 declares that when we accept Jesus as our Saviour, His Spirit and our spirit are joined together as one spirit. Technically, what happens is that Jesus' Spirit makes our spirit alive to His Spirit realm. This results in the Spirit of God, the Spirit of Jesus, and the Holy Spirit being one with our spirit.

The influence of God's Spirit through Jesus continues in our lives as long as we keep the connection or relationship alive and well between our spirit and God's Spirit. God's Spirit, Jesus' Spirit, and the Holy Spirit are all one and the same, even though they are three different beings and each one has different functions. Regardless, Jesus' Spirit is for all intents and purposes living in us.

So how does Jesus live in our heart? Since our spirit becomes one with Jesus' Spirit, at our point of receiving salvation our spirit becomes subject to Jesus' influence, which affects our spirit, soul, heart, and mind; thus, we can say that we have Jesus dwelling in our heart.

Just as a point of clarification, Jesus is our avenue of connection to God's Spirit. Even though God, Jesus, and the Holy Spirit are one Spirit, Jesus is still the only way to get to Father God. Jesus is the only way we can receive salvation and connect to God.

To minimize confusion, most of the time I will use "God's Spirit" or the "Spirit of God" rather than use all three references: God, Jesus, and Holy Spirit. Of course, this is not to ignore or minimize Jesus or the Holy Spirit.

To make it easy to understand, I'm going to break down the process of getting saved (receiving salvation), into seven simple steps, as follows:

1. **Acknowledge.** We must first acknowledge that all of us have been (or are) sinners, and that we have not just failed God, but ourselves and other people as well.

   > ... for all have sinned and fall short of the glory of God ...
   > —Romans 3:23, NIV

2. **Repent.** This means that we must be sorry for all of the wrongdoing (sin) which we have done in our lives to this point, and we must ask Jesus to forgive us for these things.

   > Repent therefore and be converted, that your sins may be blotted out, so that times of refreshing may come from the presence of the Lord ...
   > —Acts 3:19, NKJV

   > If we confess our sins, he is faithful and just and will forgive us our sins and purify us from all unrighteousness.
   > —1 John 1:9, NIV

3. **Forsake.** This word means "to turn away from," and if we apply it or add it to the act of repenting, it means "to express regret for having done something wrong."

   > Let the wicked forsake their ways and the unrighteous their thoughts. Let them turn to the Lord, and he will have mercy on them, and to our God, for he will freely pardon.
   > —Isaiah 55:7, NIV

4. **Believe.** Next, we must believe that Jesus is the Son of God, and that the only way we can connect with God is through Jesus Christ. We must also believe that Jesus died to take away our sins, and that Jesus rose from the dead to bring us an abundant, victorious life.

> For God so loved the world that He gave His only begotten Son, that whoever believes in Him should not perish but have everlasting life.
> —John 3:16, NKJV

> *...that by the name of Jesus Christ of Nazareth, whom [you] crucified, whom God raised from the dead... Neither is there salvation in any other: for there is none other name under heaven given among men, whereby we must be saved.*
> —Acts 4:10, 12, KJV (emphasis added)

5. **Confess and receive.** Then we must invite Jesus, with the confession of our mouths, to be our Saviour and take control of our life. With this we are inviting Jesus' Spirit to connect with our spirit. This is when our spirit awakens and comes into communion and relationship with Jesus' Spirit. At this point, we receive the free gift of eternal life, and we can receive God's many available blessings.

   > *For with the heart man [believes] unto righteousness; and with the mouth confession is made unto salvation...* For whosoever shall call upon the name of the Lord shall be saved.
   > —Romans 10:10, 13, KJV (emphasis added)

   > But as many as received him, to them gave he power to become the sons of God, even to them that believe on his name...
   > —John 1:12, KJV

6. **Follow Jesus.**
   a) By getting baptized in water:

   > He who believes and is baptized will be saved.
   > —Mark 16:16, NKJV

> After being baptized, Jesus came up immediately from the water; and behold, the heavens were opened, and he saw the Spirit of God descending as a dove and lighting on Him ...
> —Matthew 3:16, NASB

b) By seeking and receiving the baptism of the Holy Spirit:

> They were all filled with the Holy Spirit, and began to speak in foreign languages according as the Spirit gave them words to utter.
> —Acts 2:4, WNT

7. **Determine.** Finally, we must determine to live a life which is totally sold out to God by obeying His Word, by asking God for help, and by never, ever going back on this commitment.

> Wherefore, my beloved ... work out your own salvation with fear and trembling.
> —Philippians 2:12, KJV

By now, I trust you have accepted the free gift of salvation, or that you will be giving very serious thought to doing so. If you would like to receive the gift of salvation, repeat the following prayer out loud wherever you are:

> Dear Jesus, I believe that You are alive and that You are God's Son. Jesus, I am sorry for the sin in my life and I'm asking you to forgive me and cleanse me from all my sin. Jesus, I believe that You died on the cross for my sins, that You were buried in a grave, and three days later You arose from the grave. Jesus, come and take control of my life and live in me. I believe that You arose to bring me abundant life and I receive that abundant life. I now believe that I have received Your free gift of salvation. I pray this in Jesus' name. Amen.

So what happens when we get connected or accept the free gift of salvation? Well, upon confessing with our mouth that we receive Jesus to come and live in our heart, our spirit connects to and plugs into the Spirit of God (Jesus' Spirit). Our spirit actually comes out of a state of dormancy, meaning that we were asleep but then made awake or alive with the power of the Spirit of God. In other words, our spirit receives the ability to relate to the Spirit of God, whereas before it could not relate to God.

We can now choose to be attuned to the Spirit of God or we can choose to live as before, in the soul realm. If we choose to live in the soul realm, our relationship and experience with God will never grow, and may eventually disintegrate to the place where we were before we accepted Jesus as our Saviour. However, if we choose to stay attuned to God, which is what we're going to discuss in the next chapter, we will experience the abundant, blessed life of a child of God.

Chapter Five:

Staying Connected

At this point, I trust that you've already made Jesus the major influence in your life by connecting your spirit to the Spirit of God through Jesus Christ. When we first connect to the Spirit of God, by believing in Jesus and confessing our commitment to Him, our spirit comes alive to God's Spirit and His realm. Wow!

Recalling the laptop computer analogy in a previous chapter, if we don't keep the power plug connected the battery soon dies. So it is with us; if we don't keep our spirit connected to God's Spirit, our spirit dies or goes back to a dormant or sleeping state. Hence, we are no longer living in touch with God's Spirit realm; we are living in the realm of the soul. I will explain how to maximize our spirit-led life as I proceed.

So How Do We Stay Connected?

I'm going to give you six ways or disciplines which will help you to keep your connection with God alive and well on a daily basis. These are not laws, but rather ways to build our relationship with God. I'm going to list them here, and then expand on each one to give insight into how to function in each area:

- Hungering after God.
- Reading God's Word.
- Prayer.
- Praise and worship.
- Dealing with sin.
- Practicing the presence of God.

1. Hungering After God

All of us have experienced hunger at some time or another: our stomachs growl and feel uncomfortable, and some of us even get faint and tired. Of course, we know that the pangs of hunger will subside and go away if we eat food and fill our stomachs. In the same way, it's important for our spiritual stomachs to growl, feel uncomfortable, and want to be fed. What do I mean by this? We need to have a hunger and desire to know God in a greater way then we currently do. In other words, we never really do arrive at knowing all there is to know about God; God is so great and vast that we can never know Him in all His fullness and greatness in this life.

Without a hunger to experience and know God, our lives as Christians will be dead and dry spiritually, lacking in God's abundance. God doesn't just lavish His blessings upon us because we are Christians; He wants to see that we really do want a closer relationship with Him.

As an example of how God works in this area, I received the baptism of the Holy Spirit with an anointing when I was thirteen years of age. I wasn't properly discipled and taught regarding this new experience from God. After a number of years, I lost the experience—and the anointing that came with it.

For many years, I lived a very mediocre so-called Christian life, never having a desire for that baptism experience to be renewed. When I began once again to put God first in my life, to live for Him day by day, I wanted the baptism of the Holy Spirit experience to be renewed in my life again. As much as I prayed for it, nothing happened. After many years of seeking the return of this experience, I finally asked the Lord what was wrong. Why was I unable to receive the renewal of this experience? God answered, "Do you really want it, and are you going to do what it takes to keep it this time?"

Finally, I knew that I had to have a deep hunger and desire for the return of this experience. Then God would restore it to me—and that's what happened! The same is true of our desire to experience and know God; we must have a deep hunger and desire within us, and when we get that desire, He will begin to fill us to overflowing. If you don't have the desire, ask God for it and He will be faithful to give it to you. Look at the following scripture for a confirmation of God's desire to fill us if we are hungry:

Blessed are those who hunger and thirst for righteousness, for they will be filled.

—Matthew 5:6, NIV

2. Reading God's Word

My people are destroyed for lack of knowledge...

—Hosea 4:6, KJV

Here are some questions I would like to ask regarding the Bible. I'm not going to answer them right now, because each is a Bible study in itself. I just want to provoke some thought.

- How can you know what God's Word says if you don't read it?
- How can God's Word be a guide for your life if you don't know what it says?
- How do you know who God is?
- How do you know who you are in God's eyes?
- How do you know what God wants to give you and do for you?

Let me see if I can challenge you further by asking some more questions about God:

- Does God do evil?
- How come God heals some people from sickness but not others?
- What does it mean to hide God's Word in our hearts?
- Does God want you to be rich?
- Do arguing, strife, and disagreements affect God's blessing on your life?
- Is revelation and new understanding from God's Word only for pastors and leaders?
- What does it mean to be worldly as a Christian?
- I'm a new creature in Christ, but I still sin... how does that work?

In order to answer these and many other questions, we must study God's Word daily, or as often as we can. It's not important to read a lot of Scripture at a time, unless you want to. It is important to meditate or think on the scriptures we read. It's important to digest what we read and begin to memorize it, especially those verses which stand out to us. It is absolutely necessary to apply the Word to our lives and begin to live it. We should speak the Word (speak it out loud, preferably) and take it as ours, as we are encouraged to do in the following verse:

> So then faith comes by hearing, and hearing by the word of God.
> —Romans 10:17, NKJV

This means that our faith ability is increased when we hear the Word of God. John 1:1 says, *"In the beginning was the Word, and the Word was with God, and the Word was God"* (KJV). When we confess the Word, we're actually speaking Jesus or God and His power into our lives. By speaking or confessing the Word, we're also building our faith to the point where we latch on to the Word as ours. This enables us to live according to the Word and what it says. When we speak God's Word, we should actually be aware that we're speaking agreement with His Word. We should be bringing His Word to mind at every opportunity throughout the day. Take God's Word as yours to live by and experience.

> But He answered and said, It is written, "Man shall not live by bread alone, but by every word that proceeds out of the mouth of God."
> —Matthew 4:4, MKJV

In the above verse, we're encouraged to know what the Word says. Look at the verse again—we are not to live by bread or food (meat and potatoes, pasta, and apple pie) alone, but by God's Word. Food feeds our physical bodies to keep us healthy. God's Word feeds our spirit to keep it in relationship with Him—to keep our spirit healthy and well. Further, the word "live" means to conduct our lives the way God has instructed us in His Word. We are to pattern our lives according to the examples and instructions God has given to us in His Word. After all, this is what Jesus is telling us to do.

In the parable of the seed and the sower, Jesus is the sower and His Word is the seed. We read:

> But the ones that fell on the good ground are those who, having heard the word with a noble and good heart, keep it and bear fruit with patience.
> —Luke 8:15, NKJV

Planting the seed in good ground is compared to planting the Word in the heart of someone who accepts it and commits to it at the initial point of salvation. This Word will begin to grow and produce God's blessings. If it is read, meditated on, and believed, just like the seed in the garden when it is watered and fertilized, it produces fruit to be enjoyed. In other words, unless we put the Word into our minds and hearts on a daily basis, by hearing and holding on to it as ours, we cannot grow in our experience with God and His blessing in our lives. It is the Word which produces God's character in our lives—evidence of our spirit being connected with God's Spirit—and which will have the effect of drawing others to Christ. Take a look at the following scripture:

> Then Jesus said to the Jews who believed on Him, If you continue in My Word, you are My disciples indeed.
>
> —John 8:31, MKJV

First let's look at the word "continue," from the Greek word *meno*. According to Strong's Hebrew and Greek Dictionary, it is defined as "to stay (in a given place, state, relation or expectancy)."[21] It follows then that the word "continue" means to stay or remain in the same place. If we apply it to this verse, it means that we are to keep on reading and applying God's Word to our lives.

So, how do we stay in God's Word? Obviously we read it, but more importantly we think on it and determine how we can apply it to our lives. We think about how can we adjust our lives to live like the Word wants us to live, and then we ask God to help us. In addition, we bring Scripture to mind throughout the day.

And what is the reward for obeying God as indicated in the above verse? It says that we are indeed His disciples. Does that mean that we may not be His disciples if we fail to read the Bible? It could be! Think about it. More than anything else, may we be encouraged to read the Bible and apply it to our lives, for then we can be assured of being His disciples.

Understanding God's Word

I'd like to share a little on three prerequisites to understanding God's Word, because I feel it is extremely important to understand and apply what we read

---

21 Ibid., "Meno."

in God's Word. The three prerequisites are hunger, our spiritual condition, and Holy Spirit understanding.

Hunger. Hunger is one of the six disciplines of staying connected, which we have already covered. So rather than repeat it, we will reaffirm our previous discussion. Without a hunger to learn and grow in understanding God's Word, we will not receive much of anything from God. He releases His revelation and understanding to those who are hungry for it.

If you don't have a hunger for the Word, ask God for it. He will be faithful to give it to you. Just look at the following scripture:

> ... but whoever drinks of the water that I shall give him will never thirst. But the water that I shall give him will become in him a fountain of water springing up into everlasting life.
> —John 4:14, NKJV

Our spiritual condition. I was a carpenter for more than twenty years, and during that time I built many houses. If a house is going to stand, it needs to have a good foundation. Houses that have a poor foundation or no foundation at all will eventually collapse, especially if the soil under them has any movement in it at all. An example of the earth moving under a house might be a frost heave or an earthquake. For us, the moving soil is like a temptation, upheaval, or problem in our lives which really affects us. The problem may shake us to our very foundation.

> If the foundations are destroyed, what can the righteous do?
> —Psalms 11:3, NKJV

What do we mean by a foundation, with respect to the Christian life? Just like with a house that has a weak foundation, if we as Christians have a weak relationship with God, we will eventually fall to pieces when problems and difficulties begin to shake and move us. A strong foundation in the things of God means that we have a strong, clear understanding of God's Word, that we know how God wants us to live our lives, that we know what we can expect from God. It also means that we have a very close friendship with God.

Holy Spirit understanding. This prerequisite is related to the second one, but it's important for me to share further on it, as you shall see.

> But the natural man does not receive the things of the Spirit of God, for they are foolishness to him; neither can he know them, because they are spiritually discerned.
>
> —1 Corinthians 2:14, MKJV

We can see from this verse that a natural man or woman cannot understand the things, ways, or Word of God. We learned earlier that a natural man is one whose life is controlled by his soul, without any influence from God's Spirit. Every man or woman born into this world lives as a natural man or woman in the soul realm. They live like this unless their spirits are connected to God by salvation. When this happens, they are able to receive revelation and understanding from God, provided they keep their spirits renewed to God's Spirit.

So how do we renew our spirits? How do we keep our souls and spirits renewed and connected to God's Spirit? We do that by engaging ourselves in the six ways or disciplines itemized above.

3. Prayer

The third discipline of keeping ourselves connected to God is prayer. We should pray or talk to God whenever we can. The Word of God says, in 1 Thessalonians 5:17, that we should *"pray without ceasing"* (NKJV). This means that we should talk to God at every opportunity throughout the day. We can talk to Him about things that are happening around us, things that are going through our minds, and issues we're facing. However, we don't just talk to God when we're having problems or difficulties. It's easy when things are going well to forget about God, and seldom include Him in our daily lives. If we haven't learned to include God in all areas of our lives, we will find it very hard to get through to God when difficulties happen. We should learn to live our lives in connection with God throughout each day. As a result, we will have His Word and His help so that we can handle problems when they come.

There are numerous types of prayer and ways to communicate with and relate to God in our personal lives. It is important to know about them and use them to increase the effectiveness of our prayer lives. Each one provides a different way of relating to God, and zeros in on a different area of our relationship with God.

First, let's deal with the three different types of prayer which we don't want to pray. They are faithless prayer, Pharisaical prayer, and repetitive prayer.

a) The Faithless Prayer

Faithless prayer is a prayer we pray without activating faith. Everything we do as Christians is accomplished with faith. Without faith, we cannot expect to get a favourable answer to our prayers. The following verse defines biblical faith for us.

> ...God, who gives life to the dead and calls those things which do not exist as though they did.
> —Romans 4:17, NKJV

What does it mean to have faith when we pray? As we see in this verse, God's way of faith is speaking that we have what we have asked for even though we cannot see it in the physical realm yet. Prayers that are accompanied by faith are the kind in which we believe that what we ask for will manifest in our lives. When we pray in faith, we speak what we expect to receive and what we're looking for. Praying without faith is really a waste of time, so we need to learn where our faith comes from, and get it working, in order to receive answers to our prayers.

b) Pharisaical Prayer

Pharisaical prayer is one which is prayed with pride and arrogance. It is the prayer of a Pharisee, a prayer to showcase how much better we can pray than others.

> But all their works they do to be seen by men... Woe to you, scribes and Pharisees, hypocrites! For you devour widows' houses, and for a pretense make long prayers... For you are like whitewashed tombs which indeed appear beautiful outwardly, but inside are full of dead men's bones and all uncleanness.
> —Matthew 23:5, 14, 27, NKJV

In Matthew 23, Jesus is exposing the terrible lifestyle of the Pharisees, and He talks about how they pray and conduct themselves. As a result, we can understand that the Pharisees' prayer is really a meaningless flow of words.

They may even be eloquent, but they lack sincerity and trust in God: true prayer comes from a heart of sincerity to God.

Many times I hear people praying to bless a meal, and you would think they were in a race to see how fast they can pray. The words are spoken quickly and with little or no sincerity. This is a type of Pharisaical prayer, which is really a form of religion that displeases God—it is a prayer in which we go through the motions and speak the words, but our hearts fail to express trust in God.

c) Repetitive Prayers

Repetitive prayer are ones in which we ask for the same thing over and over again.

> I have been young, and now am old, yet I have not seen the righteous forsaken or his children begging for bread.
> —Psalms 37:25, ESV

In this psalm, David indicates that he has never seen God's children begging for God's provision. The word "beg" means to ask for money, food, or help as charity. My picture of a beggar is one where a person sits on a street corner with his hand out asking for money. This certainly doesn't illustrate God and His provision for His children. So if we're not to beg or ask God over and over for things, what are we to do?

Well, we've covered three types of prayer we don't want to pray. Now let's look at seven types of prayer we do want to pray. They are request or petition, thanksgiving and praise, worship, agreement, confession, consignment, and authority. The first of these seven types of prayer will answer the question we posed above.

a) Prayer of Request or Petition

This is the most commonly used prayer. It is the one where people make requests and ask God for things they need in their lives. This is the prayer used most often by people who seldom pray. When people have difficulty or desperate situations in their lives, this is how they pray. If we are in the habit of talking to God and bringing our requests to Him, we will have far greater success than if we seldom talk to God. It's often very hard to get through to

God in a difficult situation if you have a skimpy prayer relationship with Him. A healthy prayer relationship with God is developed when we spend time in all types of productive prayer.

Let's look at how God wants us to pray:

> And whatever things you ask in prayer, believing, you will receive.
> —Matthew 21:22, NKJV

In this verse, we need to look at three words in relation to answered prayer. The words are ask, believe, and receive. From Strong's Hebrew and Greek Dictionary, the word "ask," from the Greek word *aiteo*, means "beg, call for, crave, desire, require."[22] From the same dictionary, the word "believe," from the Greek word *pisteuo*, means "to have faith (in, upon, or with respect to a person or thing)"[23] and the word "receive," from the Greek word *lambano*, means "to *take* (in very many applications, literally and figuratively [probably objective or active, to *get hold* of])."[24] Finally, from Webster's dictionary, the word "believe" means "to accept the word of; to accept as true."[25] Remember that it was Jesus who spoke this verse.

Let me use these definitions to paraphrase what Jesus said as follows: "Whatever you ask or make a request for, providing that you accept Jesus' words as being true, you will receive, take, or get a hold of what you asked for."

Let's take a little closer look at this verse. Jesus said that we may "ask," which means to make a request—one request. Next He says that we are to believe, not ask again. Believing means that we can trust and accept that God will come through for us, and that we know we already have what we've asked for. Finally, Jesus says that we are to receive or take whatever we have asked for. How do we take or receive what we have asked for?

The words "believe" and "receive" are linked together when it comes to faith. If we don't believe, we can't receive; and if we believe but don't receive, we can't receive either. Wow! What a mouth full! So what is it that links these two words together? We find it in the following verse:

---

22 Ibid., "Aiteo."
23 Ibid., "Pisteuo."
24 Ibid., "Lambano."
25 *Webster's Canadian Dictionary & Thesaurus* (Toronto, ON: Strathearn Books, 2011), 38.

> For assuredly, I say to you, whoever says to this mountain, "Be removed and be cast into the sea," and does not doubt in his heart, but believes that those things he says will be done, he will have whatever he says.
>
> —Mark 11:23, NKJV

In both of these cases—believe and receive—we accomplish them by the things we say. We must say what we believe, and we must say what we receive, in order to get what we ask for, according to God's Word. The last part of Mark 11:23 says that if we believe what we say, we will have or receive what we say. So in order to receive the answer we're looking for, we must speak that we believe and speak that we receive what we have asked for.

You see, we speak or declare God's Word, which produces the belief. Next, we speak or declare that we receive or have what we've asked for. Of course, our request must line up with God's Word. We get a hold of or receive what we have asked for with the words of our mouths. Therefore, the first time we ask for something, we believe that God has heard us, unless we're ignoring sin in our lives. Next, we believe and speak that we have what we've asked for. Then we take it or receive it with the words we speak with our mouths.

> Let the redeemed of the Lord say so...
>
> —Psalms 107:2, KJV

Remember the question we posed earlier: "If we aren't to beg God, how should we pray?" Here is the answer: Instead of begging God with repetitive prayer, we ask, believe, and receive. This is the best way I know of in which we can experience answered prayer.

Let's take a look at another scripture with regard to the prayer of request or petition, and take our understanding to a higher level:

> This is the confidence we have in approaching God: that if we ask anything according to his will, he hears us. And if we know that he hears us—whatever we ask—we know that we have what we asked of him.
>
> —1 John 5:14–15, NIV

This verse confirms one of the keys to answered prayer, which we have already touched on. This key to answered prayer is to make our request according to God's will. In order to do that, we must know what His will is for the situation we're dealing with. We find God's will in the Bible, God's Word. If our requests agree with God's Word, we will receive the answer we're looking for. Furthermore, this verse actually says that if we ask according to God's will, we know that we have what we've asked for; this means that it is ours.

b) Prayer of Thanksgiving and Praise

> ...giving thanks always for all things to God the Father in the name of our Lord Jesus Christ...
> —Ephesians 5:20, NKJV

Ephesians 5:20 encourages us to always be thankful to God. He does so much for us. We can thank Him all day long. Part of living by faith includes thanking God for His provision for us, even before we have received it. Instead of repetitively asking God for the same thing, we thank Him for it even before we get the answer. This is another way in which we speak and receive the answer.

There is an aspect of praising God which is important. It's essential to include this as part of your praise.

> Let the high praises of God be in their mouth, and a two-edged sword in their hand...
> —Psalms 149:6, NKJV

This verse teaches us that we need to speak our praises of God out loud. The highest form of praise is the praise which is spoken out of our mouths. So let's praise Him for the answer.

c) Prayer of Confession

This prayer is one in which we speak God's promises for and over our lives, and over situations. It increases our faith and ability to receive. If we look at Mark 11:23, we find that it's the things we speak or confess which come to pass and happen in our lives. This is why it's so important to confess or speak God's words instead of our own words.

To illustrate this type of prayer, let's say that we have a power bill to pay, but we don't have the money to pay it. The first thing we do is we find a scripture that declares God's will for the situation. For this situation, we find the following verse:

> But those who seek the Lord shall not lack any good thing.
> —Psalms 34:10, NKJV

I think most of us could agree that God would want us to have our power bill paid. It is impossible in this day and age for us to live in our homes without power. Now that we have a scripture, we begin to confess or speak this scripture for our situation. We could say, "The Lord says that I shall not lack for any good thing; therefore my power bill is paid. Praise the Lord!" There are so many scriptures to choose from, and after a while we get to have our own favourites.

d) Prayer of Agreement

The prayer of agreement is one in which people can band together in unity. They agree with the one making the request from God. They don't make the same request to God; they agree that the request being made is granted.

> And five of you shall chase a hundred, and a hundred of you shall put ten thousand to flight. And your enemies shall fall by the sword in front of you.
> —Leviticus 26:8, MKJV

The above verse describes, by way of illustration, what happens when believers band together in prayer. When God is on your side, five people's prayers are twenty times more effective than one. Effectively, the banding together of just two people in prayer creates a fourfold multiplication of power and effectiveness to succeed in prayer. Wow! What power!

e) Prayer of Worship

The prayer of worship is one in which we give credit to God for who He is with the words of our mouth, like in the following verse:

> For I proclaim the name of the Lord: ascribe greatness to our God. He is
> the Rock, His work is perfect; for all His ways are justice, a God of truth
> and without injustice; righteous and upright is He.
> —Deuteronomy 32:3–4, NKJV

We can use verses like this one to acknowledge God and who He is. We express honour, esteem, and respect for God. We talk about His marvellous works in the universe and in our lives. We speak His name and talk of His great goodness. This is the prayer of worship.

f) Prayer of Authority

A prayer of authority is a prayer that uses the power and authority God has given us through Jesus' name.

First of all, who are we going to exert authority over? We exercise authority over the evil spirit realm. Why? It is our mandate as believers to stop or bind up evil. Where does evil come from? It comes from Satan and his evil spirit realm. What are some examples of evil which we can bind or stop?

- An evil spirit of depression upon someone.
- An evil spirit causing someone to be addicted to something.
- Someone disrupting a godly assembly of believers.

Where do we get the authority to deal with the evil spirit realm? Let's look at the following verse:

> Behold, I give you the authority to trample on serpents and scorpions,
> and over all the power of the enemy, and nothing shall by any means
> hurt you.
> —Luke 10:19, NKJV

From this verse, we can see that we have authority over Satan and his evil spirit realm, and we can stop him from doing evil. In order to exercise our authority, we need to have faith. If we have never used our faith, we need to build our faith ability with the Word of God. Once we are truly confident in the Word of God and the name of Jesus, we can begin to take authority over the evil spirit realm.

We take authority by telling the devil or evil spirit realm what we want him or them to do. Next, we follow our instructions to the enemy with our stamp of authority, the name of Jesus. Let me give you an example: "Satan, take your depression from Johnny and get out of here in the name of Jesus." Once we have spoken to the evil spirit realm in the name of Jesus, we can believe in faith that our command is obeyed and that the depression is gone. Praise God!

Let's look at the prayer of authority a little further:

> For assuredly, I say to you, whoever says to this mountain, "Be removed and be cast into the sea," and does not doubt in his heart, but believes that those things he says will be done, he will have whatever he says.
> —Mark 11:23, NKJV

This verse illustrates God's faith principle of ask, believe, and receive; however, the principal words change from ask, believe, and receive to confess, believe, and receive. First of all, we speak and declare what it is we want to accomplish. Next, we believe that what we spoke is done. Finally, we receive the results by words of confirmation from our mouths. The result is that we get what we speak.

To illustrate, let's say that the devil is tormenting us with fear about something. In this case, we tell Satan to take his fear and leave in the name of Jesus. Notice that we speak this under the authority of the name of Jesus. In order for us to speak with this authority, we must believe that we have the authority of the name of Jesus. Once we speak to Satan, we can affirm that Satan has taken his fear and is gone. Finally, we praise God that the fear is gone and declare that we are filled with the peace of God. Let's look a little further at declare, believe, and receive:

> You will also declare a thing, and it will be established for you; so light will shine on your ways.
> —Job 22:28, NKJV

As we have shared previously, we already know that God will provide what we have requested, because it is His will. When we declare something we cannot yet see, we're essentially expecting that our request has been granted. For example, let's say that we've ask God to heal our back. Next, we begin to praise him for the healing. We declare that by Jesus' stripes our back is healed. Essentially we're declaring what God's Word has already said, and as a result, we will have what we have declared. Isn't it wonderful that God has made it so easy for us to receive from Him if we follow His directions?

We will delve into the area of authoritative prayer in greater detail in Chapter Fourteen.

g) Prayer of Consignment

What does the word consignment mean? To illustrate, let's say that we decided to sell some of our used clothing. We could put an ad on the internet and sell the clothes ourselves or we could take the clothes down to a used clothing store and consign them to the store. By consigning the clothes, we give the store the right to sell them for us, and we share in the proceeds of the sale. Effectively, the store takes over the sale of our clothes. The benefit to us is that we don't have to do the work of selling, but we still get some of the proceeds. Now let's look at the Word and see how to pray prayers of consignment.

> ... casting all your care upon Him, for He cares for you.
> —1 Peter 5:7, NKJV

This verse is the scriptural basis we use when we pray a consignment prayer. Just like the illustration above, we're really consigning or giving the problem over to God. We're letting God do the work, and then we're sharing in the benefits or rewards. What kind of things can we consign to God? An example of something which we should consign or give to God is a bad relationship because of unforgiveness, a lie, gossip, slander, etc.

Anything you cannot resolve on your own is a candidate for consignment to God. So how do we go about consigning things to God? First of all, we forgive whoever is involved in the situation in order to free up God to work. Secondly, we speak and pray blessings on those involved, which helps us to get and keep our hearts right. Finally, we cast or give the situation to God for His resolution of it. Again, we give or consign the situation to God with the words of our mouths.

Let me illustrate what we might say: "God, I have forgiven Mary for gossiping about me. I bless her in the name of Jesus, and I give that situation into Your hands. It is Yours to take care of. It is no longer mine to deal with.

God, thank You that I can depend on You to work out everything for the best, according to Romans 8:28: *"And we know that all things work together for good to those who love God, to those who are the called according to His purpose"* (Romans 8:28, NKJV)."

Prayer in the Spirit

This is another type of prayer which we didn't include earlier, because it is prayed without understanding. All of the ten prayers above were prayed with understanding—we know and understand what we're praying. For those who are baptized in the Holy Spirit, they are encouraged to pray in the spirit, in the following verse:

> But you, my dearly-loved friends, building yourselves up on the basis of your most holy faith and praying in the Holy Spirit ...
> —Jude 1:20, WNT

It is important for us to pray in the spirit daily in our heavenly language, because this is one way that we're able to build up our spirit in the ways of God. By faith, we talk to God in an unknown tongue or language about the things of God, even though we don't know what we're saying. God knows what we're saying, and by faith we understand that we are growing in God, since His Word says so.

The baptism of the Holy Spirit is very important for the Christian life, because it helps us to be able to live and walk according to God's Word in a more powerful way. This gift also opens the opportunity to experience many of the ministry gifts of the Spirit, such as words of knowledge or wisdom, prophecy, and tongues and interpretations.

As much as it is very important to talk to God, it's just as important to listen to Him. We need to take time to be quiet and listen for God's voice, because a balanced friendship or relationship occurs when both parties to the relationship are able to talk and listen. (For more on hearing from God, see Chapter Six.)

Years ago, I had no idea there were seven different kinds of prayer which are prayed with our understanding, and that they can be used in different situations. As a result, many times I ended up approaching God incorrectly. When we pray the right kind of prayer, we are able to pray more effectively.

This enables us to immensely improve our success in receiving positive answers to our prayers.

4. Praise and Worship

Let's deal with these two words—praise and worship—separately. Regarding the word "praise," let's refer to the International Standard Bible Encyclopedia: "The word comes from the Latin pretium "price," or "value," and may be defined generally as an ascription of value or worth."[26] Praise may be bestowed upon unworthy objects or from improper motives, but true praise consists in a sincere acknowledgement of a real conviction of worth.

The following verse is an illustration of praise to God:

> I will bless the Lord at all times; His praise shall continually be in my mouth. My soul shall make its boast in the Lord; the humble shall hear of it and be glad.
> —Psalms 34:1–2, NKJV

In the above verse, the psalmist expresses his purpose in praise. He is determined to constantly speak praises and give thanks always to God. When people are truly committed to praise God, they tend to praise Him more often. True praise is praise which comes from the heart of a person. Of course, we know that the heart is the character of a person.

Those people who have little integrity are disposed to praise God in good times. Sometimes they may even pretend to praise, to give a good impression. True commitment and praise to God mean that we praise Him in difficult times as well as in good times.

I don't think the word praise could be summed up any better than this.

Are there different ways in which to praise God? Let me share some scripture in that regard and elaborate on each verse:

> Sing to Him, sing psalms to Him; talk of all His wondrous works!
> —1 Chronicles 16:9, NKJV

---

26 *International Standard Bible Encyclopedia*, "Praise" (Grand Rapids, MI: Wm. B. Eerdmans Publishing Co., 1979).

Singing choruses, hymns, and psalms to God are several ways we can praise Him. Singing in the spirit is also a way to give praise to God. Another way is to give praise reports and testimonies of God's marvellous works in our lives.

> Shout for joy to the Lord, all the earth, burst into jubilant song with music; make music to the Lord with the harp, with the harp and the sound of singing, with trumpets and the blast of the ram's horn—shout for joy before the Lord, the King.
> —Psalms 98:4–6, NIV

We can shout to the Lord or we can whisper His praises, and we can play musical instruments of all kinds to praise Him.

> I will sing of the mercies of the Lord forever; with my mouth will I make known Your faithfulness to all generations.
> —Psalms 89:1, NKJV

Not only are we to sing praises to God, but we are to speak them audibly out of our mouths. One thing I used to have a problem with, and which seems to be very common amongst some Christians, is a fear of praising God out loud. Many will clap their hands to give praise but hardly ever speak a word of praise out of their mouths. It's very important to let our mouths declare the praises of God. Of course clapping is okay, but we should not default to clapping all the time and leave out audible praise.

> But whoever denies Me before men, him I will also deny before My Father who is in heaven.
> —Matthew 10:33, NKJV

When we fail to give God praise because we're afraid of what others will think, in a sense we're indicating that we are ashamed to praise God out loud. As long as it's done decently and in order, who cares what others think? It's more important to let God know that we love Him by expressing our praise to Him with our mouths.

Let's look at worship next. The International Standard Bible Encyclopedia defines worship as

Honor, reverence, homage, in thought, feeling, or act, paid to men, angels, or other "spiritual" beings, and figuratively to other entities, ideas, powers or qualities, but specifically and supremely to Deity.[27]

In my words, worship of God would be described as showing and expressing respect, reverence, and honour to God.

There is only one Supreme Being, God. Everything else that's worshiped is an idol, a false god or material thing, and worshiping an idol is called idolatry, which is sin. God's requirement for man with respect to worship is seen in the following verses:

> ... for you shall worship no other god, for the Lord, whose name is Jealous, is a jealous God ...
> —Exodus 34:14, NKJV

> You shall have no foreign god among you; you shall not worship any god other than me.
> —Psalms 81:9, NIV

As Christians, we seem to ignore the fact—or maybe we don't understand—that anything we do that exalts itself above God is idolatry. What does God's Word say about it?

> Their land is also full of idols; they worship the work of their own hands, that which their own fingers have made.
> —Isaiah 2:8, NKJV

Examples of some things that could be classified this way are sports, cars, houses, money, music, and pleasure, to name a few. What does it mean to exalt something above God? It means that we spend most of our time participating in and talking about those things, and very little time participating in and talking about the things of God. It means that our heart's desires are mostly focused on the things of the world and hardly on the things of God. When we put all our energy into the things of the world and leave God out, we are committing idolatry. We must learn how to include God in everything we do in life.

---

27 Ibid., "Worship."

One further issue I need to clarify regarding worship is found in the following verse:

> Yet a time is coming and has now come when the true worshipers will worship the Father in the Spirit and in truth, for they are the kind of worshipers the Father seeks. God is spirit, and his worshipers must worship in the Spirit and in truth.
>
> —John 4:23–24, NIV

Worshiping in spirit means that the worship flows out of our spirit, which is connected to the Spirit of God. If we have not taken the time each day to keep our spirit in touch with God, our worship will flow out of the soul (the flesh), and this kind of worship isn't pleasing to God, as we can see in the following verse:

> So then they that are in the flesh [a soul lacking in contact with God's Spirit] cannot please God.
>
> —Romans 8:8, KJV

Here are some of the ways we can worship God:

- We can get down on our knees as an act of submission to the Lord.
- We can raise our hands as an act of surrender to the Lord.
- We can bow our heads in reverence to God.
- We can take time to be quiet and wait on the Lord.
- We can express the scriptures in an attitude of worship (an example would be to personalize or pray the scriptures).

Now, let's consider the words praise and worship together. As children of God, it's important for us to take time to worship and praise God on a daily basis. It's especially important for us not to be afraid to give our praise and worship out loud, with our mouths. This is something many Christians struggle with. When we utter praise and worship out loud, we put the devil on the run, because praise and worship releases the power of God in our lives. Singing, clapping our hands, dancing, and playing instruments are also ways to praise and worship God, but they should not replace audible praise and worship, since this is the highest form of praise and worship.

> Let the high praises of God be in their mouth, and a two-edged sword in their hand...
> —Psalms 149:6, NKJV

We build our faith and confidence in God, and in the marvellous promises in His Word, when we praise and worship God for the good things which He has done. We praise and worship God for things we believe for in faith and things which we haven't yet experienced in the natural realm. This is a good way of confessing our confidence in the answer we expect to receive and experience.

Finally, praise and worship of God during times of difficulty or trial are a way for us to express our faith. By this, we're affirming that the Word of God is working in our lives to bring about the victory we're looking for. This builds confidence in the fact that God is going to work out the difficulty for our good, just like His Word promises:

> Now thanks be to God, who always causes us to triumph in Christ...
> —2 Corinthians 2:14, MKJV

Why wouldn't we want to praise and worship God? Just think of all the wonderful things He has done for us, and then think of the marvellous things He is going to do for us in the days ahead, according to His Word. We have every reason in the world to praise and worship God. Begin to do it often every day, and just watch what God will do in your life!

5. Dealing with Sin

This is an extremely important area of our lives that is often overlooked. If we don't deal with the sin in our lives, we certainly will not stay connected to the Spirit of God—and we certainly will find it hard to hear from God.

> If I regard [have] iniquity [sin] in my heart, the Lord will not hear me...
> —Psalms 66:18, KJV

If we have offended the Lord or another person, if we have unforgiveness against God or someone else, or if we have known unrepented sin in our lives, we will not hear from God. If God has asked us to do something and we have not done it, we become guilty of the sin of disobedience to God. Again, we should not expect to receive from God. The Holy Spirit will not stop doing His work of bringing our sin to mind, however, so that we can deal with it.

Let's take a look at the following scripture regarding offences and unforgiveness:

> ... but if you do not forgive others their offences, neither will your Father forgive yours.
>
> —Matthew 6:15, WNT

According to the above, if we don't forgive others for the things they have done wrong against us, our sins will not be forgiven either. This means we have not been redeemed and aren't entitled to enter the Kingdom of Heaven. I think you would have to agree that this is pretty serious stuff.

Let's just read through the following parable, which Jesus shared:

> Therefore, the kingdom of heaven is like a king who wanted to settle accounts with his servants. As he began the settlement, a man who owed him ten thousand bags of gold was brought to him. Since he was not able to pay, the master ordered that he and his wife and his children and all that he had be sold to repay the debt.
>
> At this the servant fell on his knees before him. "Be patient with me," he begged, "and I will pay back everything." The servant's master took pity on him, canceled the debt and let him go.
>
> But when that servant went out, he found one of his fellow servants who owed him a hundred silver coins. He grabbed him and began to choke him. "Pay back what you owe me!" he demanded.
>
> His fellow servant fell to his knees and begged him, "Be patient with me, and I will pay it back."
>
> But he refused. Instead, he went off and had the man thrown into prison until he could pay the debt. When the other servants saw what had happened, they were outraged and went and told their master everything that had happened.
>
> Then the master called the servant in. "You wicked servant," he said, "I canceled all that debt of yours because you begged me to. Shouldn't you have had mercy on your fellow servant just as I had on you?" In anger his master handed him over to the jailers to be tortured, until he should pay back all he owed.

> This is how my heavenly Father will treat each of you unless you forgive your brother or sister from your heart.
> —Matthew 18:23–35, NIV

We see that the unforgiving servant was delivered to the torturers (the devil and his angels). Then, in the last verse, Jesus says that the same thing will happen to us if we're not willing to forgive those who have sinned against us. Once again, we see that the sin of unforgiveness draws us away from God and His kingdom, into the kingdom of darkness. There are very serious consequences to the sin of unforgiveness! This is a good example of how we can give Satan an opportunity to oppress or afflict us because we have sin in our lives.

So we have dealt with the sin of unforgiveness, but what about the sin of disobedience? Let me share with you an experience from my own life in which I disobeyed God and paid the price.

Many years ago, when my older children were in high school, my wife and I sold our travel trailer. It was getting old and we wanted to replace it. We decided that we would like to have a motorhome. Upon looking around, we found a place that rents motorhomes. With this company, we could purchase the motorhome, they would rent it out, and then we would split the revenue with the company. In this way, we wouldn't have to make payments on the motorhome.

To make a long story short, I asked God if we should buy the rental motorhome. His answer was no. I called the salesman with the purpose of telling him we would not proceed. However, he invited us down to discuss the matter and we made the mistake of going to meet him. As a result, he talked us into purchasing it. Well, most of the things he promised us didn't happen. Instead we only got to use it in the off-season; otherwise we wouldn't earn enough rent to make our payments.

Next thing you know, there wasn't enough rent anyway, and we couldn't afford the motorhome anymore. We ended up selling it for a big loss and having to carry a loan with the bank even after we had sold it. All of this happened at a time when we were struggling financially. When we're disobedient to God and His Word, and not paying attention to His voice, sometimes our sin allows the enemy to bring difficulty or even tragedy into our lives.

> But Jeremiah said, "They shall not deliver you. Please, obey the voice of the Lord which I speak to you. So it shall be well with you, and your soul shall live."
>
> —Jeremiah 38:20, NKJV

From the above, it's safe to conclude that we must make sure we are hearing the Lord when He speaks to us, and most importantly obey Him. It is especially important for us to become aware of sin in our lives so we can deal with it immediately. God is very merciful and patient, but if we ignore the Lord's repeated attempts to get our attention with regard to sin, it can have dire consequences. If we make the effort and our hearts are right, God will reward us with His blessing and a long life.

Now that we have dealt with offences, unforgiveness, and disobedience to God, let's turn our attention to *"the lust of the flesh"* (Galatians 5:16). This issue seems to be misunderstood by some Christians, and I believe God would have me deal with it here. "The lust of the flesh" has been interpreted by many to mean sexual sins only, but that is not so. Let's look at the meaning of the word "lust" as found in Strong's Hebrew and Greek dictionary. It comes from the Greek word *epithumia* which means "a *longing* (especially for what is forbidden) ... concupiscence, desire, lust (after)."[28] The word concupiscence, also from the Greek word *epithumia*, means "to set the *heart upon*, that is, *long* for (rightfully or otherwise) ... covet, desire, would faint, lust (after)."[29] Therefore, the phrase "the lust of the flesh" encompasses much more than sexual sin. It includes longing for and setting one's heart on things that please the soul (the flesh)—things like sports, money, music, toys, sex, and worldly pleasures. Anything we desire more than God is the lust of the flesh, and it is sin.

The best plan I've found is to ask God, on a regular basis, if there is any sin or offences in my life that should be dealt with. If so, we must be quick to repent (be sorry for and turn away from the sin). As well, we must ask for forgiveness of God and of people, if they are involved. When the Holy Spirit impresses a sin or offence upon your mind, don't procrastinate; deal with it as soon as possible. Immediately is better.

---

28 James Strong. *Strong's Dictionaries of the Hebrew and Greek Words*, "Epithumia" (Nashville, TN: Abingdon Press, 1890).
29 Ibid.

If the name of a person, or an action that occurred with that person, comes to mind, deal with it by asking for God's forgiveness. As well, contact that person and ask for forgiveness and make amends. When sin, names of people, and events come to mind, the Holy Spirit is speaking to you. You may want to do this several times a week for the first while. Afterward, it would be a good idea to keep this practice in mind and maybe do it once or twice a month. I still ask God on a regular basis if there's sin in my life, even after having done this for many years. It's important for us to keep our lives clean and pure before God.

Dealing with sin in our lives is a very important aspect of our relationship with God. Sin hinders the relationship and stops the flow of God's blessings in our lives. We must keep our lives free from sin by repenting of sin as soon as we're aware of it.

Finally, in an effort to keep our lives pure, we should ask the Lord to show us things He wants to change or improve in our lives. We should also ask for His help in making the changes. Then, at every opportunity, we should express thanks and praise to God for all He has done and is going to do in our lives.

6. Practicing the Presence of God

Practicing the presence of God is the process whereby we discipline ourselves to be aware of God's presence in our lives, moment by moment, every day. There are many places in the New Testament where we are urged to walk in the Spirit, the awareness of God's presence, throughout every day, such as in Galatians 5:16:

> I say then: Walk in the Spirit, and you shall not fulfill the lust of the flesh. (NKJV)

To be more specific, the process of keeping ourselves in the presence of God is accomplished with the mind. Let me share seven steps that will help us be successful:

- We need to have a desire to live in the awareness of God's presence.

- We start off the day by spending time in the first five steps of staying connected, especially Bible reading and prayer.
- We keep our minds aware of God by purposely talking to Him about everything in life, by thinking on His Word, and by applying His Word to our lives.
- We learn scriptures that apply to our daily lives and practice confessing or speaking them often throughout the day.
- We practice bringing God into our decisions and directions, even the small ones, where the right decision or direction is not obvious in His Word.
- As well, the awareness of God's presence is heightened by praise and worship and by thanking God for His presence throughout the day.
- A further increase in experiencing God's presence is brought about by praying in our heavenly language every day.

Earlier in this chapter, I mentioned a number of excuses or reasons for not having time for God. It would be good for believers to spend a couple of hours every day taking time for God. However, those who have busy lives, with families to raise, jobs, businesses, and other activities, don't have time to block off a couple of hours every day to seek God. I have found that spending thirty minutes to an hour every morning, in the first five steps of staying connected, gets the day started right. Throughout the rest of the day, I take every possible moment to acknowledge God and practice His presence in my life. This adds up to a fair amount of time. It's a matter of disciplining ourselves to experience God's presence and recognize that He is present with us by His Spirit all the time.

As we purposely do the things in the above paragraphs, they become commonplace every day in our lives.

We must choose to invite God's Spirit into our every situation, and thus we will experience a life that's led by God's Spirit. Whatever you do, don't allow these things to become an action without heart and meaning. This is how I and many other men and women stay in touch with God most of the time and keep our spirits connected to the Spirit of God. So take these things I have shared and begin to do them. You will experience the abundant blessing of living in God's presence on a daily basis.

Six Areas of Concern

Before we go any further, I would like to bring some clarity and understanding to six areas of concern which are important with regard to staying connected to God. These concerns will confirm our need to live in the six disciplines of the Christian life.

The six areas of concern are:

1. Work out your own salvation
2. Eternal security
3. Greasy grace
4. Deceptive Christianity
5. Repetitive sin
6. Our free will

1. Work Out Your Own Salvation

In order to bring clarity to God's gift of salvation to us, we must understand the subject of salvation by works. Salvation is a gift from God, the gift of His Son Jesus coming into our lives by connecting our spirit to His Spirit. This gift is not obtained by any work or effort from us, the recipients. The only thing we have to do is to receive the gift. This is confirmed in the following verse:

> If you declare with your mouth, "Jesus is Lord," and believe in your heart that God raised him from the dead, you will be saved.
> —Romans 10:9, NIV

Salvation is a totally free gift from God; however, the works part of salvation begins after we have received the free gift. It means we have to do something: we are not given this free gift just to sit on it and do nothing. From the very first moment we receive salvation, we are to begin the works part of salvation. This means that we are to begin to pursue a close relationship with God and His Son Jesus. Let's look at this verse first:

> Jesus said to him, You shall love the Lord your God with all your heart, and with all your soul, and with all your mind.
> —Matthew 22:37, MKJV

A close relationship requires love and the need to live that love in the relationship. Think of how we relate to our close friends for a moment. We call them by phone, we text them, we Facebook them, we play games, and we get together to talk to them in order to get to know them. We do acts of kindness and help them in times of need. Developing a close relationship with God is very similar, but instead of phoning God we talk to Him or pray to Him. We ask Him for direction in our lives. We worship, praise, and thank Him for all the things He has done and is doing for us. As well, because God is our Heavenly Father, we respect Him for who He is.

> But He answered and said, It is written, "Man shall not live by bread alone, but by every word that proceeds out of the mouth of God."
> —Matthew 4:4, MKJV

The words that proceed out of God's mouth are found in the Bible. We shouldn't just be filling our stomach with food to live by; we should be feeding on the Bible, which is God's Word. We need God's Word to feed our spirit. Feeding on it means reading the Bible, thinking on what we have read, and applying it to our lives. We read God's Word so that we can learn about God and how to live God's way.

> Therefore be imitators of God, as His dear children.
> —Ephesians 5:1, WNT

> But be doers of the word, and not hearers only, deceiving yourselves.
> —James 1:22, NKJV

Have you ever had a child repeat every word you said? This is how we are to live our lives. We are to say what God says and do what God does. Let us be imitators, followers of God. After all, Jesus Christ is the head of the church. Who is the church? God's children, the believers in Jesus, are the church. We should be looking to imitate the head, or the leader. God and Jesus have provided the example as to how we are to live. We should be following them as outlined in the Word.

What if we don't take time to get to know God? What if we don't do the things which I have just shared above, such as communication with God, reading His Word, and saying and doing life God's way? To answer these question, let's look at the following scripture:

> For I say to you, that unless your righteousness exceeds the righteousness of the scribes and Pharisees, you will by no means enter the kingdom of heaven.
> —Matthew 5:20, NKJV

In examining this scripture, let's take a look at the word "righteousness." After seeing the definitions from Strong's Dictionary and the International Standard Bible Encyclopedia, I have come up with a paraphrase for the word "righteousness." It is the action flowing from a willing heart, empowered by the Spirit of God to do and live right according to God's Word. According to this scripture, it would appear that we need to live better than the way the scribes and Pharisees lived in order for us to enter the Kingdom of Heaven. This is kind of a sobering thought, isn't it? How did they live? If we look at Matthew 23, we find many of the characteristics of these people. They were critical, proud, religious, lacking in love, judgemental, unforgiving, and causing offenses. We need to evaluate our lives often to see if these things are prevalent in our lives.

> Wherefore, my beloved, as ye have always obeyed, not as in my presence only, but now much more in my absence, work out your own salvation with fear and trembling.
> —Philippians 2:12, KJV

What does it mean to work out your own salvation? To answer this question, let me list some things we should be doing to work out or build up our salvation experience:

- Reading and meditating in God's Word daily.
- Communicating with God as often as we can throughout the day.
- Praising and worshiping God often.
- Dealing with sin in our lives.

What about the fear and trembling part of Philippians 2:12? The word "fear," from the Greek word *phobos*, in Strong's Dictionary means "morally reverent."[30] In Webster's Dictionary, "fear" means "reverence towards God,"[31] and "reverence" means "awe mingled with respect and esteem."[32] If we apply these meanings to the "fear of the Lord," the definition would go like this: thinking of and treating the Lord with awe, mingled with respect, esteem, and affection.

Let me paraphrase Philippians 2:12. Before I do, let me say that I'm going to use the name Jesus, because it is through His name that we receive salvation. So here is my paraphrase: "We are to live our lives in a way that draws us closer to Jesus, our Saviour. We are to have a healthy respect and honour for our Saviour, Jesus, as indicated by fear and trembling." This is my simplified way of stating how we are to grow in our salvation experience.

> But speaking the truth in love, may grow up into him in all things, which is the head, even Christ...
> —Ephesians 4:15, KJV

What does it mean to grow up into Him in all things? To answer that, let me list some things we should be doing to grow in our salvation experience and walk with Jesus:

- Reading and meditating in God's Word daily.
- Communicating with God as often as we can throughout the day.
- Praising and worshiping God often.
- Dealing with sin in our lives.

I might sound like a broken record, but these are extremely important parts of a healthy Christian life, which is why I have repeated them.

Finally, in Philippians 2:12, working out our salvation means to begin to live a life of faith in God's abundant provision, not toiling or striving but resting in God's Word, blessing, and provision.

---

30 Ibid., "Phobos."
31 J.B. Foreman, MA, *The Webster Worldwide Dictionary* (Great Britain: William Collins Sons & Co. Ltd., 1960), 192.
32 Ibid., 414.

The just shall live by faith.

—Galatians 3:11, KJV

This particular directive from the Lord is found four times in the Bible, which seems to indicate its importance. It means that as Christians, our lives are to be lived out by faith in God and His Word. We begin the faith walk when we first accept Jesus Christ into our lives, by connecting our spirit with His Spirit, as previously discussed.

The next step we should take is water baptism. Again, in faith, when we go down under the water, our old life (soul man) dies and we come up out of the water as a new creature (spiritual man) in Christ. This act of obedience to God is part of our spirit awakening. However, it doesn't mean that we are now living fully spirit-led lives.

Next, we seek the baptism of the Holy Spirit, which empowers us spiritually to live the Christian life to the fullest. This is also received by faith. Spiritual growth, healing, financial abundance, protection, and emotional balance are all received by faith.

I would like to reiterate that upon receiving the free gift of salvation, we are expected to pursue, obey, and serve God in every area of our lives. This is the works part of our salvation journey.

2. Eternal Security

Our ability to live as believers and receive God's promises is affected by some of the things which have been taught in some churches and denominations over the years. There is a way of teaching many of us have been exposed to, with respect to our relationship with God, which I would like to deal with here.

I want to expose some shortcomings in the way some of the Word is presented, because it tends to lead to false hope and expectations by those who hear it. These teachings give the impression that in order to be spiritual and have a close relationship with God, all we have to do is get saved, attend church services, and read the Bible and pray once in a while. Some even go so far as to say that once you accept Christ as your Saviour, you can never be lost; in other words, you will go to heaven or enter the Kingdom of God regardless of how you live your life on earth. These teachings do not line up with the Bible, as we shall see.

I know that most teachers and preachers don't intend to create this perception, but it happens because they don't place enough emphasis on having a daily relationship with the Lord. People tend to get the "once saved, always saved" impression.

Some whole denominations believe that once you are a believer in Jesus Christ, you can live however you want and still go to heaven; they call this being eternally secure. Don't get me wrong; I believe in eternal security, too, but only for those whose hearts' desire is to have a close relationship with God. As well, they don't just desire a close relationship with God; they develop one.

Many people believe that going to church services, ushering, watching Christian TV programs, and teaching Sunday school will keep them in tune with God. Not so! Don't be deceived. The only way to keep in tune with God is to have a personal, individual relationship and friendship with God. Many think that they are on their way to heaven because they live a good life. We cannot live a good life without being a regular partaker of God's Spirit—preferably daily.

> But we are all [in the soul realm] as an unclean thing, and all our righteousnesses are as filthy rags; and we all do fade as a leaf; and our iniquities, like the wind, have taken us away.
> —Isaiah 64:6, KJV

Upon meditating on this scripture, I've discover that we who are living in a natural, soulish, carnal state are not embracing God's righteousness. Instead, it says that we're unclean and like filthy rags in the way we live. We tend to think we live pretty good lives in our own ability, but not according to this verse.

Now let's look at the following scriptures:

> But he who is joined to the Lord is one spirit with Him.
> —1 Corinthians 6:17, NKJV

> ...even the righteousness of God through the faith of Jesus Christ, toward all and upon all those who believe. For there is no difference...
> —Romans 3:22, MKJV

In 1 Corinthians 6:17, we see that as soon as we accept Christ as our Saviour, our spirit becomes one with His Spirit. Also, in Romans 3:22, when we commit to having faith in Jesus as our Saviour, we become pure and righteous because of that connection; this is available to us because Jesus, God, and the Holy Spirit are one Spirit. We become one in spirit with them. However, this righteousness doesn't manifest in our lives unless we choose to live under the direction of our renewed spirit.

I pray for five minutes every morning, and I get God's Word from my pastor on Sunday. I ask the blessing on our meals at home and I pray when we have needs. Isn't that enough? I have a busy life, and it's hard for me to find time to pray and read God's Word. Between my work, family, social activities, and going to church, my life is full. Did I cover all of the excuses we Christians use? Maybe not, but I think I've covered the most common ones. This is how I lived for too many years, and I know there are a lot of people who profess Christianity who live just like I did.

Don't be deceived! We cannot keep up a relationship with God and His Son Jesus with this kind of lifestyle. Brothers, sisters, and friends, you are in jeopardy and walking on dangerous ground. You are in danger of losing your salvation. You may not lose your salvation, but you certainly will have little or no reward in heaven, and you certainly won't experience much of God's blessing here on earth.

Once you get to know God's Word well enough, you will discover for yourself what your spiritual condition is really like. Just read and meditate on the scriptures that follow. They will help you to understand your spiritual condition. I've had to make many changes in my life to align myself with the Word of God and be obedient to live the way He wants me to live. We need to make some changes when we are convicted, changes that will move us closer to God.

> For if we would judge ourselves, we should not be judged.
> —1 Corinthians 11:31, KJV

In this verse, we are encouraged to examine ourselves and look at how we're living our lives in the light of God's Word. As well, in order to be effective in judging ourselves, we need to be objective and make the changes revealed to us through God and His Word.

> If, however, we estimated ourselves aright, we should not be judged. But when we are judged by the Lord, chastisement follows, to save us from being condemned along with the world.
> —1 Corinthians 11:31–32, WNT

In this verse, the writer reminds us that if we always think we're right in the things we do and say, and don't judge ourselves, we will come under God's judgment. God will have to discipline us simply because He is merciful and doesn't want us to be condemned with the world. To be condemned with the world means that we will not be redeemed from the sin of this world, and we will not have eternal life.

Let's get into the Word a little deeper by taking a look at the following verses regarding eternal security:

> Not everyone who says to me, "Lord, Lord," will enter the kingdom of heaven, but only the one who does the will of my Father who is in heaven. Many will say to me on that day, "Lord, Lord, did we not prophesy in your name and in your name drive out demons and in your name perform many miracles?" Then I will tell them plainly, "I never knew you. Away from me, you evildoers!"
> —Matthew 7:21–23, NIV

Matthew 7:21 says that only those who do the will of God will enter the Kingdom of Heaven. What does it mean to do the will of our Father which is in heaven? Jesus did the will of His Father, God, who is our Father as well. Doing the will of God really means living and obeying the Word of God on a daily basis. It means living our lives the way God directs us with His still, small voice. Furthermore, it means that when we serve God in His work, we know undoubtedly that He has asked us to do it.

> A Song of Ascents. Of Solomon. Unless the Lord builds the house, those who build it labor in vain. Unless the Lord watches over the city, the watchman stays awake in vain.
> —Psalms 127:1, ESV

It doesn't matter what we say or how much we've asked God to bless our work if we haven't heard from God. If we haven't been told by Him to do the work, it isn't His work. As we can see in Psalms 127:1, any work we do outside God's will is useless; it will accomplish nothing. God is not in that work with us, and therefore the work will not bear fruit. Can you see how important it is that we know undoubtedly that we are in God's plan and doing God's will?

Now, let's look to the one from whom we are to take our example—Jesus. In the following verse, we will see how we can determine undoubtedly that we are doing God's will and work.

> But the testimony which I have is weightier than that of John; for the work the Father has assigned to me for me to bring it to completion—the very work which I am doing—affords testimony concerning me that the Father has sent me.
> —John 5:36, WNT

First of all, here we see that the very work Jesus was doing gave testimony that God had called and sent Him to do that work. What was the testimony Jesus alluded to regarding the work He was doing? His testimony was one of deliverance, salvation, and healing. Everywhere He went people were set free from darkness, disease, and bondage into the glorious light and liberty of God. What a testimony! Our fruit or testimony will show whether our work has been sanctioned by God.

> Do you not believe that I am in the Father, and the Father in Me? The words that I speak to you I do not speak on My own authority; but the Father who dwells in Me does the works.
> —John 14:10, NKJV

Secondly, in John 14:10, Jesus indicates that He is not speaking His own words with His own authority; rather, God was doing the work through Him with God's authority and words. This means that we need to be speaking God's words with God's authority in the things we do for God. So how do I know that it is God's words I'm speaking? Furthermore, how do I get God's authority in the things I do for Him? These are both very good questions that need to be addressed in order to understand how we know whether we're in God's will.

Let me answer the first question. In order to speak God's words, we need to know His Word as found in the Bible. We must also be spiritually at the place where we're able to hear God's still, small voice.

Now let me answer the second question. In order to operate in God's authority, we need to understand who we are in Christ. We need to be able to operate in faith, we must be spiritually rich in our relationship with God so He can speak and work through us, and we need Holy Spirit boldness to perform God's works with authority. In both cases, speaking God's Word and operating in His authority require us to spend considerable time with God, preparing our spirit for God's work through us.

Let me summarize what we have just covered with respect to knowing that we're doing God's work:

- We must know that it is God's work.
- The words we speak must come from God.
- The testimony and results of our work will reveal if it is God's work.
- We will have God's authority in the work if we prepare ourselves spiritually.

In Matthew 7:23, the Lord says, "I never knew you." Obviously these people didn't have a relationship with the Lord. It appears that these people who thought they were working for God were doing it in their own natural strength without God, because they never knew Him. Then how can they do miracles when they're operating in the soul or natural realm? Let's read on:

> But I will persist in the same line of conduct in order to cut the ground from under the feet of those who desire an opportunity of getting themselves recognized as being on a level with us in the matters about which they boast. For men of this stamp are sham apostles, dishonest workmen, assuming the garb of Apostles of Christ. And no wonder. Satan, their master, can disguise himself as an angel of light. It is therefore no great thing for his servants also to disguise themselves as servants of righteousness. Their end will be in accordance with their actions.
> —2 Corinthians 11:12–15, WNT

Here, Paul is saying to the Corinthian church that he will continue his work as an apostle; however, it appears that those who were ministering in his absence were boasting that they could minister just as well as Paul. They were trying to build themselves up in the eyes of the Corinthians. Paul calls these braggarts, false apostles who were making themselves look like apostles of Christ. Paul then explains that Satan does the same thing; he parades around looking like he has the light. He performs miracles which appear to come from God.

From these verses, we learn that not all miracles are of divine origin—and not all miracle workers are empowered by God. A miracle simply means that a supernatural power is at work. The power may be divine or satanic. Satan may empower his workers to prophesy and do miracles in order to create the illusion that the miracle is from God. Some may think that he is dividing his kingdom, but Satan is a master at deception. He is not dividing his kingdom against itself, but he is plotting an even worse invasion of demons, or an even worse situation in the future.

Therefore, with regard to people doing miracles, people in general (including those who call themselves Christians) can be used by Satan to perform miracles. They have opened themselves up to Satan's spiritual influence because of their lack of relationship with God. The devil can make the work appear like God's work. These people operate under Satan's authority to perform miracles. They actually work or operate in the evil realm, with Satan's spiritual influence, instead of in the realm of the Spirit of God. The result of this work is deception, and it eventually leads to the death and destruction of the soul.

Once again, in Matthew 7:23 we see that Jesus refused to give these so-called Christian workers entrance into the Kingdom of Heaven, because they were working in sin, not doing God's will. What does it mean to work in sin or iniquity, even when we think we're serving the Lord? It means that God didn't ask us to do the work we're doing. Therefore, this work is being done because we want to do it, and it isn't God's work or will at all. Since we call the work God's work when it isn't, we are misrepresenting God and profaning His name. We are calling evil good and perpetrating deception upon those who experience and see the works. When we do work outside God's will, we don't come under the influence of God's Spirit to accomplish the work; we do the work in our own natural strength. The people referred to in Matthew 7:23 were operating largely in the realm of the soul, or the natural man, with the assistance of the evil spirit realm, pleasing man or themselves rather than God.

Attempting to do God's work without His power and approval is a recipe for disaster. It places one at the disposal of Satan and his deceitful devices. Eventually it leads to death. Ultimately, professing Christians and church workers who aren't in the will of God are not destined for the Kingdom of God, and therefore they are not eternally secure.

In sharing on the subject of eternal security, we had to take a side trip to deal with the issue of people who perform miracles but aren't getting into the Kingdom of Heaven. Now let's get back to the subject of eternal security more directly. If you're not sure and are wondering whether a saved soul can lose his or her salvation, look into the many scriptures which refer to that situation. I have included references from eight different books in the New Testament:

> And you will be hated by all for My name's sake. But he who endures to the end will be saved.
>
> —Matthew 10:22, NKJV

> I am the true vine, and My Father is the vinedresser… If anyone does not abide in Me, he is cast out as a branch and is withered; and they gather them and throw them into the fire, and they are burned.
>
> —John 15:1, 6, NKJV

> God "will repay each person according to what they have done." To those who by persistence in doing good seek glory, honor and immortality, he will give eternal life. But for those who are self-seeking and who reject the truth and follow evil, there will be wrath and anger. There will be trouble and distress for every human being who does evil: first for the Jew, then for the Gentile.
>
> —Romans 2:6–9, NIV

> For if God did not spare the natural branches, He may not spare you either.
>
> —Romans 11:21, NKJV

> Now, brothers and sisters, I want to remind you of the gospel I preached to you, which you received and on which you have taken your stand. By this gospel you are saved, if you hold firmly to the word I preached to you. Otherwise, you have believed in vain.
>
> —1 Corinthians 15:1–2, NIV

Take heed to yourself and to the doctrine. Continue in them, for in doing this you will save both yourself and those who hear you.
—1 Timothy 4:16, NKJV

Therefore, since a promise remains of entering His rest, let us fear lest any of you seem to have come short of it.
—Hebrews 4:1, NKJV

And having been perfected, He became the author of eternal salvation to all who obey Him ...
—Hebrews 5:9, NKJV

It is impossible for those who have once been enlightened, who have tasted the heavenly gift, who have shared in the Holy Spirit, who have tasted the goodness of the word of God and the powers of the coming age and who have fallen away, to be brought back to repentance. To their loss they are crucifying the Son of God all over again and subjecting him to public disgrace.
—Hebrews 6:4–6, NIV

For if we go on sinning deliberately after receiving the knowledge of the truth, there no longer remains a sacrifice for sins, but a fearful expectation of judgment, and a fury of fire that will consume the adversaries.
—Hebrews 10:26–27, ESV

See that you do not refuse Him who speaks. For if they did not escape who refused Him who spoke on earth, much more shall we not escape if we turn away from Him who speaks from heaven ...
—Hebrews 12:25, NKJV

For if after they have escaped the pollutions [wickedness] of the world through the knowledge of the Lord and Saviour Jesus Christ, they are again entangled therein, and overcome, the latter end is worse with them than the beginning. For it had been better for them not to have known the way of righteousness, than, after they have known it, to turn from the holy commandment delivered unto them. But it is happened unto them

according to the true proverb, The dog is turned to his own vomit again; and the sow that was washed to her wallowing in the mire.
—2 Peter 2:20–22, KJV

Blessed are those who do His commandments, that they may have the right to the tree of life, and may enter through the gates into the city.
—Revelation 22:14, NKJV

To conclude this section on eternal security, let me share eight points which will keep us eternally secure:

- Every believer is a builder; the house he builds is the salvation of his soul.
- The act of receiving salvation initially for our soul is just the beginning of a journey, a journey wherein we are to live in a relationship with God all of our lives.
- We need to grow in our relationship with God until we finally meet with God and His Son Jesus. When Jesus comes to get His saints from this earth, the salvation of our soul will be complete, as we can see in the following verse:

That the trial of your faith, being much more precious than of gold that perisheth, though it be tried with fire, might be found unto praise and honour and glory at the appearing of Jesus Christ… Receiving the end of your faith, even the salvation of your souls.
—1 Peter 1:7, 9, KJV

- In order to stay connected to the Spirit of God, we need to dig deep until we come to a rock, a good foundation; that foundation is Jesus and the Word of God.
- We need to search diligently into Scripture for truth.
- Constantly attend the ministry of the Word.
- Inquire of gospel teachers and other saints the deeper way of salvation. Having found it, we must lay the whole success of our salvation on the rock of ages, which is Christ.

- We make Him the foundation of all our hopes, of our future, and of eternal life, which is the foundation God has laid in Zion, the heavenly city.

This is how we stay eternally secure.

3. Greasy Grace

What is greasy grace? It's the slippery slope of carelessly continuing to sin and expecting God's grace to cover for you. Several years ago, a Christian brother said to me, "We have God's grace to fall back on when we sin." He felt that we are going to sin anyway, so we shouldn't worry about whether we sin or not, but rather just do it and get it over with. After all, God's grace will cover for us.

First of all, we shouldn't even have a desire to sin, and if it happens we should be quick to repent and ask for forgiveness. Our hearts should contain the desire to live without sin if we truly have the love of God dwelling within us. Let's look at the following scripture:

> What shall we say then? Shall we continue in sin that grace may abound? Certainly not! How shall we who died to sin live any longer in it?... What then? Shall we sin because we are not under law but under grace? Certainly not!... But now having been set free from sin, and having become slaves of God, you have your fruit to holiness, and the end, everlasting life. For the wages of sin is death, but the gift of God is eternal life in Christ Jesus our Lord.
> —Romans 6:1–2, 15, 22–23, NKJV

You might want to read that whole passage from Romans 6:1–23. It starts by saying, *"Shall we continue in sin that grace may abound? Certainly not!"* The apostle Paul couldn't have stated it any clearer than this. We can certainly see that it is wrong to continue to live in sin, and therefore it is wrong for us to misuse the grace of God by continuing to sin.

> Don't you know that when you give yourselves to obey someone you become that person's slave? You can be slaves of sin. Then you will die. Or you can be slaves who obey God. Then you will live a godly life.
> —Romans 6:16, NIrV

In this verse, we find that when we sin we actually become a slave, in bondage to sin, which leads to death. Instead we are encouraged to become slaves of God, which leads to a godly life. Sin leads to death, and we have been delivered from sin by the grace of God and the precious work of Jesus on the cross. If we continue to live in sin, we will die (go to sleep) spiritually. How far can we push the grace of God until it no longer covers us?

> And the Lord said, "My Spirit shall not strive with man forever…"
> —Genesis 6:3, NKJV

God is very gracious, no doubt, but there does come a time when He says enough is enough. This is sometimes the reason some Christians die premature deaths. Why would we want to live in sin, produce death in our lives, and miss out on God's abundant blessings?

4. Deceptive Christianity

I've chosen this heading to share what God has laid on my heart by way of revelation. I have lived a deceptive Christian life in the past, and therefore I'm sharing from my experience. If this subject speaks to you, talk to God and ask Him to make the changes He wants in your life. I had to make a lot of changes in mine.

First of all, what does the word "deceive" mean? Webster's Dictionary defines it like this: "to cause to believe what is false, or disbelieve what is true."[33] The word "deceive" means to lead someone to believe something is truth when it is not true.

Next, let me define the term "deceptive Christianity." It's the belief that once we have accepted Jesus as Saviour we are living as spirit-led, godly people all the time. Let us explore this subject from the vantage point of God's Word:

> Therefore, if anyone is in Christ, he is a new creation; old things have passed away; behold, all things have become new.
> —2 Corinthians 5:17, NKJV

---

33 Noah Webster, *American Dictionary of the English Language*, "Deceive" (1828).

When the Bible says that we have become a new creature or creation in Christ, or a new spiritual person in Christ, we have to be careful to understand what it's saying. We effectively become a new creature in Christ when we become believers in Jesus Christ. At this point, our spirit becomes connected to Christ's Spirit, God's Spirit, and the Holy Spirit, which are all one and the same. What actually happens when we become a new creature in Christ is that our spirit is activated to the Spirit of God, or our spirit becomes one with God's Spirit.

Allow me to draw an analogy. A person preparing to drive a car for the very first time must put the key into the ignition and start the motor. When the motor is running, they have to put the car in gear and begin to drive it. In order to learn how to drive the car, they must practice driving the car. Finally, they must show competence by passing a driver's test. If they don't pass the test, they won't be able to drive the car.

Let's relate learning to drive a car to our salvation experience. Starting the car is like accepting Jesus as Saviour—our spiritual motor is ready to run. We are connected to the Spirit of God. Next, we need to put gas into our spiritual tank so that our spiritual motor will run. The kind of gas it needs is found through Bible reading, prayer, praise and worship, and dealing with sin in our lives on a daily basis.

Now that we've fuelled up our spirit, we can begin to drive the car with plenty of fuel to reach our destination. Of course, we must make conscious choices throughout the day to use our spirit and not the natural man, the soul, which is fuelled with the fuel of the world. We can either let our soul or natural man lead our lives or we can let our spirit lead us; it's our choice. We will discuss this in greater depth later in the book.

Many Christians believe that the minute they become a believer, they are spiritual persons, and that all the words they speak and things they do are spiritual, originating from God. That is not the case. The experience of being spirit-led all the time doesn't happen immediately as soon as one becomes a believer, or as soon as one is baptized in water. We learned this from the example of learning to drive a car. The process of becoming a spiritual person who speaks and acts in a godly manner requires the discipline of staying spiritually connected to God—putting spiritual fuel in the tank.

Because it's so important, I'm going to repeat those disciplines again. They are: hungering and desiring after God, being a student of God's Word, communicating with God, praising and worshiping God throughout the day, dealing with sin in our lives quickly, and practicing the presence of God every day. Moreover, our ability to be led by the Spirit is immensely improved after we receive the infilling of the Holy Spirit.

The words "in Christ," found in 1 Corinthians 5:17, mean that we must keep our spirits connected to His Spirit in order for us to speak and act in the realm of Jesus' Spirit. The more we exercise the disciplines of staying connected, the more we will live in the realm of the Spirit of God and not the soul realm.

It seems there are as many opinions on most portions of God's Word as there are Christians. Opinions come from the soul, the natural or carnal man, not the Spirit of God. Differing opinions result from people not having their spirit properly fed by the Spirit of God. In fact, many so-called Christians have little or no connection to God's Spirit. Remember, these things are very hard for me to write; I have been there myself!

It isn't this way with everyone, but it seems like going to church and hanging out with other people of like belief has a tendency to teach the soul how to live rightly or wrongly. It doesn't matter if the pastor is preaching under an anointing of the Holy Spirit; if we haven't taken the time daily to keep our relationship fresh with God's Spirit, we will only be receiving the pastor's message into our soul.

> But the natural man does not receive the things of the Spirit of God, for they are foolishness to him; nor can he know them, because they are spiritually discerned.
>
> —1 Corinthians 2:14, NKJV

Without our spirit being regularly fed and fuelled by God, we cannot really comprehend the Word of God. You see, if we haven't kept ourselves spiritually in tune with God, we will be trying to understand the things of God with the natural man or the soul. This only produces a carnal, soulish understanding of God.

> ...having a form of godliness but denying its power. And from such people turn away!
>
> —2 Timothy 3:5, NKJV

According to this verse, we can go through all the right motions in the soul realm and still lack the power available to us in God's Spirit realm. Without the Spirit of God activated in our lives regularly (preferably daily) and connected to our spirit, we cannot comprehend the Word of God. This is why we have dozens of opinions from churchgoers on almost every portion of the Bible. When Christians are truly connected by their spirit to the Spirit of God, the understanding of the Word will come from God. This is how unity happens among Christians, as we see in the following scripture:

> But he that is joined unto the Lord is one spirit.
> —1 Corinthians 6:17, KJV

No longer are there multiple opinions in understanding the Bible. There is one truth, one interpretation, one understanding, one mind, and one accord, all because of the Spirit of God. This is why the things we have covered in this chapter are so important for all Christians!

It is such a treat to fellowship and share with believers in Christ who have taken the time daily to keep themselves connected to the Spirit of God. We have such a unity and oneness as we talk together about the things of God. It is so sweet! This is how it will be in the Kingdom of God—no divisions or arguments over God's Word, just pure, holy unity in the Spirit. Praise God!

5. Repetitive Sin

Why do so many Christians continually fail in their daily lives by committing the same sins and offences over and over again? I've been there. If you'll be honest with yourself, you have probably experienced repetitive sin as well. Maybe you're still experiencing the problem of committing the same sin over and over again. You're not alone; most Christians do. Let's look at the following scripture:

> And if I do what I do not want to do, I agree that the law is good. As it is, it is no longer I myself who do it, but it is sin living in me. For I know that good itself does not dwell in me, that is, in my sinful nature. For I have the desire to do what is good, but I cannot carry it out. For I do not do the good I want to do, but the evil I do not want to do—this I keep on doing. Now if I do what I do not want to do, it is no longer I who do it, but it is sin living in me that does it.

> So I find this law at work: Although I want to do good, evil is right there with me. For in my inner being I delight in God's law; but I see another law at work in me, waging war against the law of my mind and making me a prisoner of the law of sin at work within me. What a wretched man I am! Who will rescue me from this body that is subject to death? Thanks be to God, who delivers me through Jesus Christ our Lord!
>
> So then, I myself in my mind am a slave to God's law, but in my sinful nature a slave to the law of sin.
>
> —Romans 7:16–25, NIV

The problem of repetitive sin has been with mankind since Adam and Eve sinned in the Garden of Eden. As we can see in these verses, even the Apostle Paul admitted to his weakness in this area. This problem with Christians is largely due to the reality that they're living a mostly soul-directed life with little influence from God and His Spirit.

Adam fell from God's blessing in the Garden of Eden when he committed sin by disobeying God. As a result of this, his soul took on a sin nature which he didn't have before. Adam's sin nature has been passed down to all mankind throughout the generations. After all, where does the sin of speaking nasty words come from? Where does vengeance and hatred come from? Where does unforgiveness come from? It can't come from God, because God is love, so obviously it has to come from the soul of human beings, or sometimes it comes from the devil.

So what is the answer to repetitive sin? In Romans 7:25, the Apostle Paul gives us the answer. His answer is Jesus Christ our Lord. What does that mean? It means that we should be seeking, as Christians, to live our lives with our spirit connected to God's (Jesus') Spirit. It means we should be living a life that's like Christ, following God's Word. As we live our lives with the spiritual man connected to God, we are able to avoid sin. Further, Romans 7:18 says that when we're living in our soulish sin nature, we do not have the power. What power is the apostle talking about? It is the power of God through Christ Jesus. This power enables us to avoid sin. We have already discovered how to live in this power, the power of God, in the six disciplines which we have just finished learning about.

If we cultivate a life in the spirit and power of God, we will turn away from sin and function with little or no sin in our lives, which will move us towards maturity as Christians. That's why I've spent so much time sharing on how we can stay connected to God's Spirit.

6. Our Free Will

I would like to touch briefly on the subject of free will, as it applies to our connection to God.

> I call heaven and earth to witness against you today, that I have set before you life and death, the blessing and the curse. So choose life in order that you may live, you and your descendants...
> —Deuteronomy 30:19, NASB

As we can see in this verse, God has given us the choice of what kind of life we want to live. God didn't make people like puppets whereby they have no control over what they speak or how they think and act.

"Free will" means that we have the ability to say or do what we want in our lives, but we must bear the consequences of our choices. God has given us a free will to choose how to live; we can choose whether or not to stay connected to God. God wants us to use our free will to stay connected to Him. He speaks through our conscience or spirit, and sometimes by His still, small voice, to try and get our attention. If we ignore Him, we open ourselves up to circumstances or difficulties in our lives. If we don't acknowledge God when He's trying to get our attention, we end up under the influence of circumstances, our human limitations, or the devil.

On the other hand, if we use our free will to include God, giving Him control of our lives, we will progress in our relationship with Him. Our progression should include decreasing our reliance on the soul, the natural man (ourselves), and increasing our reliance on our spirit, in tune with God.

As a Christian, we should choose to follow God's direction and will for our lives. This means laying down our own soulish will and desires for God's higher calling and direction in our lives. As a result, we come under God's direction for our lives, because of our obedience to Him. Of course, there is no higher fulfillment in life than to use our free will to live a life in God's will and plan.

Conclusion

In order to stay connected to God, you must be willing to discipline yourself and make it a priority to implement or increase the exercise of the six steps or disciplines I've shared in this chapter. You will be amazed at the difference it will make in your relationship with God, and in your experience of His goodness.[34]

If you've never had this type of a relationship with God, and you fail in your efforts when you try, don't beat up or condemn yourself. Rather, determine to keep trying. To begin with, work on putting one or two of the above steps into action. Maybe start with reading the Bible and praying. Once you get into the habit and become consistent in the first one or two steps, begin to add the others. If you're disciplined and committed to doing these things, you will build a strong, healthy, blessed relationship with God.

---

[34] I have published a booklet called *Tap into God's Promises*, with over three hundred scriptures categorized by life circumstances. It fits into a shirt pocket or purse. As well, I have another booklet of over twelve hundred scriptures called *Winning with God's Promises*. The verses in this booklet are also categorized by life circumstances. I have found these two booklets extremely valuable in building one's faith and seeing the results that God's Word provides.

Chapter Six
Hearing from God

It is important for us to hear from God through His Word, through preachers and other Christians, through dreams and visions sent by God, through circumstances, and finally through God's still, small voice. In order to live our lives in God's will and according to His direction, we must be able to hear from God. Let's look at these five ways by which we can hear from God.

Just as a side note, there are actually two other ways of hearing from God, which is through angels as God's messengers and God's audible voice. We will not be dealing with these in this book. I have chosen to deal with the five which are more common.

Through God's Word

Before we share on how to hear from God through His Word, let me repeat that in order for you to get anything out of the Word of God, you must have a hunger for Him and His Word. Without a hunger and desire to know Him better, the Word will seem very dry and dead. If you don't have a hunger for God's Word, ask Him to give you a hunger for it, and God will be faithful to do this for you. I know, since He did it for me. He'll do it for everyone else who asks.

> If any of you lack wisdom, let him ask of God, that [gives] to all men liberally, and [upbraids] not [does not reprimand]; and it shall be given him.
> —James 1:5, KJV

There is only one place to get true wisdom, and that is from God. The Bible is full of direction from God with regards to every circumstance and situation we might face in life. If you have questions for God about Him or His Word, or if you have questions about life, God wants to answer them.

With respect to hearing from God through the Word, at times I've sat down in need of direction or encouragement from the Lord and I've picked up the Bible and opened it up. My eyes have fallen on a scripture which was exactly what I needed for the moment. In fact, when I do that now, I open the Bible expecting to receive from God. God gave us His Word for our direction, teaching, and encouragement. Maybe I'm not sure how to walk in love with respect to something a pastor has said to me, or maybe one of my Christian friends said words of discouragement to me. Many times I will open my Bible to the place where I'm reading in my daily devotions, and I will read verses which apply directly to my current situation. As I've said before, God's Word does contain answers.

As you read God's Word, ask God to reveal it to you. He will do just that, by His Spirit, the Holy Spirit. Remember, we are only able to receive revelation from God if we take the time to keep our spirit in tune with God's Spirit.

Through Preachers and Other Christians

Many times we hear from God through preachers and other Christians, and it is important for us to remain teachable and open to receive what God is saying through them. As a word of caution, it is also important to test the words that come to us by referring to the Bible, and also by being sensitive to the witness of our spirit, properly connected to God.

> Beloved, do not believe every spirit, but test the spirits, whether they are of God; because many false prophets have gone out into the world.
> —1 John 4:1, NKJV

What does it mean to test the spirits? Basically, it means that we are to determine the spiritual origin of the words being spoken. They can come from the natural man (soul), from the spirit connected to God's Spirit, and from the evil spirit realm.

The only way we can determine which of the three voices we are hearing is to be sensitive and tuned in to the Holy Spirit. Of course, as I've said before, this requires intimacy and closeness with God. However, God looks at the heart of a person. If the heart is desirous of intimacy with God, God will respond to it. New Christians and others who have never developed a close relationship with God can begin to hear God's voice immediately; all it takes is a heart that really desires God. When someone gives us a word, supposedly from God, peace is one of the best ways to know if it is from God. If we have a feeling of turmoil and uncertainty from the word, it's probably not from God. On the other hand, a calm, peaceful feeling generally means the word is from God. However, it is important to keep a close relationship with God all the time, otherwise our own desires apart from God could be massaged by the word. Thus, we accept the word for our own reasons, not God's reasons or purpose. The following three suggestions will help us in our ability to hear from God through others:

- As we have just shared, we should have peace about the word which we've heard.
- As we come into a greater experience of hearing God's still, small voice, we will be able to receive confirmation from God that what we have heard is correct.
- God usually directs our attention to something, then He gives us confirmation through others regarding what He has already said to us.

I can remember a time quite a number of years ago when my wife and I were going through a difficult time financially. We happened to share our situation with a Christian brother at the fellowship we were attending. He proceeded to tell us that he was a prophet and that the words which he prophesied would come to pass. Well, the word of knowledge he proceeded to speak for us was partly right, in that it confirmed what we had already been contemplating. However, he said that we should drop everything and proceed with the decision, even though the timing was wrong at the moment. We did eventually move in that direction, but when the timing was right for us, eight months later. He was quite upset with us, because we didn't proceed immediately, in obedience to his word of knowledge for us.

Please don't allow this experience to prevent you from hearing prophetic words, or words of knowledge or wisdom, which come from God through other people. It is very important for us to remain teachable and open to hear from God in whatever way God chooses to speak to us.

We learned three things from this experience:

- The word of knowledge given to us was partially true. When these words are false or only partially true, they tend to create confusion.

- We learned that we had to have peace about what was spoken.
- Words which come from God can be trusted more readily if the prophet doesn't know anything about your situation.

Many times I have been listening to a preacher, or maybe sitting and having coffee with a brother or sister in the Lord, when I heard them speak a word directly to my situation, a word regarding what the Lord had already been speaking to me. The amazing thing is that these people have no idea they have just spoken into my life. Don't you just love those times?

My experience has proven that the ability to hear God's still, small voice is the best way to weed out confusion, and it's undoubtedly the best way to know God's will and direction. This is why I intend to share on the subject of hearing God's still, small voice, in depth, a little later on.

Through Dreams and Visions

Some people hear from God through dreams and visions, but again, we need to be very much plugged in to God's Spirit in order to discern whether or not the dreams or visions actually come from God.

A dream, as defined by Webster's Dictionary, is "a series of images or thoughts in the mind of a person asleep."[35] My own definition of a vision is "something imagined to be seen, though not real, and which occurs when awake." The major difference between a vision and a dream is that a dream occurs during sleep, and a vision occurs when we are awake.

With respect to dreams, let's turn to the account of Joseph and his life beginning in Genesis 37. Joseph was one of twelve sons of Jacob, who was a descendant of Abraham. Joseph dreamt two dreams in which he saw his father, mother, and his eleven brothers bowing down to him and coming under his authority. Joseph, not realizing the trouble it would cause himself, shared his dreams with his family. Needless to say, his brothers began to hate him, because obviously they were not interested in coming under Joseph's authority. The story of Joseph's life is rather lengthy, so we will try to the get to the point quickly.

As a result of Josephs brothers' hatred for him, and through some very difficult circumstances, Joseph ended up in a foreign country called Egypt. In

---

35 J.B. Foreman, MA, *The Webster Worldwide Dictionary* (Great Britain: William Collins Sons & Co. Ltd., 1960), 159.

spite of his situation, Joseph knew that God was with him. Joseph had faith that somehow the dreams he had dreamt were from God, and that the dreams would come to pass someday. In fact, even the people of Egypt could see that God was with Joseph:

> And his master saw that the Lord was with him and that the Lord made all he did to prosper in his hand.
> —Genesis 39:3, NKJV

Well, wouldn't you know it, one day Jacob and his family realized that they were running out of food because of a great famine in the land—and the only place they could get food was in Egypt. Guess who was in charge of distributing the food in Egypt? Joseph, of course. Joseph's brothers—in fact, Joseph's whole family—ended up under Joseph's authority in Egypt.

With respect to visions, I suggest that you look at Acts 10:1-19. Here, the Apostle Peter experiences two visions related to something God wanted Peter to do for him.

So here we have an example of how God sometimes brings direction through dreams and visions. Does God still do this today? Yes, of course.

Through Circumstances

Some would say that circumstances aren't really direction from God. What about the times when we're ignoring God, and He can't seem to get our attention through the other avenues of communication, such as the Bible, other people, dreams and visions, and His voice?

In the book of Jonah, we have the account of a man named Jonah, whom God asked to go to the city of Nineveh and preach against their wickedness. Jonah was disobedient, refusing to obey God, and he got on a boat going to a city called Tarshish in order to run away from the Lord. On the way, the Lord sent a great wind and the boat was in danger of capsizing. Eventually, the other people on the boat found out that Jonah was running away from God. To make a long story short, Jonah was thrown overboard and swallowed by a great big whale. He ended up staying in that whale for three days and three nights. When he was ready to obey the Lord, he was vomited out of the whale onto the shore.

This is a good example of how the Lord can use circumstances to speak to us, and give us direction. This type of hearing from God usually happens because we aren't listening to God. It emphasizes not only the importance of listening to God, but also the importance of obeying God.

Through God's Still, Small Voice

THOUGHT PROCESSES

In order to understand better how to hear from God, I feel it is necessary to delve into how our mind functions. The mind functions in two types of thought processes: analytical cognitive and spontaneous.

Analytical cognitive thought processes. Analytical refers to the breaking up of anything into its constituent elements or parts. The word cognitive means "to know."

Let's combine these two words and summarize them to produce an understanding of this type of thought process. An analytical cognitive thought process is the process of the mind taking the input from the five senses, drawing from the memory and the heart, analyzing everything, and coming to a conclusion.

Let me use an example of this type of thought process. My hand accidentally touches a hot stove element. Immediately, the sense of touch sends a signal to my mind that the element is hot and my hand is burnt. As a result, my mind causes the necessary muscles to remove my hand from the element. My memory says, "I should put my hand into cold water to help ease the pain."

Spontaneous thought processes. This type of thought is natural. It comes out of the blue and isn't forced, planned, or analysed. It just happens. A complete thought drops into our minds.

Let me share two examples:

- You just remember that you've left the garage door open at home.
- On your way home, you suddenly have the thought that you should pick up some milk at the store.

We use both types of thought process: analytical cognitive and spontaneous. We use these thought processes in everyday communication. We also use them in our communication with God.

SPIRITUAL COMMUNICATION PROCESS

So how does our spirit participate in the thought process as a Christian? First of all, in order to be a Christian, we need our spirit to be alive to God's Spirit. We call this salvation.

> And He has made you alive, who were once dead in trespasses and sins ...
> —Ephesians 2:1, MKJV

Secondly, we need to develop a hunger and desire in our heart to know God intimately— to have a close relationship with Him. Once we have this desire and are working towards it, God's Spirit, the Holy Spirit, speaks to us through our spirit to our soul (heart and mind). In other words, God can influence our thought process and speak to us.

To illustrate, let's say that you have a nasty mother-in-law staying with you. One day a fire breaks out in the house and she's sleeping in the bedroom. Your soul without the Holy Spirit's influence would just as well leave her to sleep, but your spirit in tune with God hears God whisper, "You need to walk in love." This is God communicating His will to you.

> And the second is like it. "Love your neighbor as you love yourself."
> —Matthew 22:39, NIrV

This means that you need to get our mother-in-law out of the house and save her life. Instead of hate you begin to love your mother-in-law. The Holy Spirit has had an influence on your spirit and soul (heart and mind).

This is one of the ways in which we change our thinking and living from the way of the world to God's way. God is a Spirit and all of his thoughts are spiritual. In order for us to receive a thought from God or hear His voice, it must come through our spirit.

> But the natural man does not receive the things of the Spirit of God, for they are foolishness to him; nor can he know them, because they are spiritually discerned.
> —1 Corinthians 2:14, NKJV

Even in the spiritual realm, the analytical cognitive thought process is used in a dialogue between us and God. However, the spontaneous thought process just happens.

Let me illustrate. Let's say that you're driving down the road and minding your own business. Suddenly, a thought drops into your mind to turn off the road and go another way. Later, you discover on the news that a house had blown up from a gas leak right around the time you were to drive by it. This is an example of the spontaneous way we can hear God's voice.

We find an example of God's spontaneous communication in the Bible, with the disciple Philip:

> Then the Spirit said to Philip, "Go and enter that chariot."
> —Acts 8:29, WNT

In this verse, a man is sitting in his vehicle and reading the Bible. He can't understand it and he wants someone to help him. Philip is nearby, and God tells him to go and sit with this man in his chariot. As a result, Philip was able to help this man understand what he was reading. This is a good example of how we can be used of God when we can hear His voice.

The Inner Witness

Some have indicated that the inner witness is different than God's still, small voice. On the other hand, we have concluded that they are one and the same thing. Let me explain. The inner witness is a hunch, thought, instruction, or direction that pops into the mind; it can be in the form of either the removal or the increase of peace. Regardless, it's a thought that comes from God through our spirit to our mind. Since the inner witness and God's still, small voice are translated into thoughts by the mind, I can't see any difference in these two ways of communication with God. Thus, whether it's a spontaneous thought, an inner feeling or witness, or words that just come to us, we will refer to them all as God's still, small voice.

God's Voice

God speaks to His children through His still, small voice when His children learn how to hear it. The first thing we have to ask is, "What is God's still, small voice?" Well, it's not an audible voice, since God seldom speaks that way, and it is not heard through angels, which of course God has sometimes used to bring messages to us.

> And after the earthquake a fire; but the Lord was not in the fire: and after the fire a still small voice.
> —1 Kings 19:12, KJV

God's voice is an inner voice, speaking to our spirit, which is communicated to our minds. Our spirit must be in tune with the Spirit of God in order to be able to hear and receive from God, although God does sometimes speak even though we are not in tune with Him.

Sometimes when I use the words "God told me" as a part of a conversation, I get strange looks, and sometimes even unkind comments from other Christians. It seems like they think I'm not supposed to hear God's voice. It also seems like they think that hearing God's voice is reserved only for pastors and leaders in the church. What nonsense! Every one of God's children should and must be hearing God's voice.

> My sheep hear My voice, and I know them, and they follow Me.
> —John 10:27, NKJV

There are many times when God wants to give us specific, individual directions that aren't in the Bible but are specifically meant for us. For example, God may say to us:

- "I don't want you to go to that conference."
- "Go talk to that young lady over by the stairway and tell her that God loves her."
- "Go and apologize to them for what you said."
- "I want you to spend the next three months studying My Word."

BLOCKING GOD'S VOICE

If we can't hear God's voice, we miss out on a huge part of God's blessings. So what is it that blocks us from hearing God's voice?

> If I regard iniquity [sin] in my heart, the Lord will not hear me ...
> —Psalms 66:18, KJV

Very simply, it is sin, disobedience, offences, and unbelief. If we know about unrepented sin in our lives, if we have offended someone or God, or if we have unforgiveness towards God or other people, we will find it very hard to hear God's voice. However, this doesn't stop God from convicting us of sin through the Holy Spirit, because God wants to remind us to deal with the sin.

If God has asked us to do something and we have disobeyed and not done it, that will stop us from hearing God's voice. Unbelief means that we don't believe that God wants to talk to us, and we don't believe His Word. Both of these things stop us from hearing God. God is never the problem when we can't hear His voice; the problem is always us.

FAITH TO HEAR

Before we begin talking to God, I need to deal with the faith issue. What do I mean by the faith issue? Faith is believing, confessing, and expecting that what we cannot see in the physical realm will become real in this realm. In other words, we expect that which we cannot see or experience to become what we can see and experience. This faith principle is seen in the following verse,

> ... (as it is written, "I have made you a father of many nations") in the presence of Him whom he believed—*God, who gives life to the dead and calls those things which do not exist as though they did.*
> —Romans 4:17, NKJV (emphasis added)

For example, when we experience salvation, we accept and believe that we now have eternal life, because that's what God's Word says. Even though we cannot see eternal life in the here and now, we accept and believe that we have it. By the same token, when we pray for healing for our bodies, we believe and accept that it has taken place according to God's Word even though sometimes we can't see or feel the healing. We believe and accept that it will show itself in the physical realm so that we are able to see, feel, and experience it. By faith in God and His Word, we believe and accept that when we talk to God and listen for His voice, He will respond to us.

Whose Voice Am I Hearing?

One of the most difficult things to learn in hearing God's still, small voice is knowing if it's me speaking to me, the devil speaking to me, or God speaking to me. We will be able to identify the voice if we look at the main characteristics of each one of these three voices:

Our Voice

- Our thoughts, which come from the natural mind, tend to ignore God's influence, which comes from our spirit in tune with God.
- Our thoughts tend to line up with the world and the way it thinks.
- Our thoughts tend to be self-centred.
- Our thoughts tend to come from our desires, surroundings, and circumstances.
- In our thoughts, we tend to allow our emotions to get involved.

The Devil's Voice

- His thoughts and words are always contrary to God's Word.
- He generates fear, confusion, unrest, worry, and anxiety.
- He can create a sense of hopelessness and being overwhelmed.

God's Voice

- His voice always lines up with His Word.
- He engenders faith, order, and love.
- His voice generates peace and calm.
- He speaks words which are meant for our good.
- His words always give hope and expectation.

So how do we deal with the two voices we don't want to hear from—the devil's voice and our voice? We get them out of the way.

Let's take care of the devil's voice first. God's Word says,

> Therefore submit to God. Resist the devil and he will flee from you.
> —James 4:7, NKJV

How do we resist the devil? We get rid of the devil by telling him to leave, in Jesus' name, and we should do that anytime we sense that the devil is bothering us. But what if he doesn't leave? Nonsense! The devil must leave at our command, in the name of Jesus.

> I have given you authority to trample on snakes and scorpions and to overcome all the power of the enemy; nothing will harm you.
> —Luke 10:19, NIV

In this verse, Jesus gives His disciples authority over the enemy, Satan. The name of Jesus gives us authority, by faith, to command Satan. He must obey because he is subject to the authority of Jesus Christ, having been defeated by Jesus on the cross of Calvary. Since the authority of Jesus has been given to us, the devil has no choice but to leave our presence when we tell him to do so, in the name of Jesus.

As you begin to mature in hearing God's voice, you'll find that you become more aware of the devil's interference, and thus you will only need to deal with him when this happens. After having spoken to the devil in faith, we accept and believe that he is gone because God's Word says so, as we see in James 4:7.

Now that we have eliminated the devil, the next step is to eliminate the voice of our sometimes busy natural mind; this is the voice which doesn't let God's influence happen. All of us talk to ourselves every day, and unless we have purposely chosen to include God, our natural minds will be speaking. Many times we will stop to talk to God and hear dozens of thoughts and ideas bombarding our minds. It's pretty hard to hear God's voice if our minds are busy with all these thoughts, thus we need to bring our minds to a place of quietness. In order to eliminate our voice, we need to speak to it and tell it to be still. Then we need to ask God to quiet our minds. I often confess the emphasized portion of the following verse to accomplish this:

> We demolish arguments and every pretension that sets itself up against the knowledge of God, and *we take captive every thought to make it obedient to Christ.*
> —2 Corinthians 10:5, NIV (emphasis added)

READY TO HEAR

Finally, we arrive at the place where we're ready to hear from God. We can ask questions of Him, or we can ask Him to speak to us about whatever He desires. Regardless, usually the first thing that pops into our minds is God's still, small voice. If you're unsure about which of the three voices it is, see which characteristics match the voice. If the voice we hear talks like us, it's probably us. God usually communicates in a different way than we do; His way usually, but not always, involves encouragement.

As well, if we spend too much time analysing and doubting what we have heard, we will be operating in fear, which will nullify our faith to hear God.

Do you think God wants to trick you and play games with your mind? Absolutely not! God wants to talk to you. There are examples throughout the Bible of God talking to His children:

> While Peter was reflecting on the vision, the Spirit said to him, "Behold, three men are looking for you. But get up, go downstairs and accompany them without misgivings, for I have sent them Myself."
> —Acts 10:19–20, NASB

In these verses, God spoke to the Apostle Peter to prepare him to minister to a Gentile and his family. Peter had just seen a vision from God in which God was teaching Peter not to reject any of His creation. The Jews considered the Gentiles an unclean people and preferred not to have anything to do with them. Peter didn't know that these three men were Gentiles. In this passage, God gives Peter instructions by the spirit to go and meet these three men.

Sometimes God will speak a thought into your mind out of the blue. When this happens, until you get to know His voice well, you may want to ask God if it was from Him. God will respond to you. God enjoys talking with His children.

Begin talking to God regularly throughout the day, just like you would talk to a friend or family member if they were present with you. Remember that as a believer in God and His Son Jesus, and as one who has taken time to get to know God intimately, your spirit and His Spirit are able to communicate with each other. It's your choice to be sensitive to God's Spirit throughout the day. This means that you're able to hear His voice as well as talk to

Him. If you're willing to discipline yourself and make hearing God's voice a priority, you will be amazed at how quickly God will respond to you.

For many years I have made it a practice of talking and listening to God every day. It's kind of neat to have the wisdom and direction of God available in all kinds of circumstances. It certainly helps to bring victory and success into our lives.

We can also then begin to use the ministry gifts of the Spirit, such as words of knowledge (as found in 1 Corinthians 12:8–10). This enables us to share the knowledge and wisdom of God with others, to help them through their struggles and see God's victory in their lives. We become able to receive words from God for other people and for the body of Christ. God has so much for us; let's begin to experience and live in it.

Specific and Focused Times of Hearing

There are times when we face difficulties or need some clear direction from God. Often during these times we can be too emotionally and mentally involved in our situation. In this case, there are some things we can do to make it easier to hear from God. It won't be necessary to do every one of these things every time you talk to God. The number of things you need to do will vary according to how cluttered your mind is and how focused you are on hearing from God.

First, let me mention a few things not to do.

What Not to Do

- Do not leave sin and disobedience to God in your life without repenting. (Psalms 66:18)
- Wrong motives for hearing from God will get you nowhere, such as asking God if you should divorce your wife.
- Don't expect God to answer questions that are none of your business.
- Don't do all the talking—leave time for God to talk.
- Stay away from strife and worry.
- If you hear anything, don't overanalyse where it came from.

What to Do

- Remove distractions by finding a quiet place, alone and undisturbed. No phones or texting.
- Choose a quiet time of the day to get alone with God.
- Keep a to-do list handy. This is necessary to eliminate the distractions which to-do items can create if they come to your mind.
- Tell Satan to leave in Jesus' name.
- Quiet your mind by speaking, "I take every thought captive in obedience to Christ" (see 2 Corinthians 10:5).
- Ask God to open up your spiritual hearing.
- Confess and quote scriptures which declare that God wants to talk to you, such as:

> My sheep hear my voice, and I know them, and they follow me …
> —John 10:27, KJV

> Every one that is of the truth [hears] my voice.
> —John 18:37, KJV

- Imagine that you're having a conversation with God.
- Thank God for His desire to speak to you.
- Expect to hear God's still, small voice just as if you were talking to Him face to face. (John 10:27)
- Be quiet and wait on God. Let God speak.
- If you have questions for God, write them down.
- Write down what you hear.
- Fasting from food, TV, and other distractions will also help in hearing from God.
- Pray in the spirit for a period of time, let's say for five to thirty minutes beforehand. But remember that this isn't a formula: you can pray in tongues for as little or as long as you choose.
- Try to be in a state of patience, relaxation, and rest in God.

We can do all of these things, but sometimes we may still have trouble hearing God's still, small voice. Let's now look at something else we may experience when trying to hear from God during difficult times.

THE SILENT TREATMENT

I don't know what else to call it when God is silent other than "the silent treatment." Most, if not all of God's children, go through this experience at different times in their lives. I know that I've certainly been there a number of times.

When the silent treatment happens, we need to look at our lives and see if we have missed it somewhere. Maybe we've failed to do something God has asked us to do. Maybe we have unforgiveness or some other sin in our lives and God has been trying to get our attention in regards to the situation.

> If I regard iniquity [sin] in my heart, the Lord will not hear me...
> —Psalms 66:18, KJV

During times of God's silence in our lives, He doesn't stop communicating with us totally, but He is very silent on the issues that are confronting us. It may be that one is going through a major financial crisis, and seemingly there is no direction from God. God is silent regarding what to do specifically in this difficult situation.

No, God doesn't stop encouraging us with His Word, other Christians, and His still, small voice. However, it seems like He is purposely avoiding His direction and guidance for the moment. Did I say for a moment? Sometimes it can be for a while. Yes, sometimes God does purposely avoid giving us His specifics for some time regarding our situations and trials. Why does God do this?

When we're subjected to a trial, it's usually a trial of our faith and ability to trust in Him. God is testing us as we work through a trial in a certain area of our lives, for a time, in order to build up our faith ability. God wants us to have strong faith, the kind which will move mountains. During these times of silence and faith building, if we ask God questions regarding what to do, often He's not ready to release that direction to us yet. God releases His direction and breakthrough when He knows we are ready to obey Him.

Asking God for specifics during these times of silence will sometimes cause us to be confused. We might think we have heard God's voice when in fact it is our own, overanxious desire to hear. This often results in us hearing our own voice.

The best thing to do when God is silent on specifics is:

- Examine yourself and see if there's sin or disobedience in your life, and repent if there is something.
- Just keep trusting Him because He will come through.
- Keep on praising and worshiping Him.
- Keep on exercising the six steps of staying connected.
- Keep on speaking the victory and not the problem.
- Keep on believing and speaking God's Word in Scripture, such as:

> And we know that all things work together for good to those who love God, to those who are called according to His purpose.
> —Romans 8:28, MKJV

> Now thanks be to God, who always causes us to triumph in Christ…
> —2 Corinthians 2:14, MKJV

Peace and Joy

Let me say a few things about peace and joy with respect to hearing from God. If the message you hear from God is a warning or stern message, you most likely will not have peace or joy as a result. However, if God gives you a word of encouragement or direction, you certainly should have peace or joy about that.

> For God is not the author of confusion, but of peace, as in all churches of the saints.
> —1 Corinthians 14:33, KJV

When we're looking to God for an answer to a problem, or direction for our lives, peace and joy certainly come into play. A sense of peace and joy after we've just heard a word of encouragement or direction tends to confirm that the word is from God. A troubled or anxious feeling tends to confirm that the word is not from God.

Summary

Finally, to conclude this section on God's still, small voice, I would like to remind you of some important points:

- The inner witness and God's still, small voice are basically one and the same thing.
- Don't block God's voice with sin, disobedience, offences, and unbelief.
- Learn to decipher the voice you hear by its characteristics.
- Get rid of your voice and the devil's voice before you talk to God.
- After you have talked to God or asked Him a question, the first thing you will likely hear is God's voice.
- Whatever you hear, you must have peace about it, unless of course it is conviction for sin.

Conclusion

In concluding this chapter, I would like to share three points that will help us fine-tune our relationship with God in the area of communication: be flexible, get permission, and line up with the Word.

1. Be Flexible

We have just spent a considerable amount of time sharing on the five main ways of hearing from God. Sometimes God will choose to speak to you in a different way than you're expecting. Don't put God in a box and expect Him to do it your way. God knows what's best, and sometimes He will choose to speak to you through His Word or a song rather than with His still, small voice.

If you're not hearing His still, small voice, pick up the Bible and ask God where He would have you read. Be flexible and allow God to speak to you in the way which He chooses. You will be abundantly blessed for being open and submissive to God and His ways. If you're still having trouble hearing from God, go back in your mind to the last time you heard from God when He asked you to do something. If you haven't obeyed Him, immediately repent and ask for God's forgiveness. Tell Him that with His help, next time He asks you to do something you will be obedient to do it.

2. Get Permission

When God speaks to you and gives you guidance for your life, do not share this with other people unless and until God gives you permission. God always has reasons when He requires you to keep quiet regarding what He has shared with you. It might be that you have a problem with pride, or you may not yet fully understand what He is saying to you. Or you may not have God's timing and purpose. Finally, you may bring confusion to others who aren't ready to accept what you have to share with them.

I would like to add that when you get revelation from God through His Word, the same thing applies: we should be careful to ask God's permission to share that revelation with others. Be sensitive so as to avoid an argument over the things of God. One rule I tend to live by is that I will share briefly about what God has shared with me, with God's permission. If it's well-received, I will continue; if it's not well-received, I will change the subject. We cannot force others to accept what we have received from God. Only as the Holy Spirit opens up a person's spiritual understanding will they be able receive the understanding as well.

3. Line Up with the Word

Any time we get direction or hear from God, it must never contradict the Bible. I remember a time when a friend told me that God had told her to divorce her husband. God hates divorce, thus God would not tell one of His children to divorce their spouse. This is definitely not an example of hearing from God, but rather an example of pleasing the soul, or hearing from the devil. Make sure that what you hear agrees with the Word of God.

In this chapter, we have covered five of the most common ways in which one can hear from God. Let me encourage you to begin hearing from God every day, for God is our greatest friend and ally. God's desire is for you to be fulfilled, happy, healthy, and prosperous. So get connected, begin to hear from God, and expect to be blessed abundantly.

Chapter Seven

God's Multiplied Abundance

The Blessing

The word "blessing," from the International Standard Bible Encyclopedia, means "the form of words used in invoking the bestowal of good; the good or the benefit itself which has been conferred."[36] The word "blessed," from the same source, means, "But where man is in mind it is used in the sense of 'happy' or 'favored.'"[37] Finally, the word "bless," from Webster's Dictionary, means, "To make happy; to make successful; to prosper in temporal concerns."[38]

If we were to simplify the definition of these words, it would look like this: the giving of good or favour, happiness, prosperity, and abundance. These definitions describe a giver of good gifts, one who gives awesome and plentiful gifts. The purpose of defining these words is to set the stage for the rest of the chapter, in which we will tie God to the blessing.

> Then God blessed them, and God said to them, "Be fruitful and multiply; fill the earth and subdue it; have dominion over the fish of the sea, over the birds of the air, and over every living thing that moves on the earth."
> —Genesis 1:28, NKJV

Where does the word "blessing" come from? The very first words God spoke to man were His blessing, as we see in Genesis 1:28. With this blessing, God told man that he would be a recipient of all God's goodness by bearing fruit, increasing, filling up the earth, and controlling and ruling the

---

36 *International Standard Bible Encyclopedia*, "Blessing" (Grand Rapids, MI: Wm. B. Eerdmans Publishing Co., 1979).
37 Ibid., "Blessed."
38 Noah Webster, *American Dictionary of the English Language*, "Bless" (1828).

earth. From the very beginning, God intended and planned to bestow good on His children.

Before Adam and Eve sinned in the Garden of Eden, they weren't aware of the curse and what it was. Furthermore, they were never exposed to it. After Adam and Eve sinned, they fell from God's blessing and it was no longer on them.

> Then to Adam He said, "Because you have heeded the voice of your wife, and have eaten from the tree of which I commanded you, saying, 'You shall not eat of it': cursed is the ground for your sake; in toil you shall eat of it all the days of your life."
> —Genesis 3:17, NKJV

After the fall in the Garden of Eden, man became aware of evil and the curse. As a result, man understood the difference between good and evil. Now, God's blessing on man's life became a choice; man could choose good or evil.

> I call heaven and earth as witnesses today against you, that I have set before you life and death, blessing and cursing; therefore choose life, that both you and your descendants may live.
> —Deuteronomy 30:19, NKJV

God describes the choices we have in life in the above verse, and one of them is the blessing, the choice we really want. Where do we find the blessing in the Bible? It is found in Deuteronomy 28:1–14, which says, *"And all these blessings shall come upon you and overtake you"* (NKJV). What blessings does this refer to? If we look at 28:3–14, we can see what the word "blessings" actually includes.

Let me summarize and paraphrase them as follows. God will empower us to prosper in every area of our lives, including health. He will bestow good on our children, our businesses, and our jobs. He will multiply our material goods. He will prosper the work of our hands and everything we undertake to do. We shall have plenty of money to give or lend and we shall not have to borrow. The Lord will make us leaders, and the people of the earth will respect us. In these verses, the word "blessing" really comes to life, portraying God's goodness to His children.

The Curse

The curse helps us to see the opposite of the blessing, to realize how big the blessing really is. Obviously, the curse is the opposite of the blessing and we find it outlined in Deuteronomy 28:15–68. It includes sin, sickness, poverty, lack, darkness, plagues, fear, doubt, unbelief, and every other form of evil. Since we now know what the curse consists of, and since the curse is one of the choices we can make for our lives, how does its influence come into our lives? Can we say that it is Satan who administers the curse?

> When they had returned to the people, there came to Him a man who fell on his knees before Him and besought Him. "Sir," he said, "have pity on my son, for he is an epileptic and is very ill. Often he falls into the fire and often into the water. I have brought him to your disciples, and they have not been able to cure him."
> "O unbelieving and perverse generation!" replied Jesus; "how long shall I be with you? how long shall I endure you? Bring him to me." Then Jesus reprimanded the demon, and it came out and left him; and the boy was cured from that moment.
> —Matthew 17:14–18, WNT

You see, Jesus rebuked the demon which had obviously brought this disease on the boy. The true cause of our trouble and sickness is the evil spirit realm, the curse, demons, and Satan their leader. Thus, we must conclude that Satan is the administrator of the curse.

When Adam was tempted by Satan and disobeyed God in the Garden of Eden by eating the fruit from the tree of the knowledge of good and evil, he gave up God's blessing and the spiritual authority which God had given him. Satan usurped that authority from man in the Garden of Eden. As a result, mankind became subject to Satan's influence in their lives.

Satan was thrown out of heaven because he rebelled against God. God's kingdom is the kingdom of life, and when Satan was kicked out of heaven he left the kingdom of life and entered the kingdom of death. Deuteronomy 30:19 writes about the curse and death like they're equals: the curse produces death, therefore we can conclude that Satan came under the curse as well. Satan and his evil spirit realm represent and administer the curse and all the evil that it contains. Satan became the representative of the curse and death in the earth.

If Satan can get us to believe our source of trouble is God, then he's got us in his clutches. We won't have any tools to fight against him. When we know that the source of our problems is Satan, we have all kinds of tools to defeat him. We have all kinds of powerful tools to send him away with his problems. We have tools like the name of Jesus, the Word of God, and the praise of God, which will undoubtedly defeat him and send him away with his cursed problems.

Now that we understand what the curse consists of, we can understand what we have been delivered from if we choose to live in the blessing. Praise God!

God's First Blessing

As we have already discovered, God's first blessing command to mankind is found in the following verse:

> So God created man in His own image; in the image of God He created him; male and female He created them. Then God blessed them, and God said to them, *"Be fruitful and multiply; fill the earth and subdue it; have dominion over the fish of the sea, over the birds of the air, and over every living thing that moves on the earth."*
> —Genesis 1:27–28, NKJV (emphasis added)

Many have believed over the years that when God spoke this blessing over mankind, He meant mankind should only have a lot of children. In order to see what God really meant, let's look at five keywords and define them. The words are fruitful, multiply, replenish, subdue, and dominion. The following definitions are all taken from Strong's Hebrew and Greek Dictionary:

- Fruitful (Greek word *parah*) means: "fruitful, grow, increase..."[39]
- Multiply (Hebrew word *rabah*) means: "to *increase* (in whatever respect)... [bring in] abundance."[40]

---

39 James Strong. *Strong's Dictionaries of the Hebrew and Greek Words*, "Parah" (Nashville, TN: Abingdon Press, 1890).
40 Ibid., "Rabah."

- Replenish (Hebrew words *male mala*) means: "to *fill* or (intransitively) *be full* of."[41]
- Subdue (Hebrew word *kabash*) means: "bring into bondage, force, keep under, subdue, bring into subjection."[42]
- Dominion (Hebrew word *radah*) means: "prevail against, reign (bear, make to) rule … take."[43]

Let's apply these definitions to the above scripture and see how it looks:

And God gave good and favour to them, and God said unto them grow, increase in every respect, replenish and furnish the earth, and bring it under control; and rule over the fish, the birds, and every living thing that moves on the earth.

—Genesis 1:27–28 (paraphrase)

It seems to me that this blessing is a lot more encompassing than just making more babies. In the first portion of the verse, God created man in His own image, and then God's very first words to man in Genesis 1:28, emphasized, were His blessing to man. God's expressed gifts of goodness were given to man for every area of his life. These words are to be applied to man's prosperity in intimacy with God, family, health, finances, protection, relationships, the fruit of the spirit, and in every area of man's life. You mean man was to be healthy as well? Of course, God didn't make disease to put upon man; the devil and the curse brought disease to man. Just look at Deuteronomy 28:15–68.

In addition, man was to bring the whole earth under his power and control, under God. After all, when Adam was just created he was spiritually connected to God, enjoying God's presence day by day. Then Adam sinned and gave up God's blessing of authority and dominion to Satan. Thus man messed up God's first blessing to him.

---

41 Ibid., "Male Mala."
42 Ibid., "Kabash."
43 Ibid., "Radah."

God Continues His Blessing

God did not and never will stop blessing His children. After Adam lost the blessing, God raised up another man called, Noah, a godly man on whom God bestowed His blessing once again.

> So God blessed Noah and his sons, and said to them: "Be fruitful and multiply, and fill the earth."
> —Genesis 9:1, NKJV

This is the same blessing God had given to Adam, and as long as Noah lived that blessing was with him. In fact, God even removed the curse from the land under Noah. As a result, the land would again produce an abundant harvest.

However, during Noah's time the children of God began to turn away from God. They began to live more and more in sin under the curse instead of under God's blessing.

After Noah, God chose another man called Abram. Again, God began to pour out His blessing upon Abram. It was the same blessing God had given to Adam and then to Noah. God always has a man, and He always has a people He wants to bless, as we can see in the following verse:

> I will make you a great nation; I will bless you and make your name great; and you shall be a blessing. I will bless those who bless you, and I will curse him who curses you; and in you all the families of the earth shall be blessed.
> —Genesis 12:2–3, NKJV

You see, God promised Abraham that He would not only bestow good on him, but that He would also make a great nation of Abraham, that his name would be great. If you think about it, Abraham's name is one of the most well-known of the patriarchs of the Old Testament, even unto this day. Further to that, Abraham was to be the one through whom God would extend His good to others, even to the point of providing God's goodness to the whole earth. Finally, God promised that whoever bestowed good on Abraham and his descendants would have God's goodness in their lives.

Before we move on to other matters regarding the blessing, we should look at a couple of other items in the following verses:

> No longer shall your name be called Abram, but your name shall be Abraham; for I have made you a father of many nations.
> —Genesis 17:5, NKJV

We see here that God changed Abram's name to Abraham, meaning a father of multitudes. God promised that Abraham and his descendants would be the father of many nations instead of just one nation.

> I will multiply your descendants as the stars of heaven, and will give your descendants all these lands; and by your descendants all the nations of the earth shall be blessed; because Abraham obeyed Me and kept My charge, My commandments, My statutes and My laws.
> —Genesis 26:4–5, NASB

Allow me first to identify the context of Genesis 26:4–5. In these verses, God is speaking to Isaac, Abraham's son whom God chose to carry Abraham's blessing into the next generation, and consequently to all the generations to come. The Lord appeared unto Isaac, reminding him of the covenant promises He had made with his father Abraham.

Continuing in the promises God gave to Abraham, here we read once again that Abraham was the man through whom God would extend His blessing to the whole world. In addition, God promised to give Abraham all of the land of Canaan. Many other verses in the Bible describe God's covenanted promises and blessings to Abraham and his descendants. Wow! What a blessing, and it's available to all of God's children, including the Gentiles.

As we move forward from Isaac to the next man who would receive God's blessing on his life, we come to Jacob. From Jacob, the blessing went to Joseph, and then to Moses. As we move through the first five books of the Old Testament, we arrive at Deuteronomy 28. In 28:1–14, we find the blessings that God gives to His children for their obedience to Him. In 28:15–68, we find the curses that will come on the children who disobey God. In Deuteronomy 30, God promises His Abrahamic blessings to His children through Moses as follows:

> I call heaven and earth as witnesses today against you, that I have set before you life and death, blessing and cursing; therefore choose life, that both you and your descendants may live.
> —Deuteronomy 30:19, NKJV

God gives us a choice. He urges us to choose His blessing instead of the curse. In the Old Testament, Abraham's children were the Jews. God refers to Abraham's children as those who have the choice between the blessing and the curse. However, even though God had given them the choice of His blessing, it was up to them to choose to receive it.

The Gentile Blessing

In Chapter One, we found many scriptures from God's Word which describe God as a giver of good gifts to His children for every area of their lives. We included verses from the Old Testament and the New Testament. In spite of all those scriptures, there are still those who would believe that the Gentiles are not recipients of the Old Testament blessings, such as those found in Deuteronomy 28:1–14. They believe that these blessings are only for the Jews or Israelites, natural-born Jewish people. In order to enlighten our understanding, let's go to the New Testament and see how the blessing came about for the Gentiles. But first let's define the word "Gentiles," from the Greek word *ethos*. It means "a race (as of the same *habit*), i.e., a *tribe*; specifically a *foreign (non-Jewish)* one (usually by implication *pagan*),"[44] as taken from Strong's Hebrew and Greek Dictionary.

> The just shall live by faith.
> —Galatians 3:11, KJV

> Understand, then, that those who have faith are children of Abraham.
> —Galatians 3:7, NIV

Galatians 3:11 is very clear about how Christians are to live. We are to live by faith and total trust in God and His Word. According to Galatians 3:7, those of us who live by faith in God are the children of Abraham. Therefore,

---

44 Ibid., "Ethos."

we have the blessing God gave to Abraham on our lives. As we have discussed before, the Christian life is lived by faith in God and His Word. Therefore, from Galatians 3:7 we can conclude that we are the children of Abraham.

Now let's consider further what Christ did for the Gentiles in relation to the blessings of Abraham:

> Christ redeemed us from the curse of the law by becoming a curse for us, for it is written: "Cursed is everyone who is hung on a pole." He redeemed us in order that the blessing given to Abraham might come to the Gentiles through Christ Jesus, so that by faith we might receive the promise of the Spirit.
> —Galatians 3:13–14, NIV

In Galatians 3:13, we see that Christ had become the curse for us. Previously, we discovered what the curse was. We determined that the curse, found in Deuteronomy 28:15–68, included sin, sickness, poverty, fear, doubt, unbelief, and every form of evil that exists brought on us by Satan. Jesus took all of these things on His body, for all of mankind, when He hung on the cross, shed His blood, died, and was buried in the grave. He took all of the evil which is in the curse upon His body, but He did not stay in the grave. He arose from that grave victorious, having defeated every form of evil, including Satan. He also provided life abundantly for us to experience. If we stay in a close relationship with Christ, the curse is in the grave for us, and we no longer have to accept the curse upon us.

> And if you are Christ's, then you are Abraham's seed, and heirs according to the promise.
> —Galatians 3:29, NKJV

Here we see that through Jesus Christ the blessing of Abraham has come on the Gentiles, that we might receive the covenant promises God made to Abraham by faith. It confirms that if we are Christians, we are Abraham's seed or children, heirs of God's covenant promises. In Christ, we become spiritual Jews, ancestors of Abraham, and therefore we are entitled to have the blessing of Abraham on our lives. Wow! What a plan! What a victory!

Blessing Stoppers

Up to this point, we have explored our entitlement to God's promises, but there are six major things we need to be aware of which could block the flow of God's abundance into our lives. I have listed them below, and then I will share a little on each one.

1. Unbelief, doubt, and fear.
2. Little or no faith ability.
3. Disobedience to God and His Word.
4. Offences and unforgiveness.
5. Strife and no love.
6. Sin, which includes all the other blessing blockers.

1. Unbelief towards God and His Word means that we do not really take God's Word as true. As Christians, we are to believe in and act on God's Word. Simply put, belief in God means that whatever God's Word says is not only true; it already exists, even if we can't see it in the natural realm. That's what we call faith. Doubt and fear are the opposite of faith. We doubt when we don't think God will keep His Word. We fear when we allow the enemy, Satan, to convince us that God won't come through for us. Doubt and fear in our lives cause us to believe that God's Word doesn't do what it says it will do. Thus, we cannot expect to receive from God.
2. Faith is our belief mechanism. We have little faith ability because we have allowed doubt, fear, and unbelief to cripple the measure of faith which God gave us when we became Christians. No faith ability means that we have totally ignored the measure of faith God gave us as believers, through doubt, fear, unbelief, and disobedience of God. We destroy faith by the words of our mouth and the thoughts of our mind.
3. Disobedience to God and His Word is a sure way to block His blessings, because believers in Christ are to live their lives guided and directed by God's Word. We also need to be able to hear God's voice and obey it.

4. Unforgiveness and offenses. Previously I have shared that these things would prevent us from entering the Kingdom of God. That's a sure way to stop God's blessing.
5. Strife and no love. We are to live our lives as Christians loving God and others. We are also to stay out of strife, bickering, arguing, and fighting. These things bring confusion and evil into our lives.
6. Finally, the word sin describes all the other five blessing stoppers. We recognize sin as meaning "doing what displeases God and living contrary to His Word." Sin separates us from God.

We should try to eliminate these blessing stoppers from our lives. Also, we should try not to be overwhelmed by them, but rather ask God for help. If we find that God's promises seem to be avoiding us, we should do a check-up on ourselves to see if there's anything we have neglected to deal with in our lives. When we find a failure, we need to repent immediately and ask God to help us overcome this shortcoming so that we can move back into the flow of His blessings.

How to Get and Keep the Blessing

What brings the curse into our lives? How do we protect ourselves from the curse? How do we insure that we have the blessing and not the curse? These are all good questions, so let's take a comprehensive look at God's Word to answer them.

There are three main categories which require attention by us in order to live the Christian life successfully. They are intimacy with God, our view of God, and our faith in God. I have written in some detail on each of these categories already. However, I would like to highlight and summarize each one of them to round out our findings regarding how to get and keep the blessing.

INTIMACY WITH GOD

Let me begin by listing the six disciplines of intimacy with God. They are a hunger for God, prayer, Bible reading and meditation, praise and worship of God, dealing with sin, and practicing the presence of God.

1. **Hunger for God.** We need to have a great desire to understand and know God. Without that desire, we will not grow in our relationship with Him. We will end up staying very dry and unconnected spiritually with God. In fact, we may even go backwards in our relationship with God. Look at John 6:35:

> And Jesus said to them, "I am the bread of life. He who comes to Me shall never hunger, and he who believes in Me shall never thirst." (NKJV)

You see, Jesus said that He has the spiritual food we need to live a successful Christian life. He also promised us that He would never send us away hungry or thirsty when we seek Him.

2. **Prayer.** It is paramount in any good relationship that we communicate with each other. Our relationship with God is no exception. We communicate with Him in various ways, such as asking for his provision in all areas of our lives, expressing honour and respect for Him, and listening for His voice of direction and encouragement. In 1 Thessalonians 5:17, we are encouraged to pray without ceasing. This verse means that we are to talk to God as often as we can throughout every day.

3. **Bible reading.** It says in John 8:31,

> Then Jesus said to those Jews who believed Him, "If you abide in My word, you are My disciples indeed." (NKJV)

In order to know God and what He wants to do for us, we need to read His Word. We must think and meditate on His Word and then commit to living by its directions.

4. **Praise and worship.** 1 Thessalonians 5:18 says,

> ...in everything give thanks; for this is God's will for you in Christ Jesus. (NASB)

Many times we forget to thank God for all He has done for us, even the small things. As well, we need to thank Him for what He is going to do for us in the future, because of His promises in His Word.

5. **Dealing with sin.** It says in Psalms 66:18,

> If I had cherished sin in my heart, the Lord would not have listened. (NIV)

It is important to deal with sin quickly and to ask God to forgive us. We must also repent and ask forgiveness when we hurt someone else. We should make a practice of asking God often whether or not we have any outstanding sin which needs to be dealt with.

6. **Practicing God's presence.** Acts 17:28 says,

> ...for in Him we live and move and have our being... (NKJV)

If we want to have a close relationship with God, we need to be aware of His presence throughout every day. He lives in us because our spirit is connected with His Spirit. This happened when we got saved. Thinking about God's presence in our lives and acknowledging it with our mouths is something we can do to heighten our awareness of God's presence.

OUR VIEW OF GOD

> Therefore listen to me, you men of understanding: far be it from God to do wickedness, and from the Almighty to commit iniquity.
> —Job 34:10, NKJV

The second main category for successfully living the Christian life is our view of God. How do we see God? Do we see Him as one who is good or as one who allows evil in our lives? If we are going to be recipients of His blessings and goodness, we need to see God as good, and one who gives good gifts. We must stop blaming God for evil, and put the blame on Satan, the perpetrator of all evil. As well, we must have the fear of the Lord in our lives. This means that we respect, honour, and esteem God with our words and actions.

FAITH IN GOD

Finally, the third main category for living the Christian life is having faith in God. Everything we do as believers requires us to act in faith. Our faith actions need to include:

- Walking and living in love towards all people.
- Obedience to God's voice and His Word.
- Living in peace with others.
- Being a generous giver of our resources.
- Having patience to wait for God's timing.
- Speaking faith words, God's Word, over our circumstances.
- Being a doer of God's Word.

Don't Despair

I don't think I have covered absolutely everything with respect to getting the blessing. I have, however, covered the things that are important. It seems like a long list of things to do. Maybe it even seems overwhelming, but don't despair. It is very possible to accomplish the true Christian lifestyle with success. We have God, Jesus, and the Holy Spirit to help us, as we call upon them. They want us to succeed, as we see in the following verse:

> Now thanks be to God, who always causes us to triumph in Christ...
> —2 Corinthians 2:14, MKJV

God always causes or makes it possible for us to be successful. He made our success possible through Jesus. Furthermore, God is gracious. He isn't sitting in heaven with a blessing switch in His hand, waiting for you to mess up so He can turn off the blessing.

> ...for the Lord searches all hearts and understands all the intent of the thoughts.
> —1 Chronicles 28:9, NKJV

First of all, He looks at our hearts to see if we desire to change and grow, and if we are working at it. Secondly, He allows plenty of time for us to succeed. He graciously convicts, urges, and encourages us to succeed in our walk with Him. Only when we ignore God repeatedly do we get ourselves into trouble.

In order to clearly imprint on our minds what we have just covered with respect to getting and keeping the blessing, let me summarize our findings:

- The three main categories of successful Christian living are intimacy with God, our view of God, and our faith in God.
- There are six disciplines needed in our lives to achieve intimacy with God: hungering after God, prayer, Bible reading, praise and worship, dealing with sin, and practicing God's presence.
- Our picture and view of God is very important. We must see God as good and a giver of good gifts in order to receive His blessings.
- We must not blame God for evil, in our minds or with our mouths.
- We must have a high respect, honour, and esteem for God.
- We must live by faith in God and His Word. Everything we do to live for Him requires faith.
- We must know His Word and be doers of it.

Before we conclude, I would like to share a key truth to releasing God's blessing in your life. If you didn't get anything else out of this study, you must get this.

> For assuredly, I say to you, whoever says to this mountain, "Be removed and be cast into the sea," and does not doubt in his heart, but believes that those things he says will be done, he will have whatever he says.
> —Mark 11:23, NKJV

The last part of this verse says that if you believe the things you say, you will get whatever you say. We activate the blessing in our lives with the words we speak out of our mouths. If we speak God's words of blessing, we will get them. If we speak about problems, sickness, lack, and circumstances, that is what we will get in our lives. May I encourage you to only speak God's words of blessing over your life all the time.

Conclusion

In this chapter, we have laid out the basis for God's blessing upon His children, both Jews and Gentiles, as follows:

- We have defined the blessing as God's good gifts to His children.
- We found the curse to be every form of evil on this earth administered by Satan.
- We have discovered God's first blessing to man in Genesis.
- We saw that the blessing was passed from one patriarch to another.
- In the New Testament, the blessing became available to Gentile believers through Jesus Christ.
- We have established the foundation for the blessing of God to the Gentiles and the Jews, as Abraham's seed, through Jesus Christ.
- We shared six things that will limit or stop God's blessing to us.
- We found that in order to get and keep the blessing in our lives, we need to develop an intimate relationship with God, see God as a giver of good gifts, and live our lives by faith in God and His Word.

I have put together two books of scripture which will abundantly enlighten you as to the magnitude of God's many blessings. One is called *Tap into God's Promises*, and it contains more than three hundred scriptures categorized for one's circumstances. It is easy to carry with you because of its small size. The other one is called *Winning with God's Promises*, and it contains well over twelve hundred scriptures in twenty-three categories such as healing, direction, faith, finances, and protection, among others.

Both of these books have helped me immensely to put God's Word into my heart. As a result, I have His Word deeply embedded in my heart in many areas of my life. What does that mean? First of all, my heart is who I am. My heart is my personality and character, will, desires, and emotions, as we previously learned. Consequently, the Word has become who I am in many areas of my life. As I continue to feed my heart with the Word, other areas of my life are coming under God's influence and direction as well. You are also able to experience God's promises as you put His Word into your heart.

Chapter Eight

Triumphant Faith

God's mandate to Christians is to live by faith, and in order for us to receive God's promises it is important for us to take an in-depth look at faith. It's important for us to understand what it looks like to live by faith. Furthermore, it is far more important to live by faith than just understand it.

Before we get into the meat of this subject, there are two things we need to deal with that keep our faith from producing results:

- Does God do evil?
- Does God really give good gifts?

We will deal with each question separately.

Does God Do Evil?

I want to speak to a perception a lot of people have with respect to God. Many believe that God puts or allows evil on His people. I've often heard Christians say things like,

- "God is in control of everything, so it may not be His will to heal me."
- "God took that young pastor and his family to heaven, except for their three-year-old son."
- "If God doesn't heal them, we have to accept that His answer is that He took them to heaven to heal them."
- "It is such a wonderful testimony when Christians can give God praise, because they continued to be strong in God during their horrible suffering, until they died."
- "He was a pastor, a great man of God. I don't believe that he didn't know how to use his faith."

There probably are others, but I would like to deal with the attitude and beliefs that these words produce. Can you imagine the negative testimony these words produce for those who do not know Jesus? Nonbelievers already blame God for tornados and earthquakes and all the bad things that happen. When we speak words that suggest God did the evil deed, we are blaming God. Nobody thinks it is wonderful to have an evil deed happen to them.

> For unclean spirits, crying with a loud voice, came out of many who were possessed; and many who were paralyzed and lame were healed. And there was great joy in that city.
> —Acts 8:7–8, NKJV

It is love and good that draws people to Jesus, not bad and evil. It is healing and deliverance that brings great joy to the people. By the time we are finished this section, there should be no doubt that God does not do evil.

Many Christians hold to the belief that since God is sovereign, almighty, and in control of everything He actually brings evil upon His children to destroy them. Many believe that God puts cancer on people to kill them. Some believe that God allows calamity and tragedy to happen to His children. In other words, God would allow a parent to drive over and kill their child. What kind of a God do they think we serve? Would you allow someone to drive over your child? Would you put cancer on your wife to kill her? Need I answer these questions?

Is God really in control of everything? Is God in control of the husband who kills his wife? Is God in control of the mother who drowns her two boys in a bathtub? Is God in control of the teenager who bullies one of his peers until he commits suicide? Since when is God in control of evil?

> Then God blessed them, and God said to them, "Be fruitful and multiply; fill the earth and subdue it; have dominion over the fish of the sea, over the birds of the air, and over every living thing that moves on the earth."
> —Genesis 1:28, NKJV

This verse says that Adam was to have dominion over every living thing on earth. He blew off that blessing to the devil in the Garden of Eden, but God got that dominion back for us through Jesus on the cross. This means that we do have dominion. What? You can't be serious! Yes, I am.

> I call heaven and earth as witnesses today against you, that I have set before you life and death, blessing and cursing; therefore choose life, that both you and your descendants may live.
>
> —Deuteronomy 30:19, NKJV

Here God is indicating that He has asked heaven and earth to watch and see what you choose. You have the choice of life or death, blessings or the curse. He wants us to choose life and the blessing. Which one do you choose? Who has control here, you or God? You do, of course. So how do we choose life and the blessing? We choose it by lining up our words with God's Word. We speak God's Word into and for our lives everyday. Who is in control? We are.

Of course, God is sovereign and almighty, but God's Word provides us with the foundation for successful Christian living. If we violate His Word, we are subject to the consequences of our actions. Sin, disobedience, doubt, fear, unbelief, and not living according to the Word of God eventually opens the door for the devil to bring calamity into our lives through affliction and oppression.

> The thief comes only to steal and kill and destroy: I have come that they may have Life, and may have it in abundance.
>
> —John 10:10, WNT

This verse says that the devil comes to steal, kill, and destroy. So how can we say that the thief in this verse is the devil?

> Inasmuch then as the children have partaken of flesh and blood, He Himself likewise shared in the same, that through death He might destroy him who had the power of death, that is, the devil...
>
> —Hebrews 2:14, NKJV

The last part of this verse says that the devil had the power to destroy. How can we say that the thief in this verse is the devil? It says that the devil has the power of death. Thus, we can conclude that it is the devil that comes to steal, kill, and destroy us. He is the thief. If we let the devil have the power, he still has the power of death today, but we don't have to let him have that power. It is the devil who brings calamity, sickness, poverty, and every evil thing that happens on this earth.

> Put on the whole armor of God, that you may be able to stand against the wiles of the devil. For we do not wrestle against flesh and blood, but against principalities, against powers, against the rulers of the darkness of this age, against spiritual hosts of wickedness in the heavenly places.
> —Ephesians 6:11–12, NKJV

This portion of scripture makes it pretty clear who our enemy really is. Ephesians 6:11 says that we are to stand against the tricks of the devil. 6:12 says that we are fighting against the rulers of darkness and spiritual wickedness. It's pretty clear that the devil is our enemy. The major enemy or thief Christians have is the devil, or the evil spirit realm.

Of course, we can't eliminate our soul, which is us, our natural man. We can sometimes be our own worst enemy. The devil is the only one who can steal our salvation. The devil, outside of us, is the only one who can destroy our relationship with God. It is the devil's nature to lie, steal, kill, and destroy. It is God's nature to lavish His pure love on His children; God desires to bless His children and give them life, as we can see in the following verse:

> For You, O Lord, will bless the righteous; with favor You will surround him as with a shield.
> —Psalms 5:12, NKJV

In God's great plan and order for mankind, He has put principles into place in His Word which we are to live by. God never violates His principles, otherwise they wouldn't be principles. A principle is a fundamental truth or moral rule that God will not break.

Let's apply God's principle of sowing and reaping in the area of sin or unbelief and see how it works.

> Whoever sows to please their flesh, from the flesh will reap destruction; whoever sows to please the Spirit, from the Spirit will reap eternal life.
> —Galatians 6:8, NIV

When we live to please our flesh, soul, or natural man, we plant seed, or do and say things which produce death. If we live to please God and do His Word, we plant seed that produces life. If our words and actions line up with God's Word, they produce life.

If we sow seeds of sin in our lives—in other words, commit sin in our lives—we will experience (reap) the grief and heartache it brings. If we have (sow) unbelief towards God's Word, we will not see (reap) the blessings of His Word in our lives. For example, if we don't believe that God heals every one of His children from all disease, we probably won't get healed if we get sick. God lets His principle of sowing and reaping run its course, and He does not interfere. God's principles must and do work all the time.

If we continue to live in sin, we will break our spiritual connection with God.

> If I regard iniquity in my heart, the Lord will not hear.
> —Psalms 66:18, NKJV

Sin results in us opening the door for the devil to release the curse and bring tragedy into our lives. The door for the devil is open because we no longer have the Word protecting us. This doesn't mean that the door to Satan is wide open the minute we sin. God is gracious and gives ample time for us to repent when we have sinned. It is usually after ignoring our conscience, and God's repeated attempts to get our attention, that the door to the devil is opened. Let me give you some examples of how we open the door for the devil:

1. We get into strife, arguments, and disagreements with others without making up.
2. We carry unforgiveness against others who have hurt us.
3. We break the Ten Commandments of the Old Testament and the Two Commandments of the New Testament.
4. We fail to walk in love towards others according to God's Word.
5. We use our mouths to speak doubt and unbelief of God and His Word:
    - "My mother wasn't very bright in school, so I won't be either."
    - "Asthma and allergies run in our family, so I'm bound to get them."
    - "We just won't have enough money at the end of the month."
    - "The roads are icy. I just know I'm going to have an accident."

Do any of these words line up with God's Word? No, not at all! So we have activated the principle of sowing and reaping in a negative way. When we speak these kinds of words for our lives, we are speaking contrary to God's Word. By these words we bring the curse into our life. The blessing from God does not include these kinds of words. Just look at Deuteronomy 28:1–14 and see if you can find negative, harmful words in the blessing. Of course you can't, but just look at the curse in Deuteronomy 28:15–68. This is where you find sickness, harm, poverty, and tragedy. God does not operate under the curse; God operates under His blessing.

Finally, to add to what we have already concluded, let's look at the following verse:

> Therefore listen to me, you men of understanding: far be it from God to do wickedness, and from the Almighty to commit iniquity.
> —Job 34:10, NKJV

You might say, "Yeah, but look at all the people who got killed by God in the Old Testament; this proves that God does evil." No, it doesn't. First of all, God did destroy evil, and people died in the process. You see, destroying evil is a good thing. We destroy or remove evil from our streets when we put robbers in jail; we destroy or remove evil from our society when we confiscate drugs and put the drug dealers behind bars. When there's no evil present, good is present. God destroying evil is a good thing. But God is not evil because He destroys evil. God is a good God! In the Old Testament, God destroyed the sinners, the wicked, and the evil people over and over when they failed to respond to Him. The destruction of evil is a good thing.

In the New Testament, God continued to destroy evil. This time He used His Son Jesus to destroy evil. He sent Jesus to the cross to shed His blood for us to destroy sin, evil, the devil, death, and hell. Did God do evil by sending His Son to the cross? No, God did the greatest good He could have ever done for us. Why? Because He loves us so much! In the New Testament, God provided a different plan. God's plan of love for mankind included giving His Son to destroy evil for us.

Maybe you noticed while reading Deuteronomy 28:15–68 that the writer, Moses, indicates that it is God who carries out the curse against the people. Let's take a little side trip to explain this and shed some light on the issue.

Let's think back to the time of Moses and see what kind of resources he had at his disposal. Moses didn't have the New Testament, which deals extensively with Satan and the evil spirit realm. In fact, Satan is only mentioned in three places in the Old Testament, and mainly in the book of Job, and even there it only records his conversation with God. Nothing is mentioned regarding Job and his awareness of Satan or the evil spirit realm. I believe that men like Moses weren't aware of Satan the way we are today. Their understanding of the spiritual realm was mainly focused on God. As a result, they attributed everything that happened to God. Basically, they were ignorant of Satan and his place in this world.

Secondly, God did destroy evil, and it was a good thing He did. However, it's sin and rebellion against God which brings about the destruction of sinful and disobedient people. Disobedience to God opens the door for Satan to come in and do his dirty deeds. Just as we saw in Deuteronomy 30:19, we have the choice of the blessing or the curse. When we disobey God, we choose the curse, and as a result we get Satan performing in our lives.

Let's pick up from where we left off regarding the things we sow or speak with our mouths. We must conclude that God's principle of sowing and reaping does work. It works to bring evil upon us when we're speaking (sowing) against God's Word and living in sin. Further, when we speak negative words of unbelief, we open the door for Satan to work. Consequently, let us lay the blame for evil on sin and unbelief, not on God.

When our faith is being tested or we're being disciplined by God, we can make good or bad choices. We can make the choice to cooperate with God and learn from the discipline and increase our ability to use our faith. On the other hand, we can choose to ignore God and reap the consequences. This is how evil is sometimes able to have influence in our lives. When God removes some of His hedge of protection from around us, it gives the devil an opportunity to influence our lives. You see, God wants us to learn how to handle the devil and win. We can't do that if we're totally shielded from Satan all the time.

Again, remember that Satan only wants to destroy us. In everything, God always provides a plan of success for us over the devil and his evil devices. As long as we cooperate with God in what He wants to accomplish in us, God will always provide a way to victory for us, as we can see in the following verse:

> Now thanks be unto God, which always [causes] us to triumph in Christ, and [makes] manifest the savour of his knowledge by us in every place.
> —2 Corinthians 2:14, KJV

In conclusion, I think we have to agree that it's our sin and Satan which activates the curse and evil. God doesn't activate the curse and do evil. He's a good God! Praise His name!

Does God Really Give Good Gifts?

Some people think that healing, for instance, is a hit and miss thing: some get it and some don't. They think, "Well, maybe God doesn't like the way I comb my hair, or maybe He doesn't like the colour of my eyes, so He won't heal me." You probably think I'm being ridiculous. Not really. Whole religious denominations believe that God only heals some and not others, and they can't understand why.

Some Christians say that God is sovereign, and that God inflicts cancer or other tragedies on His children so that they'll die. I asked this before and I'm going to ask it again: would you place a tragedy or sickness upon your children so that they end up dying? No, of course not! You love your children and want the best for them. Well, you know God's love for His children is so much greater than our love for our children. How can we blame God for sickness and tragedy that brings death? It's not God who brings sickness and tragedy to kill His children; it's the devil.

> The thief comes only to steal and kill and destroy: I have come that they may have Life, and may have it in abundance.
> —John 10:10, WNT

Every time we tell someone that God is in control of everything, we include tragedy in that statement. Effectively, we're saying, "God caused the tragedy since He could have prevented it, but He didn't." Violations of God's principles—unbelief, disobedience, doubt, fear, and sin—bring tragedy via the devil. The devil brings evil, for it is the devil who comes to kill, to steal, and to destroy. We as Christians must stop blaming God for evil if we are to see God as a giver of good gifts.

Some people believe God pours out His blessings on some of His children but not others.

> Then Peter began to speak: "I now realize how true it is that God does not show favoritism."
>
> —Acts 10:34, NIV

This verse indicates that He is no respecter of persons, therefore I believe God's blessings are available to every one of His children in the same measure. The only thing that limits God's children from receiving His overflowing abundance is their ability to know how to receive from God.

To reiterate what I've just said, God does not give His blessings to some and not to others. However, we can learn how to receive God's blessings, since they are available to all those who live according to His Word. A good part of this book shares exactly that—how to receive God's multiplied abundance.

If we were to live perfect godly lives, there would be no need for trials and difficulties in our lives, but of course that isn't realistic. In spite of all this, God's plan for us is to:

- deliver us from trials victoriously.
- redeem us from sin, the curse, death, and hell.
- build our ability to live by faith in Him.
- provide the blessing, His power, and eternal life.

If we don't believe that God is the giver of good gifts, we can't have faith to believe for good things from Him. Look at the following scriptures for a moment:

> Every good and perfect gift is from God. It comes down from the Father. He created the heavenly lights. He does not change like shadows that move.
>
> —James 1:17, NIrV

> Charge them that are rich in this world, that they be not highminded, nor trust in uncertain riches, but in the living God, who [gives] us richly all things to enjoy.
>
> —1 Timothy 6:17, KJV

Begin to see God for who He really is: loving, caring, and a giver of good gifts, as we see in James 1:17. In the last portion of the verse, we see that God never changes; He has always and will always give us good gifts. Furthermore, in 1 Timothy 6:17, Paul reminds us again that God gives us all things in abundance to enjoy them.

The Old Faith Way

Let's begin our study on faith. Faith is not a mind game where we simply say in our mind, or with our mouth, that we believe. Let's say we believe God is going to heal our blind eye. On what basis are we thinking or saying that? Is it because we heard that someone else was healed? Maybe it's because we read a story about someone's blind eyes being healed. Better still, maybe in our minds we actually think we believe Jesus heals the sick. We need to have a basis, a firm foundation, for the things we believe, think, and speak if they're going to happen.

We live in such an I-want-it-now society that it's hard to have the patience it takes to live by faith. For instance, I remember a time when my wife and I were struggling financially and our truck was on its last legs. When we drove it, we were never sure if we would make it to our destination. Under our old way of living by faith, which doesn't work very well, we asked God to provide us with a newer, reliable truck—and then we believed with our minds for it to happen. Next thing you know, the old truck gave out again and the bill to fix it was going to be five hundred dollars. Well, it seemed the only option available for us was to spend the money to fix the truck. Wouldn't you know it, the truck broke down again, and this time we're asking, maybe even begging God, for a better truck.

We ask God for things and hope He'll give us the answer we're looking for. We think, "Maybe it will be our turn to hit it lucky! Just maybe God will see things our way!" By the way, I don't believe in luck.

Our patience was getting very thin, so my wife and I went out and bought a new truck. We got into debt and became servants to the loan company. That's what I used to call living by faith. I gave that up because it doesn't work very well. Why didn't it work? It didn't work because my focus was on the truck and not God's Word. It's not the exercise of my mind believing for the truck which produces faith; rather, it is the total focus of our minds and hearts on the Word of God which produces the kind of faith that generates results. The firm foundation I'm going to establish here is that God's Word is the only basis on which to operate in faith.

Another thing that doesn't work very well is repetitive prayer. Four of my wife's relatives died of cancer, even after I and many people prayed for them hundreds of times, asking God for their healing.

> And when you pray, do not use vain repetitions as the heathen do. For they think that they will be heard for their many words.
> —Matthew 6:7, NKJV

The prayer of request or petition is one of seven different types of prayer we have identified. It's the type of prayer in which we ask God for something we need or desire. Many times this type of prayer is used to ask God over and over for the same thing. This action fosters doubt and unbelief, since operating in faith means that we believe we have what we've asked for the first time.

What about 1 Thessalonians 5:17, where it says, "Pray without ceasing"? If we look at the psalms, we see that David employed all kinds of different ways to talk to God. He used thanksgiving, praise, and worship prayers. In the Lord's Prayer in Matthew 7, we are encouraged to worship and praise God as a part of our prayers to God.

If this is the case, how do we get our belief to translate into reality? Well, after asking God for something once, according to His Word, we need to employ other types of prayer, such as prayers of confession and prayers of praise. As well, we should believe that He has heard us the first time and expect that His provision is already there for us. I will explain this in more detail as I proceed.

What Is Faith?

Webster's Dictionary gives a rather generic definition of the word "faith," but I like the one provided in Romans far better:

> ... (as it is written, "I have made you a father of many nations") in the presence of Him whom he believed—*God, who gives life to the dead and calls those things which do not exist as though they did.*
> —Romans 4:17, NKJV (emphasis added)

The emphasized portion says that God, who makes the dead alive, speaks or declares those things that He cannot see as if they are visible, and that the result exists even though He cannot see it. In other words, in order to live by faith we must speak the things we want to see in our lives according to God's Word. We must expect them to happen, and act and talk as though we have them.

Some would say that God is all-powerful and that He is the only one who can just speak things into existence. However, in Genesis 1:26 we see that we're made in the image and likeness of God. God established patterns as to how we were to live. One of God's patterns, the faith pattern, tells us to speak what we want according to God's Word, and to speak that it already exists.

As we said before, the things we speak into our lives must line up with the Word of God. This gets right back to our relationship with God and our spirit being connected with God's Spirit. If we're living in a way that keeps us connected to God, such as reading the Word, praying, praising, and dealing with sin, we will get to know what God expects from us. We will also know what we can expect from God with regard to His blessings. If we don't know God's Word and what He wants to do for us, we cannot know God's will regarding our lives. We must get to know God's will for every area of our lives. How can we live by faith if we don't know God's Word and what it says?

So How Do We Get Real Faith?

So how do we know if we or someone else has real faith?

> Therefore by their fruits you shall know them.
> —Matthew 7:20, MKJV

This verse indicates that if someone says they're living by faith and that they believe, we will know if they truly are by the results or fruit they get from their prayer life. If they release their faith and believe for healing, they will get healing. If they exercise their faith and believe for a financial miracle, they will get the financial miracle. This is how we know if someone truly knows how to live by faith. If a Christian is truly living by faith, the results or fruit will manifest in and through their lives.

So how do we get this real faith? Do we have to work for it? Is it a gift? To answer these questions, let's begin with this verse:

> ...according as God [has] dealt to every man the measure of faith.
>
> —Romans 12:3, KJV

The words "the measure" here indicate one measure. It doesn't say many measures, or different measures. It says one measure of faith. This means that we as God's children all get one measure of faith—the same amount.

The word "measure" in this verse comes from the Greek word *metron*. According to Webster's Dictionary, "measure" means "a limited or definite quantity; full or sufficient quantity."[45] From these definitions and the above verse, we see that God has given every one of us a definite, sufficient quantity of faith which is more than adequate to live a life of faith. God is a good, generous God.

Also, God is no respecter of persons, which means He doesn't play favourites with His people. As believers, we are all given the same measure of faith.

> For God does not show favoritism.
>
> —Romans 2:11, NIV

As indicated in this verse, He doesn't choose to heap an abundance of faith on one person over another. God gives every believer the same, sufficient quantity of faith. As a result, we realize and accept the fact the God has already given us the faith we need. Don't confuse the measure of faith with the ministry gift of faith. The ministry gift is just that: an extra gift of faith to minister to others.

An abundance of faith in our lives grows as we're able to build our ability to use our faith. We build our faith awareness by speaking God's Word for and over our lives, by hearing God's Word and letting it dominate our hearts, and by receiving the work of the cross as ours. As well, our faith awareness is increased when we see the fruit happen, and when we receive what we have asked for. Great faith is released from within us as we believe God for bigger things day by day.

Faith Comes by Hearing

The following verse provides one of God's principles for us to live by. It indicates how we are to build our faith.

---

45 Noah Webster, *American Dictionary of the English Language*, "Measure" (1828).

> So then faith comes by hearing, and hearing by the word of God.
> —Romans 10:17, NKJV

To start with, we must commit this and other verses to memory, and we must meditate and think on these verses. We must continue to speak and confess them with our mouths, and then, with eyes of faith, we must see ourselves as the scriptures describe us. By speaking God's Word out loud, we follow the principle of building our faith ability by hearing the Word.

It is very clear that it is with the Word of God that our faith ability is built up. It's also very clear that we need to hear the Word. The only way we can hear the Word is to get the sound waves out there where our ears can pick them up. It means that we have to speak the Word out loud with our mouths. Really! Yes, really! The more we speak the Word, the more it will become a part of our heart, and the more it will become a part of who we are. The more we confess the Word for our lives, the stronger our faith skills will grow and the quicker we will receive and participate in God's blessings.

As well, we can apply the principle of sowing and reaping to increase our faith ability, because faith comes by hearing and hearing by the Word. By speaking and confessing the Word, we can sow or put God's Word, with our mouth and mind, into our heart.

> Do not be deceived, God is not mocked; for whatever a man sows, that he will also reap.
> —Galatians 6:7, NKJV

The principle of sowing and reaping is very important. It applies to so many areas of our lives. What it really means is that if you sow or plant a garden, you will reap or harvest the fruit. We can plant good or bad gardens with our mouths and actions. What we say and how we act will produce either good or bad results.

I would like to use this principle of sowing and reaping to draw an analogy, to make the process of living by faith easier to understand. When a gardener plants a seed of corn, waters it, and fertilizes it, she expects the corn seed to grow into a mature plant. She expects it to produce more corn. When the corn is ripe, she will harvest it and enjoy eating the corn.

In the same way, we sow the Word of God into our hearts by committing it to memory, meditating on it, thinking on it, speaking it aloud, believing what it says, and expecting to receive what it offers. When we do this, we are planting (sowing) the seed of the Word into our hearts (which is who we are) so the Word becomes who we are. When we plant the Word into our hearts, it sprouts and grows until it is ready for the harvest, or for us to use.

Let's say, for example, that we have been speaking into our hearts Psalms 103:3—

> Who forgives all your iniquities, who heals all your diseases... (NKJV)

The enemy (Satan) comes along and tries to afflict us with sickness. The minute we become aware of the enemy's devices, the Word spoken into our heart begins to produce the harvest. As we continue to confess the Word with our mouths, the harvest bursts forth into healing. We get healing for the sickness the enemy has tried to bring against us. In other words, the Word begins to operate because of all the planting, fertilizing, and watering which we have done to produce the harvest. The harvest is the healing we are looking for, which is contained in the Word. The Word has become so real to us that we can actually declare by faith that we are healed, even before we experience it.

To add a little extra touch of confidence, we can sow or plant the scriptures into our lives by personalizing them. For example, we can say "By Jesus' stripes, I am healed" and "My needs are supplied by God according to His riches in glory by Christ Jesus." By sowing or speaking the Word into our hearts this way, we build our faith skills in the Word. Thus, when an opportunity to exercise our faith comes, we can speak with confidence in the Word of God. We can speak that we are healed and that our needs are abundantly supplied.

Let me repeat Romans 4:17:

> Even God, who quickens the dead, and calls those things which be not as though they were. (KJV)

From this verse, I'm rehearsing God's pattern, which is to speak what the Word says is yours. See yourself in your mind as having already received it. Expect to experience it in the physical realm. Act and talk like you already have it. Why is it important to speak God's Word aloud? It's important since faith comes by hearing the Word of God.

The Work of the Cross

Let's continue to discover how we build our faith ability by looking at another aspect of this subject: the work of the cross.

> ...so that it might be fulfilled which was spoken by Isaiah the prophet, saying, "He took on Himself our weaknesses and bore our sicknesses."
> —Matthew 8:17, MKJV

The Prophet Isaiah is speaking about the work Jesus accomplished when He shed His blood and died on the cross. Jesus took all of our sicknesses and infirmities on His body, and His body was nailed to the cross. He took *all* of our sin, sickness, and poverty upon His body, thus we don't have those things anymore.

Regardless, some of you are going to ask, "Why do I still feel this pain?" or "How come my bills aren't paid yet?" Well, that's a good question. The reason is that our level of faith awareness has not yet been built up to the place where we can embrace the work of the cross.

When Jesus arose from the grave, did He give the sin, sickness, and poverty back to us? No! No, not at all! Jesus took it all to the grave, and when He arose from the grave in resurrection power He came to give us life and that more abundantly. John 10:10 says,

> I have come that they may have life, and that they may have it more abundantly. (NKJV)

Sin, sickness, and poverty stayed in the grave, never to be ours again. The cross did a complete work for all of our ills and problems. Just like Jesus took all of our sin on the cross, He also took all of our sickness and disease. It was a complete work for us.

> For sin shall not have dominion over you, for you are not under law but under grace.
> —Romans 6:14, NKJV

In this verse, we see that sin no longer has any dominion or rule over us unless we allow it to. We don't have to participate in sin anymore. We can choose to refuse to sin. In the same way, we have been delivered from sickness at the cross, as we see in Matthew 8:17. This means that sickness can no longer rule over us either, and we can choose not to participate in it. Now, that's a pretty strong statement, but the work of the cross redeemed us from sin and we no longer have it. The work of the cross has redeemed us from sickness, too, thus we don't have to have it anymore either. Can you see the similarity here? Redemption didn't just happen for sin; it happened for sickness and poverty at the same time.

Most Christians have only known a part of the work of the cross. If they only knew they didn't have to be sick, they would probably choose to live in divine health. You see, your faith will only produce results to the degree that you understand the Word of God. As you accept the truth that Jesus not only bore your sins on the cross but He also bore all your sicknesses, your days of sickness will be over.

> The one who does what is sinful is of the devil, because the devil has been sinning from the beginning. The reason the Son of God appeared was to destroy the devil's work.
>
> —1 John 3:8, NIV

Jesus came to destroy the works of the devil. The works of the devil are revealed in Deuteronomy 28:15–68, and they include every kind of evil which happens on this earth. The evil of sickness is included in the curse, as we can see in the following verse:

> …then the Lord will bring upon you and your descendants extraordinary plagues—great and prolonged plagues—and serious and prolonged sicknesses.
>
> —Deuteronomy 28:59, NKJV

In case you are bothered by the fact that Moses credited the Lord with the plagues and sickness described in Deuteronomy 28:59, please reread the beginning of this chapter. It is explained fully there.

We don't have to experience and receive the curse in our lives, because we have been delivered from the curse.

> Christ redeemed us from the curse of the Law, being made a curse for us (for it is written, "Cursed is everyone having been hanged on a tree").
> —Galatians 3:13, MKJV

How do we arrive at the conclusion, from Galatians 3:13, that we are delivered from the curse? The key words are *"being made a curse for us"* and *"having been hanged on a tree."* Let's look at the word "curse" for a moment. Webster's Dictionary defines it as "evil or misfortune that comes as if in answer to someone's request."[46] Jesus was made evil and bad for us, and went to the cross with all the evil of this world upon Him. Therefore, all the evil has been taken care of by Jesus when we embrace His work on the cross.

So who makes the request for the curse to happen in our lives?

> But it shall come to pass, if you do not obey the voice of the Lord your God, to observe carefully all His commandments and His statutes which I command you today, that all these curses will come upon you and overtake you…
> —Deuteronomy 28:15, NKJV

Disobedience to God's Word—in other words, sin—makes the request for the curse to happen in our lives, because of our choice to disobey God. In the first part of Galatians 3:13, we see that Christ has redeemed us. Further on, we see that He was made a curse for us. When Jesus was made the curse for us, He took on His body every evil represented by the curse. This curse was nailed to the cross, and then went to the grave with Him. As a result, we don't need to have the curse on us anymore. It has been taken away by Jesus. We have been delivered and set free from all the evil contained in the curse! Praise God!

Since sickness, poverty, and all evil are part of the curse, we have been delivered from them as well. Praise God! Therefore, when the enemy comes with sickness, we declare by faith the work of the cross, the grave, and the resurrection. If we believe and confess with our mouths this marvellous redemptive work which Christ did for us, that work becomes our very own. According to that work, we have no sickness, our sins are forgiven, and we are not living

---

46 *Webster's Canadian Dictionary & Thesaurus* (Toronto, ON: Strathearn Books, 2011), 107.

in poverty. By faith, we can see ourselves as healed, free from sin, and living in God's abundance. Why? Because God's Word declares it, that's why.

Real Faith Summary

Let's recap briefly what we have discovered under this subject of how we get real faith:

- We know that someone has faith by the results their faith produces.
- God gives each one of His children the same amount of faith, a plentiful portion. We have all that we need.
- All believers are urged to live by faith in God and His Word.
- We build our faith ability by hearing God's Word.
- In order to hear God's Word, we have to speak it out of our mouths.
- God's Word has to become who we are, by us getting it into our hearts.
- The Word gets into our hearts when we read it, meditate on it, and speak it out loud.
- As well, we build our faith skills by using the principle of sowing and reaping, or speaking and receiving.
- Faith is activated and increased by speaking God's Word and expecting to obtain God's blessings, such as healing.
- Our faith ability is also built when we recognize that the work of the cross didn't just deliver us from sin; it also delivered us from sickness, poverty, and every other evil.

Living Our Faith

> For in it the righteousness of God is revealed from faith to faith, as it is written, "The just shall live by faith."
> —Romans 1:17, MKJV

All Christians are required, according to this verse, to live by their faith in God and His Word. It's not an option. I have already shared on how to build strong faith ability, so let's get right into living by faith and see how it is done.

To begin with, I would like to briefly share a faith prayer principle the Lord gave me:

> And all things, whatever you shall ask in prayer, believing, you shall receive.
> —Matthew 21:22, MKJV

We previously discussed this verse and how to apply it to our lives in Chapter Five. However, I would like to remind us of this prayer principle again. Let me paraphrase what Jesus said: "Whatever you ask or make a request for, providing that you accept My words as true, you will get what you asked for."

Let me refresh your memory regarding this verse. Did Jesus say *ask* or did He say *asks*? Of course He said *ask*, which means to make a request—one request. Next He says that we are to believe, not ask again. We are to believe. Believe means that we know that we already have what we've asked for. Finally, Jesus says that we are to receive or take whatever we asked for. How do we receive what we have asked for?

> Let the redeemed of the Lord say so, Whom He has redeemed from the hand of the adversary...
> —Psalms 107:2, NASB

Just like this verse says, we get a hold of it or take it with the words of our mouth. We speak that we have it. We say so. Of course, our declaration must line up with God's Word.

In addition, we should use the prayer of praise as a form of receiving what we've asked for from God.

> Now thanks be to God, who always causes us to triumph in Christ...
> —2 Corinthians 2:14, MKJV

This verse encourages us to thank God for the success, provision, or healing even before we experience it, because God is going to cause us to triumph and be successful. He is going to see that we get what we have asked for because it lines up with His Word. Therefore, part of the process of receiving from God is not only to declare it, but also to thank God for it even before we can see and experience it in this life. Praise produces victory!

Let me just clear up a misconception that some have expressed to me. The misconception is that we can't thank God for something we can't see, because we would be lying or not telling the truth. Basically, the real truth is that when we speak what God says in His Word, we are telling the truth. God's Word is truth. Saying that we are healed, for example, is true because God's Word says that by Jesus' stripes we are healed. When we live by faith, we speak that which God's Word says we can have as though we already have it. That's called faith and that's how faith works.

To recap, the first time we ask for something in faith, we believe that God has heard us, because He is not deaf. Then we take the answer with the words of our mouth.

Let us expand on this faith prayer principle of ask, believe, and receive by looking at the following verse:

> Now this is the confidence that we have in Him, that if we ask anything according to His will, He hears us. And if we know that He hears us, whatever we ask, we know that we have the petitions that we have asked of Him.
> —1 John 5:14–15, NKJV

First of all, the above verse uses the words *"this is the confidence."* When we have confidence, it means that we believe in something enough that we expect it to happen. This is just another way of saying that we know we have what we've asked for as soon as we finish asking for it.

How do we get to the place of knowing that we really believe? Let's use the area of healing to illustrate the steps of believing. There's no better scripture to use then this one:

> But He was wounded for our transgressions, He was bruised for our iniquities; the chastisement for our peace was upon Him, and by His stripes we are healed.
> —Isaiah 53:5, NKJV

If we are to operate in belief, we must first believe that what God is saying in this verse is true. In order for this to happen, we must engrave this verse into our hearts so that it becomes a part of us. It must be so much a part of us that when a pain or sickness tries to come on us, we automatically think of and speak verses like this one.

I previously shared about the heart in Chapter Three, but I would like to do a little review here to remind us of how our hearts reveal what and how we believe.

> For out of the abundance of the heart the mouth speaks. A good man out of the good treasure of the heart brings out good things; and an evil man out of the evil treasure brings out evil things.
> —Matthew 12:34–35, MKJV

Let me just take a little time to explain this verse. Your character and personality, which you received from birth, is contained in your heart. As well, whatever circumstances of life you have experienced help to shape your heart and make you who you are. Matthew 12:34–35 indicates that your heart will reveal your character, will, beliefs, and desires by the words you speak. If you have good stored up in your heart, good will come out of your mouth, because that's who you are. When you store God's good words in your heart, they will automatically come out of your heart, revealing what you really believe. Do you believe people, the world, and circumstances, or do you believe God? Our words will portray who we are—believers of God, or not! Our hearts give evidence of who we are by our actions and what comes out of our mouths.

When God's Word gets into our hearts, we are at the place where the Word becomes ours. It's now part of us, so whenever we speak, our words will be what God says and not what we or the world says. When we arrive at this point in faith, we have arrived at the point where we believe, and our faith will begin to produce great results.

Let's go back to 1 John 5:14–15 for the second step in this faith prayer principle. We've already discovered that we only need to ask God once for anything. Asking God over and over for the same thing introduces doubt, because obviously we don't believe God heard us the first time. This verse confirms that if we ask God for anything according to His will, He hears us. Okay, that's settled! Next, it says that we have whatever we asked for; it is ours! So if we ask according to God's will, He hears us, and we get what we have asked for.

Up to this point, we have shared the faith process of believing and asking. Now let's go a little further and look at the process of receiving. As indicated above, the word "receive" means "to take, or to get a hold of."

> For assuredly, I say to you, whoever says to this mountain, "Be removed and be cast into the sea," and does not doubt in his heart, but believes that those things he says will be done, he will have whatever he says.
> —Mark 11:23, NKJV

This verse is one of my benchmark scriptures with regards to faith. It describes how we are to use our mouths to receive what we have asked for in prayer. It demonstrates an authoritative type of prayer—the process of declaring something that we already know is God's will instead of asking for it.

First of all, Jesus says that we are to tell the problem to leave. Secondly, we must not doubt in our heart. Thirdly, we must believe that what we say will be done, and that we will have what we say. Fourthly, we receive or take the answer to our prayer by declaring with our mouths that we already have what we've asked for. This verse clearly indicates that we get the answer we're looking for with the words of our mouths. To further confirm what we are talking about, let me repeat Romans 4:17:

> Even God, who quickens the dead, and calls those things which be not as though they were. (KJV)

From this verse, we can see that we're rehearsing God's pattern, which is to speak what the Word says is ours. You see yourself in your mind as having already received it, expect to experience it in the physical realm, and act and talk like you already have it.

Let me just clarify something here. The faith prayer principle we're discussing is not an exact formula. If you wish to believe and then ask God for something, that's just fine. On the other hand, if you decide to ask God for something and then believe, that's okay, too. Sometimes instead of asking for something you may declare that you have it because it's God's will, as found in His Word. The most important thing to remember about the faith prayer principle is that these three actions—ask, believe, and receive—are key to receiving God's promises.

Faith and Healing

To demonstrate practically how this faith process actually works, let me give you an example from my own life. Many years ago, when I was a teenager, my family stored gas in the garage in a forty-five-gallon drum. I remember that one of our vehicles was to be filled with gas, and I was asked to fill it. The pump was out of the barrel, standing upside-down in between a number of barrels. I couldn't get at it from the floor, so I climbed up on top of the barrels, about three and a half feet off the floor. I proceeded to bend over completely and pull this heavy gas pump up so I could install it in one of the barrels of gas. The gas pump weighed approximately sixty pounds.

I was maybe 120 pounds and built pretty light. Well, bending over and pulling up this pump was very bad for my back. I did considerable damage to my back, and from that day forward my back was a mess. There were many days when I couldn't get up off a chair or the bed without hanging on to something because of all the pain.

Eventually, my parents decided to take me to a chiropractor, but the closest one was a hundred miles away. We made this trek a number of times, and as a result I was able to function somewhat better. However, I had to be very careful how I bent over, how I got up from a chair, and how I lifted anything. Many times the pain would cause me to drop to the floor.

Finally, when I was about forty, I was offered a power belt by one of the chiropractors I was seeing. From that point on, I was able to function fairly normally with the belt around my hips. I also made numerous visits to the chiropractor every month for most of my adult life.

I wore out numerous power belts over the many years until the summer of 2010. For quite some time, I had been studying and researching the Bible to determine how to get healing for my body. What led me to do this is another story in itself, and I won't share it here. Needless to say, I had learned how to receive healing for a number of smaller things in my life, such as macular degeneration, sleep apnea, and bursitis. I decided that I was going to apply the same principles and methods in my prayer life and relationship with God to receive healing for my back as well.

I began to speak healing scriptures over my back, scriptures I had been focusing on and studying for some time, until they became very much a part of me. In other words, I was so familiar with these scriptures that I actually believed I could have what they said was mine. I asked God to heal my back, and from that point on I considered it to be healed. How could that be, you might ask? It's because I began to believe I was healed regardless of what I felt like. The other thing I did was to thank God for my healing. Even though I hadn't experienced the healing in a way I could feel yet, I declared that I was healed. I never declared anything else—I never spoke negative words about my back. I only declared what God's Word said about my back.

Another thing I should mention is that I had been working on my relationship with God for a number of years previously. Even though I had been a Christian for many years, I didn't have an intimate relationship with Him.

I realized that part of receiving God's blessings, such as healing, required me to get to know Him in a personal way. Even though I wasn't perfect in my relationship with Him, God saw that in my heart I desired to have that relationship. As a result, God began to release His blessings in my life in a greater way than He had in the past.

I had been using these faith principles to provide for my healing for a couple of months when one day I noticed something different about my back. I took the power belt off and noticed that I didn't have to be careful when I bent over, because there was no pain. I didn't have to hang on when I got up out of the chair. I could bend over and lift things with no pain! Suddenly, I realized that God had healed my back! Praise God!

From that point on, I was able to function like a normal human being. I never had to wear the power belt again, and I could lift things without experiencing any pain. Praise God! Years later, my back is still very much healed! Bless the Lord!

Faith and Finances

We have largely used the example of healing to demonstrate faith, so let's look at the area of finances. In order for faith to work in our lives, especially in the area of finances, we must be cheerful givers. This is confirmed in the following verses:

> So let each one give as he purposes in his heart, not grudgingly or of necessity; for God loves a cheerful giver. And God is able to make all grace abound toward you, that you, always having all sufficiency in all things, may have an abundance for every good work.
> —2 Corinthians 9:7–8, NKJV

Let me paraphrase the above scripture. God expects us to give of our resources and increase with a kind, loving, giving heart. When we are obedient in this way, God's grace and favour abounds toward us. He will make sure we overflow with His abundance in every area of our lives. This enables us to produce good works for Him.

In order for us to live under the influence of God's blessing, we must be givers. We must be givers of our financial resources.

"Bring the whole tithe into the storehouse, that there may be food in my house. Test me in this," says the Lord Almighty, "and see if I will not throw open the floodgates of heaven and pour out so much blessing that there will not be room enough to store it."

—Malachi 3:10, NIV

The storehouse referred to in Malachi 3 refers to the assembly you attend and where you receive some of your spiritual teaching or food. We are instructed to give tithes, ten percent of our increase, to the assembly in order that God will release His abundant, overflowing financial blessing upon us. The tithe belongs to God. The ten percent figure is found elsewhere in the Bible, which is a subject for another time. However, in order for your offerings (or sowing gifts) to produce a harvest or increase in your life, you must be a tither! Furthermore, your tithe is not your offering or seed to sow. Next, let's look at this verse:

"And I will rebuke the devourer for your sakes, so that he will not destroy the fruit of your ground, nor shall the vine fail to bear fruit for you in the field," says the Lord of hosts.

—Malachi 3:11, NKJV

If we rob God of the tithe, we bring the curse upon us. This allows Satan to devour or destroy our finances. However, if we're faithful to bring our tithe to the church, God will put the hedge of His blessing around us. The blessing will prevent Satan from destroying our finances. How important it is for us to be faithful in giving of our tithe, because God will open up the windows of heaven and bless us so abundantly that we will have an overflow of His abundance, financially.

As a part of faith and finances, we must look at the process of sowing our offerings as a seed. This action involves the principle of tangible, actual, physical giving or sowing in order to receive or reap a harvest. Let me clarify what I mean:

Give, and it shall be given unto you; good measure, pressed down, and shaken together, and running over, shall men give into your bosom.

—Luke 6:38, KJV

This verse clearly reinforces the principle of giving in order to receive. It means that we must willingly give something from our own belongings or resources in order to receive an abundant financial blessing in return. Let me say it plainly. In order to receive a thousand dollars, for instance, to pay off a bill, we must willingly give a ten dollar offering if possible, where God directs us to give it. Some might say, "Oh, but that's a hundred times more than we gave. I don't think it's right to expect that kind of increase." Why not? Let's look at,

> A farmer went out to sow his seed. As he was scattering the seed, some fell along the path; it was trampled on, and the birds ate it up… Still other seed fell on good soil. It came up and yielded a crop, a hundred times more than was sown.
>
> —Luke 8:5, 8, NIV

The principle of planting the seed and expecting to get a huge crop is the principle of sowing and reaping. This principle works in every area of life; it works in the words we speak, the things we do, and the finances we give. If we plant good words in a relationship, we will have a good relationship. If we plant seed by helping others, we will get help when we need it. If we give of our finances to help others, we are planting or sowing seed. This seed will produce a financial harvest of one hundred times, sixty times, or thirty times more than what we gave, depending on our level of faith ability.

All seed produces more of itself, as we can see in the following verse:

> Then God said, "Let the earth sprout vegetation: plants yielding seed, and fruit trees on the earth bearing fruit after their kind with seed in them"; and it was so.
>
> —Genesis 1:11, NASB

A carrot seed produces a carrot harvest. Likewise, a financial seed or gift produces a financial harvest. This is why it's important to name our seed. For example, we may give an offering of a hundred dollars and call it our 2015 summer vacation seed.

Let's get back to a statement I made earlier, which was that we need to give in order to receive. We need to give a financial offering in order to receive a financial harvest. The offering should be given to whoever God directs you to give it. Pray and ask God for direction and then listen for His answer.

In addition, to giving of our resources, we need to sow or put the Word of God into our hearts. We must put scriptures regarding finances into our hearts by speaking them, so that we can hear them, as we are directed to do in the following verse:

> So then faith comes by hearing, and hearing by the word of God.
> —Romans 10:17, NKJV

So when we discipline ourselves to sow or give financially, and sow or put God's Word into our hearts, we are preparing ourselves for an abundant financial harvest. When we do these two things, we are preparing to see our finances and grow and increase.

Since understanding how to live by faith in the area of finances is very important in order to experience God's blessings, I'm going to share an example of how to live by faith. Let's start small, because that's where all of us have to start. Great faith ability doesn't happen right off the bat; it builds and grows as it is exercised. Let's say you need a job, you have rent to pay, and you have very little or no money. What does God's Word say about this situation?

> And my God shall supply all your need according to His riches in glory by Christ Jesus.
> —Philippians 4:19, NKJV

Did the above verse say that God might supply some of your needs, but not all? No! I see the word "all" in that scripture, and to me that means total and complete supply of our every need.

What about the word "your?" Who is that referring to? In this scripture, Paul is writing to the Christian church at Philippi; that's us. We, as Christians, are part of the body of Christ just like the Christians at Philippi.

Next, we have the word "need," from the Greek word *chreia*, which means "occasion, demand, requirement"[47] according to Strong's. Webster's

---

47 James Strong. *Strong's Dictionaries of the Hebrew and Greek Words*, "Chreia" (Nashville, TN: Abingdon Press, 1890).

defines it as "some things necessary or desired."[48] These definitions are the opposite of the traditional teaching, by which we were told that need in this verse meant provision of just enough to fulfill a desperate lack. Instead, God shall supply our wants, demands, and requirements. What a generous God we have! Praise His name!

Finally, in reference to Philippians 4:19, what does Paul mean when he writes, *"according to his riches in glory"*? The word "riches" means God's abundant fullness and His endless supply. God's supply is so abundant that He has more than we can handle, and it comes through Jesus Christ, His Son.

Now that we know that it's God's will to provide for us abundantly, we put that Word into our hearts by confessing it aloud with our mouths as much as possible, until it becomes part of our hearts. Actually, we should really be putting the Word into our hearts long before we have a need. We should be prepared in advance, all the time, in the event that the devil tries to afflict us in some way.

Next, we need to sow or give a financial seed. We ask God how much to give and where to give it, and then we listen for the answer. Sometimes God will tell us out of the blue to sow a seed or give away something we have, because He has something bigger for us. As well, we should name the seed. Let's call this one our February rent seed.

Now that we have sown our seed, we are ready to receive God's provision. We ask God for His provision first, then we thank Him for His provision. We continue by speaking financial scriptures over our life and situation. Finally, we receive the answer by the words we speak from our mouths; we speak that we have His provision. We don't speak anything negative or contrary to God's Word regarding our request to God. We see with our eyes of faith that we already have our wants supplied, and this will be followed by the physical evidence of a job and the finances we asked for, because God's Word says they are ours.

Let me reiterate: it is very important for us to have an attitude of praise and thanksgiving to God at all times.

> ...giving thanks always for all things to God the Father in the name of our Lord Jesus Christ...
>
> —Ephesians 5:20, NKJV

---

48 *Webster's Canadian Dictionary & Thesaurus* (Toronto, ON: Strathearn Books, 2011), 281.

In the midst of operating in and living by faith, we should take time to praise and thank God for what we have received by faith, even though we cannot see it yet in the physical realm. Of course, once faith manifests and the answer appears in the physical realm, we must be thankful and give testimony of God's provision and blessing in response to our faith.

Faith and Relationships

I want to share one more example of living by faith from my own experience. For many years, my oldest daughter never went to church. She seemed to be slipping in her Christian life, and I was concerned about her. I had been living by faith for some time regarding health, finances, and my character, but I never thought to apply the same principles to my daughter's situation.

One day as I was praying for my children, which I do daily, it occurred to me that I should see my daughter, in faith, as a woman of God. As well, I should see her reading the Word, spending time in prayer, and fellowshipping with the saints (attending church services). I realized that I should speak what I wanted to see in my daughter's life. I should speak that she is a woman of God. I used the following scripture as part of the basis for my faith:

> Train up a child in the way he should go, and when he is old he will not depart from it.
> —Proverbs 22:6, NKJV

We had trained up our daughter in the right way, God's way. Thus we could use this verse and stand on it to believe that our daughter would return to the ways of God.

Only several weeks later, when we were away for a winter holiday, we got an email from our daughter in which she informed us that she wanted to change her life. She wanted to start going back to church and be part of the family of God again. Wow! We were thrilled! Now she reads the Word regularly, listens to messages, serves God, and attends church services regularly. As a result, with regard to the rest of my children and their spouses who are not believers yet, I see all of them in faith as believers in Christ, living according to God's Word. We've already begun to see some fruit beginning to mature in this act of faith.

Faith Works through Love

Let's look further at how important love is to a successful faith life.

> We know that we have passed from death to life, because we love the brethren. He who does not love his brother abides in death.
> —1 John 3:14, NKJV

If we look at the last part of the above verse, we note that without love for others we are living under the influence of death, or the curse. In that situation, faith is certainly not going to work.

> I call heaven and earth to witness against you today, that I have set before you life and death, the blessing and the curse. So choose life in order that you may live, you and your descendants...
> —Deuteronomy 30:19, NASB

Here we see that God gave us the choice of the blessing (life), and the curse (death). Therefore, if we live without love we fall under the curse, and faith doesn't work in our lives.

> For in Christ Jesus neither circumcision nor uncircumcision avails anything, but faith working through love.
> —Galatians 5:6, NKJV

Let me paraphrase the above verse as follows: "In Christ, neither the law nor the gift of salvation accomplish anything towards faith, but faith accomplishes things when it works through love." Without love, faith does not work. What kind of shortcomings demonstrate a lack of love and keep faith from working in our lives?

- Offences or unforgiveness with others.
- Critical or judgmental attitudes or expressions towards others.
- Bickering and strife in your relationships with friends, your spouse, family, etc.

Any of these things will block God's blessings. God's blessings come to us through living by faith, but faith works through love to release those blessings.

Love is so important to a successful faith life. We know that love dwells in us by our spirit being connected to God's Spirit, so why not declare the release of that love into our souls, for us to use and experience in our daily lives? Remember, you get what you say!

Joy Brings Success

Joy is another aspect of faith that will propel us to success in our Christian lives. It will help us to get better results with our prayer lives.

First of all, let's define the word "joy" by referring to Webster's Dictionary. It means "a feeling of pleasure or happiness that comes from success, good fortune, or a sense of well-being."[49] Now that we have defined joy, let's look at Isaiah 12:3:

And with joy you shall draw water out of the wells of salvation. (MKJV)

Most Christians think that salvation only provides redemption from sin and a ticket to heaven. Let's see if this is so. From Strong's Hebrew and Greek Dictionary, we find the following definition, from the Greek word *yshuah*: "something *saved*, that is, (abstractly) *deliverance*; hence *aid, victory, prosperity... deliverance, health, help.*"[50] According to this definition, it seems to me that salvation includes prosperity, health, and deliverance—deliverance from the curse and sin.

So if we look at Isaiah 12:3 again, we discover that joy enables us to draw upon an abundance of prosperity, health, eternal life, deliverance from the curse, and deliverance from sin. Wow! That's big! What an amazing God we serve!

Count it all joy, my brothers, when you meet trials of various kinds...
—James 1:2, ESV

---

49 *Webster's Canadian Dictionary & Thesaurus* (Toronto, ON: Strathearn Books, 2011), 232.
50 James Strong. *Strong's Dictionaries of the Hebrew and Greek Words*, "Yshuah" (Nashville, TN: Abingdon Press, 1890).

In this verse, James encourages us to be joyful when we experience trials and difficulties in our lives. This means that even though the trial may be very difficult, we should force ourselves to be joyful. Better yet, we should declare that we have joy until we actually feel it. Remember, we get what we say. Let's speak the release of joy.

Why should we be joyful when we're possibly going through great pain?

Do not be grieved, for the joy of the Lord is your strength.
—Nehemiah 8:10, NASB

The joy which God provides gives us the strength to not only endure trials, but it gives us the strength to stand on God's Word. Joy gives us strength to believe and not doubt. Joy gives us the strength to speak God's promises and wait patiently for them to manifest in our lives. You see, if we don't have joy, we may not have God's strength, which is available to us. Sometimes this could mean the difference between success and failure in our prayer lives.

Joy is within us by our spirit being connected to God's Spirit. Let's speak the release of it in our lives. Let's use all the tools and receive the victory, which is ours in Christ Jesus.

Faith Without Works

There's another aspect of faith which we need to discover:

So also faith by itself, if it does not have works, is dead.
—James 2:17, ESV

Okay, what does this verse really mean? We have already defined and discovered how to activate faith. So what is the works part of faith which we see in this verse? First, let's define the word "works," from the Greek word *ergon*, according to Strong's Hebrew and Greek Dictionary. It means "an act... deed, doing, labour, work."[51] From this definition, it appears that we have to do something or take some action in order for our faith to work. What kind of actions should we take? Here are a few:

---

51 Ibid., "Ergon."

- Thank God for the result even if it's not evident in this realm yet.
- Think and act as if you've already received what you have asked for. Again, it doesn't matter if you can't see or access it yet. Do it anyway!
- Confess and speak the scriptures over your life, especially the one you are standing on for the answer.
- Declare the promises of God (Scripture) as yours. After all, you are an heir of God and a joint heir with Jesus Christ.
- Don't speak about or affirm the problem.
- Tell the devil to leave and take the problem with him in Jesus' name.
- If you couldn't previously do something, begin to do it. For example, if you couldn't raise your arm above your chest, begin to do it. At the same time, declare the victory: "By Jesus' stripes, my arm is healed."
- If you're short of money to pay a bill, give an offering to a ministry. Ask God where you are to give it. It doesn't have to be a big offering—even one or two dollars will do. If God asks you to give more, do it, even if it means sacrificial giving on your part.

All of these actions are about us putting feet to our faith. By these actions, we're saying that we expect to receive what we have asked for. We're expecting to get what we have confessed or declared as ours according to God's Word. This is what is called putting works or actions to our faith, in order to produce the results we're looking for.

The Faith Fight

For quite some time, I have discovered that there are many Christians who have a hard time getting aggressive with Satan. They have a hard time winning against Satan, especially in the more difficult trials of life. If you're one of those, let me give you some help.

My wife was struggling with this situation and it really bothered me. I asked God, "Is it only possible for aggressive people to get their healing according to Your Word?" After a lot of thought and consideration, God turned the light on in my mind.

I remembered what happened to my wife and her twin brother when they were growing up in a small village beside Lake Winnipeg. Their family was the only white Protestant family in this area attending the elementary school. The other children were all native and Catholic. Regardless, my wife and her brother were bullied and discriminated against terribly by the boys. These children would beat them up, drag my wife in the dirt by her hair, and feed their lunch to the dogs. This went on for some time.

My wife was twenty-three years old and 105 pounds with a twenty-one-inch waist when I married her. As you can see, she was no powerhouse because of her size. In addition, her twin brother was much smaller than her and unable to defend himself.

One day, my wife decided that if they were going to win this struggle, she would have to begin to fight. Her dad was an Army veteran and he gave her some tips on how to fight to win. She began to stand her ground. It wasn't just one boy who would come after them, but rather two or three at a time. She kicked, punched, and threw them on the ground. She even threw several of the boys over school desks and broke the desks. They got a real taste of their own medicine real quick. From then on, they left her and her brother alone.

This is exactly what happens when you're in a fight with Satan. The only differences are that you can't see your enemy (Satan) and you don't fight him physically. The differences don't matter; you still have to fight if you're going to win. God has given us two major tools, as Christians, to use in the battle: the Word of God and the name of Jesus.

So how do we fight Satan? Let's say that he's trying to steal your health with cancer. We begin punching with our fists and kicking with our feet. Really? How do we do that? We fight with our words, which we take from God's Word. We might land the following punch: "Satan, it is written in God's Word that by Jesus' stripes, I am healed. Therefore take your cancer and get it out of my body now, in Jesus' name." We say this aggressively and emphatically out loud.

You see, we have just thrown two punches. The first punch was the Word of God and the second was the name of Jesus. When you're fighting like this, imagine yourself in a physical fight for your life. In order to win, you have to give it everything you have. So when you're punching with your words, do it with everything within you. Speak the words with intensity, passion, and determination. Determine to let Satan know that you really mean business.

We don't have to fight Satan like this every time. Eventually he'll get the picture that you mean business and that you will win, because God is on your side. At that point, it will require less intensity in order to win the battle against Satan.

In conclusion, let me say that a fight is a fight. You never want to lose to Satan. You will have to fight verbally against him every time if you're going to win. Don't ever give up, but become more determined to win, as long as it takes. Don't forget to ask God to help you to be determined and confident in the fight. In the following verse, God promises us His help and the victory—just thank Him for it.

> Now thanks be to God, who always causes us to triumph in Christ...
> —2 Corinthians 2:14, MKJV

Faith Killers

There are nine actions we can participate in which will limit or stop our faith ability. These actions will either prevent us from getting answers to our prayers or they will severely limit positive results when we pray. I'm going to list them and deal with each one individually.

1. Doubt and unbelief.
2. Fear.
3. Disobedience to God and His Word.
4. No respect for God.
5. No generosity or giving.
6. No love.
7. No patience.
8. Strife, discord, and envy.
9. Sin.

Don't let this list discourage you or scare you away from living by faith. God will enable you. All He needs is a willing heart and a desire to make it happen.

All of these actions are serious faith killers, so let's start with doubt and unbelief.

1. Doubt and Unbelief

Living with doubt and unbelief in your life will kill your faith and your blessing. Let's look at doubt first as we consider the following verse:

> And if any one of you is deficient in wisdom, let him ask God for it, who gives with open hand to all men, and without upbraiding; and it will be given him. But let him ask in faith and have no doubts; for he who has doubts is like the surge of the sea, driven by the wind and tossed into spray. A person of that sort must not expect to receive anything from the Lord ...
> —James 1:5–7, WNT

The word "doubt" from Webster's Dictionary means "to be in a state of uncertainty (especially in religious matters)."[52] The word doubt really means "to be undecided with regard to what we believe, with respect to a certain event or thing." The rest of James 1:5–7 says that if we waver or doubt in our faith walk, we shouldn't expect to receive anything from God. This means that we won't receive a positive answer to our requests. Some examples of doubt in the things we might say or think are:

- "I'm not feeling good today. Maybe I didn't get healed."
- "My mother had heart problems, so I'm bound to have them too."
- "I'm afraid the bank is going to foreclose on our mortgage."
- "The traffic is so busy that I'm afraid I'm going to have an accident."

There are many more examples of doubtful words and statements which express indecision or a doubting attitude. I'm sure you can think of some as well. When you speak words of doubt and uncertainty, you're sowing that doubt and uncertainty into your heart.

> For as he [thinks] in his heart, so is he ...
> —Proverbs 23:7, KJV

> Do not be deceived, God is not mocked; for whatever a man sows, that he will also reap.
> —Galatians 6:7, NKJV

What you put in your heart, through your mouth and mind, will be who you become and what you get in life. If you plant or speak doubtful, negative

---

52 J.B. Foreman, MA, *The Webster Worldwide Dictionary* (Great Britain: William Collins Sons & Co., 1960), 157.

words for your life, you will harvest or experience those things. The principle of sowing and reaping works with positive and negative words. Doubtful, indecisive words reap a harvest of doubt and indecision, which only kills our faith and accomplishes nothing toward answered pray. The words of our mouth and the thoughts of our mind are very powerful, and they need to be taken captive in obedience to Christ when we find ourselves operating in doubt and negativity. I use the following verse to get rid of negative thoughts and negative spoken words:

> ...casting down arguments and every high thing that exalts itself against the knowledge of God, bringing every thought into captivity to the obedience of Christ...
> —2 Corinthians 10:5, NKJV

We must cast and turf out every thought, argument, or imagination that goes against God's Word. We must keep every thought under control in order to make it obey Christ and the Word of God. It really bothers me when I join together with other Christians to pray for someone's healing and after we've just finished praying, someone says, "Well, if they're not healed, they only have two months to live." Those negative, doubtful words just cancelled all the faith for the one who spoke them, and for those who didn't reject these negative words. Doubt is the opposite of faith. It is important that we speak against words of doubt, even if, due to the situation we may be in, we quietly renounce them.

On the other hand, unbelief amounts to the fact that we really don't believe that God's Word is true. If we refuse to believe what God tells us in His Word, we certainly cannot expect to receive anything from Him.

2. Fear

Fear is the opposite of faith. Let's look at the account of Peter walking on the water as an example:

> "Lord, if it's you," Peter replied, "tell me to come to you on the water."
> "Come," he said.

> Then Peter got down out of the boat, walked on the water and came toward Jesus. But when he saw the wind, he was afraid and, beginning to sink, cried out, "Lord, save me!"
>
> —Matthew 14:28–30, NIV

Peter, a disciple of Jesus, was in a boat with the other disciples on the lake, and he saw Jesus coming to the boat, walking on the water. Peter asked Jesus if he could walk on the water too, and Jesus told him to come. Peter did fine walking on the water until he got his eyes on the water and wind instead of on Jesus. As soon as he took his eyes off Jesus, fear rose up in his mind. What did the fear do? It cancelled his faith to walk on the water and he began to sink. The same is true for us when we take our eyes and attention off the Lord and focus on our problems. Dwelling on the problem creates fear, and fear cancels our faith, and our prayer requests go unanswered.

Let's say you have to walk down an icy sidewalk to get to your home in winter, and in the process you ask God to keep you from falling. Before you step out, you speak this verse:

> For He shall give His angels charge over you, to keep you in all your ways. In their hands they shall bear you up, lest you dash your foot against a stone.
>
> —Psalms 91:11–12, NKJV

Now you're ready to tackle the icy sidewalk. However, just before you step out, you say, "I'm afraid I'm going to fall." What did you just do? You've just destroyed and nullified your faith and your prayer for protection. Expressing any doubt or fear will nullify and destroy faith, which results in your prayers going unanswered.

3. Disobedience to God or His Word

This is something most of us are pretty good at, unfortunately. Sometimes we're not aware of disobedience, because of our ignorance of the Word. However, God expects us to get to know His Word and obey it. He is pretty gracious and patient, but don't push Him too far (see James 1:22).

4. No Respect

Respect for God means that we treat God with esteem and honour. It means that we're careful about how we speak to God and what we say about Him. Again, God is very gracious, but don't forget to repent when you fail—it's very important (see Hebrews 12:28).

5. No Generosity or Giving

Giving is in God's nature, and He wants to develop that same nature in us. If we're stingy, our blessings will also end up being stingy. God loves and rewards a cheerful giver (see Proverbs 22:9).

6. No Love

Walking or living in love with everyone around us is very important. Galatians 5:6 tells us that faith works through love. If we fail to treat others with love, our faith will not work.

7. No Patience

It takes patience and perseverance to continue to speak the Word and confess the answer, even though you haven't experienced it yet. Sometimes you will experience the results immediately while other times it takes a day, a month, or even years, but God is faithful and He always comes through. The time it takes to get results is directly related to the level of your faith ability, which is based on your words and actions. Faith is talking and acting as though you already have what you believe to receive. Never give up speaking the Word and believing that it will happen for you. As you begin to see results, living by faith will come easier.

Most people give up on their faith just before their breakthrough. Don't give up! Hang in there! Keep speaking faith words! The Word has already completed what you believe to receive. Keep on speaking it. It will happen!

> Rest in the LORD, and wait patiently for Him.
> —Psalms 37:7, NKJV

8. Strife, Discord, and Envy

These will kill your faith. They are the opposite of love and need corrective attention. James 3:16 tells us that these things cause confusion and every evil work. These actions are certainly not faith producers.

9. Sin

This is the umbrella for all these faith-killers we're dealing with. More specifically, the sin I'm referring to is disobedience to the Ten Commandments of the Old Testament and the Two Commandments of the New Testament (Ephesians 5:1).

The Trial of Our Faith

Hardships, trials, and difficulties happen in all of our lives. It isn't that God wants us to have trials, but that we seem to need them in order to grow and mature in the Christian life. God allows the trials, but it's our need for growth and maturity which actually brings the trials.

> That the trial of your faith, being much more precious than of gold that [perishes], though it be tried with fire, might be found unto praise and honour and glory at the appearing of Jesus Christ …
> —1 Peter 1:7, KJV

God's ultimate purpose in trials is to sharpen and mature us in our Christian lives and faith walk as we cooperate with God in the midst of the trial. The devil is our greatest enemy in the Christian life. We have been empowered by the name of Jesus and the Word of God to defeat the devil. We must be able to overcome and defeat him any time we need to do it. Not only do we defeat Satan, but we get to experience God's power in our lives. We also get to experience an increase in our level of faith ability as we succeed. Praise God!

The difficulties (trials) are usually things we cannot fix ourselves. These trials are the kind that need God's supernatural fixing power. So how do we deal with trials?

- We embrace the trial as an opportunity for us to grow.
- We recognize that God gives every believer in Christ a sufficient measure of faith to deal with every trial.
- We put God's Word into our hearts by speaking it out loud as often as we can, to build our faith in every area.
- We have patience without fear and doubting.
- We expect God's Word to happen in our lives, to produce results as promised in His Word.
- We thank and praise God for the victory.
- We retain an attitude of joy, happiness, and contentment.
- We speak and declare that we have the victory we are looking for and that God is making a way for us.

As we live our lives by faith, we experience greater victories. These victories catapult our faith ability to greater heights.

The Communion Table

There's no better way to exercise or increase our faith than by celebrating the Communion Table, or the Lord's Supper. This celebration is practiced by Christians in their assemblies, usually on a monthly basis. Nothing is stopping us from celebrating this table at home or at work if we choose.

Before getting into the understanding of the Communion Table, let's read the following:

> So then, whoever eats the bread or drinks the cup of the Lord in an unworthy manner will be guilty of sinning against the body and blood of the Lord. Everyone ought to examine themselves before they eat of the bread and drink from the cup. For those who eat and drink without discerning the body of Christ eat and drink judgment on themselves. That is why many among you are weak and sick, and a number of you have fallen asleep.
> —1 Corinthians 11:27–30, NIV

There are two things we need to do before partaking of the Lord's Supper. First, we shouldn't treat it as an ordinary meal. We need to be in awe of what Jesus did on the cross for us. Secondly, we should ask God if we have any sin in our lives; if we do, we should repent and ask for forgiveness. If we omit these steps, we open up ourselves to the curse, which results in judgment, sickness, and death. So examine yourself and repent before you partake.

Next, let's look at where the Lord's Supper came from:

> So God took an oath when he made his promise. He wanted to make it very clear that his purpose does not change. He wanted those who would receive what was promised to know that. God took an oath so we would have good reason not to give up. We have run away from everything else to take hold of the hope offered to us in God's promise. So God gave his promise and his oath. Those two things can't change. He couldn't lie about them. Our hope is certain.
> —Hebrews 6:17–19, NIrV

In this verse, God is assuring us of His promise, confirmed by an oath. What is His promise? God's promise delivers us from the curse into His blessing. His promise delivers us from death into life. On the other hand, God's oath is His unchangeable declaration that His promise is sure and trustworthy. To further enhance His promise, God sealed His oath with the blood of His Son Jesus. Jesus' blood sealed the promise which God made with us, redeemed us from sin and the curse, and delivered us into life, God's blessing, and His Spirit. What a sacrifice!

So how did God fulfill His promises to us? Let's look at our deliverance from sin first:

> But if we walk in the light, as He is in the light, we have fellowship with one another, and the blood of Jesus Christ His Son cleanses us from all sin.
> —1 John 1:7, MKJV

This verse confirms that Jesus shed His blood on the cross and died to cleanse us and set us free from the bondage of sin in our lives. From the moment Jesus died on the cross, our sins were forgiven. The only thing we have to do to receive it is ask for forgiveness from God. From that point on, we can say that we are forgiven, totally cleansed from our sin by the blood of Jesus.

Next, let's look at our deliverance from the curse:

> Christ [has] redeemed us from the curse of the law, being made a curse for us: for it is written, Cursed is every one that [hangs] on a tree: That the blessing of Abraham might come on the Gentiles through Jesus Christ; that we might receive the promise of the Spirit through faith.
> —Galatians 3:13–14, KJV

These verses indicate that Jesus became the curse for us. He became sin, sickness, poverty, and every evil thing for us. He became the curse so we wouldn't have the curse in our lives. As well, Jesus redeemed us from the curse of the law. God knew that we couldn't keep the law, and that it had become a curse to us for that reason. Therefore, Jesus redeemed us from the curse of the law. In addition, Jesus redeemed and delivered us into the blessing of Abraham and the promise of the Holy Spirit.

When God sent Jesus to the cross and the grave, He made an unbreakable agreement or covenant with us through the body and blood of Jesus. God's people no longer had to sacrifice animals to be redeemed, because Jesus once and for all poured out His blood and went to the grave for us. He provided a New Testament blood covenant for us. So what does God's oath, covenant, and promise mean for us? His covenant delivers us from:

- Sin.
- Sickness.
- Poverty.
- The curse and all its evils.

Furthermore, we have been redeemed into the blessings of God, which are numerous and cover every area of our lives. When we begin to realize what this covenant has done for us, it produces a change in our lives. His covenant delivers us into:

- Health and healing for us, His children. Receive it; it's yours!
- Financial prosperity for us. Receive it; it's yours!
- The fruits of the spirit, including love, joy, peace, patience, and kindness. Receive them; they're yours!
- Eternal life and every blessing contained in His Word. Receive them; they're yours!

Jesus said, "It is finished." His covenant is complete and it's for you and me as believers right now. These things are ours right now!

So what is the Communion Table or the Lord's Supper? We find reference to it in the following verses:

> For I received from the Lord what I also delivered to you, that the Lord Jesus in the night in which he was betrayed took bread; and giving thanks, He broke it and said, "Take, eat; this is My body, which is broken for you; this do in remembrance of Me." In the same way He took the cup also, after supping, saying, "This cup is the New Covenant in My blood; as often as you drink it, do this in remembrance of Me." For "as often as you eat this bread and drink this cup, you show" the Lord's death until He shall come.
> —1 Corinthians 11:23–26, MKJV

To celebrate the Lord's Supper, we use two emblems: bread and wine (or grape juice). These represent Jesus' body and blood, respectively. As part of our celebration, we take the bread by tearing a piece off the loaf or we pick up a cracker, which we break. The act of tearing a piece off the loaf or breaking the cracker represents Jesus' broken body. This action reminds us that He took thirty-nine lashes on His back. With this suffering He took our sickness and pain on His body. He took them to the grave so we wouldn't have them anymore. As we partake of the bread, we must not forget to give our heartfelt thanks to Jesus for the sacrifice of His body on the cross.

The wine (or juice) represents Jesus' blood that was shed or poured out that we might be set free from sin and the curse. As we drink in remembrance, we give thanks to God for the blood that His Son Jesus poured out for us.

If you are experiencing a need or are going through a trial in your life, celebrate the Lord's Supper over that situation. Take communion over your tithes and offerings and see what God will do for you. When you celebrate the Lord's Supper in these things, you're confirming God's covenant to you and affirming God's blessings in your life. Wow! What a marvellous provision God has made for us.

My wife and I celebrate communion together over our needs and wants on a regular basis. When we do, we record all of our requests to God on a piece of paper which we place on the table in front of us. After we have celebrated communion, we focus on the items we have recorded on the paper. We thank God for the finished work of the cross, which has provided for every one of our requests. Since we know that our requests are in line with God's Word, we declare and affirm that these things are already ours.

To conclude, I want to reiterate that this celebration and remembrance of the Lord's Supper must come from your heart in order to produce results, because God blesses a heart that is fond of Him. So make it a point to celebrate the Lord's Supper as often as you are able to do it.

Pleading the Blood of Jesus

Many of us have heard the phrase "pleading the blood of Jesus over a person or a circumstance." Let's look into this for a few moments. I can't find the words "plead the blood" anywhere in the Bible, but I'm going to refer to Exodus 12 regarding this statement. In this chapter, God asked Moses to lead the children of Israel out of Egypt. Moses went to Pharaoh and asked him to let the Israelites go, and Pharaoh's heart became very hard against Moses. After the many plagues which were brought by God against Egypt, with no success, God told Moses that He was going to send a death angel. The death angel would kill all of Egypt's firstborn in one night, after which Pharaoh would let them go.

In order to protect the Israelites' firstborn children from the death angel, God gave Moses specific instructions. They were to put the blood of a lamb on the sides and top of the exposed door frame or trim outside of each of their homes. When the death angel came to kill all the firstborn, he would see the blood and pass over that house without killing the Israelites' firstborn children. This was an exercise in faith. The Israelites obeyed God and put the blood on the doorframes of their homes, and in faith, because God said it, they knew their firstborn children would be safe. In addition, God told them that they had to celebrate this day and event forever. As a result, it became a celebration feast called the Feast of Passover.

In relation to this feast, the blood of Jesus has done the same thing for us today.

> For our Passover Lamb has already been offered in sacrifice—even Christ.
>
> —1 Corinthians 5:7, WNT

Jesus' shed blood covers us (shields or protects us) from the death angel (Satan). We are redeemed and protected from sin, sickness, darkness, evil, poverty, and every other affliction Satan would try to perpetrate upon us, because of Jesus' blood. Praise God! We have been redeemed from the curse and all that it entails by the precious blood of the lamb, Jesus Christ. We need to speak that marvellous work and sow it into our hearts as often as we can.

Let's see if we can find a way to use the Passover event in our lives today. First of all, the word "plead," according to Webster's Dictionary, means "to ask for in a serious and emotional way."[53] In the context of pleading the blood, what are we really doing when we speak the blood of Jesus over our lives or circumstances? We are effectively speaking and confessing the blood of Jesus over our lives, possessions, and circumstances. When we declare the blood of Jesus in this way, the death angel (Satan) can no longer destroy any of those things. This is an act of faith, since we're speaking with our mouths that the Passover ordinance or ceremony, of which Jesus is the Passover lamb, is covering us and protecting us from the evil spirit realm. Praise God! We can't see the evil spirit realm, but we can experience the fruit of our faith because of the protection we receive.

The ordinance of speaking the blood over our families' lives is very important since we can use it daily to protect our loved ones from harm and danger. We can also plead the blood of Jesus over our bodies, finances, homes, vehicles, travel, circumstances, and events. Accordingly, we can attest to the marvellous protection that is ours through this ordinance. This is just another way that God pours out His blessings upon us. Praise His name!

Triumphant Faith Conclusion

We start off with the plentiful measure of faith God gives to every believer in Christ, and then life happens and we sometimes face hardships, trials, or difficulties. Sometimes the difficulties are things we cannot fix ourselves. These difficulties need God's supernatural fixing power. God allows the trials, but it is our need for growth and maturity that actually brings the trials.

Let me summarize what we can do when life happens:

---

53 *Webster's Canadian Dictionary & Thesaurus* (Toronto, ON: Strathearn Books, 2011), 321.

- We start off by recognizing the sufficient measure of faith that God gives to every believer in Christ.
- Next, we put God's Word into our hearts daily, as often as we can, to build our faith ability.
- We put God's Word into our heart by speaking it out loud and hearing it, because faith comes by hearing.
- We ask God to help us to walk in love with everyone around us, because faith does not work without love.
- We become cheerful givers of our finances and resources.
- We wait on God for answers with thanksgiving and praise.
- We have patience without fear and doubt.
- We take communion, the Lord's Supper, to remind us of what Jesus did for us on the cross.
- We plead the blood of Jesus over our families, circumstances, possessions, and any area of our lives. This affords us the blessing of God's protection over these things.
- We expect and look for God's Word to happen, to produce the answer from what we have planted in our hearts.
- We speak that we already have the thing which we have asked for.
- We expect God to provide the pathway to success, because He always causes us to triumph in Christ.

As we live our lives by faith, we experience greater and greater supernatural events in our lives. What a wonderful plan God has for our lives as we live by faith!

Finally, I encourage you to begin a walk of faith in your life today. It won't be easy at first, but it will get easier as you keep exercising your faith. If you have already walked in the faith way of living, I encourage you to step out into greater challenges and see the fruit of God's faithfulness in your life. God wants to bless you abundantly. Just begin to apply the principles I have shared from His Word and you will be amazed at what God will do!

Chapter Nine
Walking in Love

In Matthew 22:36–40, Jesus gives us the two commandments of the New Testament, which, by the way, do not replace the Ten Commandments of the Old Testament. By their nature (love), these two commandments encompass all of the Old Testament commandments. The New Testament commandments call for us to love the Lord our God with all our heart, soul, mind, and strength, and to love our neighbours as much as we love ourselves.

Let's take a look at what is known in the Bible as the love chapter:

> If I can speak with the tongues of men and of angels, but am destitute of Love, I have but become a loud-sounding trumpet or a clanging cymbal. If I possess the gift of prophecy and am versed in all mysteries and all knowledge, and have such absolute faith that I can remove mountains, but am destitute of Love, I am nothing. And if I distribute all my possessions to the poor, and give up my body to be burned, but am destitute of Love, it profits me nothing. Love is patient and kind. Love knows neither envy nor jealousy. Love is not forward and self-assertive, nor boastful and conceited. She does not behave unbecomingly, nor seek to aggrandize herself, nor blaze out in passionate anger, nor brood over wrongs. She finds no pleasure in injustice done to others, but joyfully sides with the truth. She knows how to be silent. She is full of trust, full of hope, full of patient endurance. Love never fails.
> —1 Corinthians 13:1–8, WNT

From these verses, it's pretty clear that no matter what kind of spiritual giants we think we are, if we don't have love we have absolutely nothing, and can accomplish absolutely nothing of any value in the kingdom of God. If we as believers were to apply these verses to our lives and actually live them, what a difference it would make in the church and the world today!

In order to obey the two New Testament commandments God gave us, we must realize who we are in Christ: children of God, heirs of God, and joint heirs with Jesus Christ in God's heavenly kingdom. Once we understand in our hearts who we are in Christ and are able to appreciate ourselves in that light, we can fulfill the commandment to love others just like we love and appreciate ourselves. We cannot love others if we haven't learned to appreciate who we are in Christ. If we think back over what we have read in this book so far, we should be very aware of who we are in Christ. We are so loved and valued by God that He wants to bless us immensely. This should tell us something about who we are in Christ.

Rather than speak in generalities, I have pinpointed five major areas of concern with regards to walking in love towards others.

1. Forgiving Others

Most of us know that we are to forgive everyone who hurts or offends us in any way, whether we want to or not. On the other hand, when we hurt someone we are to be sorry and ask forgiveness of that person. There is no doubt that operating in forgiveness isn't easy. Many of us think like the world (non-Christians) when we entertain such thoughts as the following:

- "I have my rights."
- "They sure deserve to be punished."
- "I can't forgive them for what they did to me."
- "They've wrecked my life."

There are many more such attitudes I could come up with, but this is not our focus here. Our focus is to see what the Word of God says, to do what the Word says, and to be obedient to God. Obedience to God means that we walk in love towards everyone around us, as God commands us to do.

> For we know Him who has said, "Vengeance belongs to Me, I will repay, says the Lord." And again, "The Lord shall judge His people."
> —Hebrews 10:30, MKJV

You see, God wants us to let Him work with and discipline those who have wronged us. When we forgive someone for an offence they have committed against us, we release God to do His work in their lives. Unforgiveness blocks God from working in their lives, because we still have the attitude that we want to hurt them back. Once we forgive them, we no longer have that desire and we release God to do His work in their lives. Also, we release God to bring good out of the situation and we release ourselves to receive God's promises once again.

Next, let's take a look at the following scripture regarding forgiveness:

> Then Peter came and said to Him, "Lord, how often shall my brother sin against me and I forgive him? Up to seven times?"
> Jesus said to him, "I do not say to you, up to seven times, but up to seventy times seven."
> —Matthew 18:21–22, NASB

When Peter asked the Lord how many times he had to offer forgiveness to his brother after his brother had sinned against him, Jesus virtually indicated that Peter had to forgive his brother every time. No matter how many times his brother sinned against him, he had to forgive him. This doesn't just apply to Peter; it applies to us as well.

2. Offences

Offenses fall in the area of unforgiveness, but let's look at it from a little different slant. It's not about us being offended, but rather about us being the offender.

When we say and do nasty things to other people, we create offenses. These people become offended and annoyed with us. First of all, we need to stop doing these kinds of things. But secondly, when we offend someone, we must make amends.

> Therefore if you are presenting your offering at the altar, and there remember that your brother has something against you, leave your offering there before the altar and go; first be reconciled to your brother, and then come and present your offering.
> —Matthew 5:23–24, NASB

This is why it's important to ask God regularly whether you have offended Him or anyone else. We aren't even supposed to give our offering if we have outstanding offenses. We must apologize and make our relationships right again before we bring our offerings to God. It's not easy to eat crow, tell someone else that you were wrong, and ask to be forgiven. However, in order to walk in love we must be obedient to God's Word and follow through when we are aware of offenses we have committed.

3. Suffering Wrongfully

> If you do wrong and receive a blow for it, what credit is there in your bearing it patiently? But if when you do right and suffer for it you bear it patiently, this is an acceptable thing with God.
> —1 Peter 2:20, WNT

God calls us to be willing to suffer hurt or offences at the hands of others, and still take it patiently without returning the hurt. When we forgive and take our hands off the situation, we release God to bring good in both of our lives. It's difficult for us to suffer when the situation isn't our fault, but our obedience in this area releases tremendous blessings from God.

4. Loving the Unlovely

> But I say unto you, Love your enemies, bless them that curse you, do good to them that hate you, and pray for them which despitefully use you, and persecute you.
> —Matthew 5:44, KJV

This act of love is particularly difficult, since it goes a step further than just suffering wrongfully. In this verse, we are instructed to literally take verbal and emotional abuse from our enemies and those who hate us. Instead we are to return love, good deeds, and prayer for them. Wow! That's a challenge, but the rewards are amazing!

Does this mean to say that we need to be a doormat, letting people walk on us and hurt us all the time? No, it does not! We need to stand strong and firm, knowing who we are in Christ. We need to realize that most of the time the abuse is coming from Satan and not the person. More than anything, we need to respond in a loving, kind, firm manner.

5. Loving the Brotherhood

> Therefore, as we have opportunity, let us do good to all people, especially to those who belong to the family of believers.
> —Galatians 6:10, NIV

This step of love really seems to be neglected in the church of the free world today. 1 Peter 2:17 says, *"Love the brotherhood"* (NKJV), and Galatians 6:10 instructs us to especially do good to our Christian brothers and sisters. The brotherhood is the body of Christ, the Christian church, our brothers and sisters in Christ.

I recently heard of a situation that happened to a dear brother of mine in a local church in our city. This brother, who was very active and giving of his time to that assembly, was asked to quote on a construction job for the assembly. The church had asked other contractors to bid on the same job as well. This brother had done significant volunteer work for the church, and had even been called on many times to give his expert advice with respect to the church's construction needs. The job was given to another contractor because the brother's bid was a little higher than the other contractor.

It's important as a church family to look out for our brothers and sisters in the Lord. Therefore, the loving, brotherly thing to do would be to give the work to the fellow brother, even if it meant paying a little more money. This gesture would have demonstrated the love principle of putting people before money. God will release His blessing upon the church when good things are done amongst the brotherhood. Some would say, "Oh yes, but we have to be good stewards of the church's money." Looking after our brothers and sisters is the best way in God's eyes to be a good steward.

I included this true story to give an example of how we as Christians treat our brothers and sisters. Many good things happen in the church as well, but far too many bad things happen in the church with regards to how we treat our spiritual family. It usually happens because we put things, money, and ourselves ahead of our brothers and sisters. I've often said, and I believe it's true of too much of the church in North America, that the Lions Club (a secular club) looks after their members better than Christians look after their brothers and sisters in Christ. What a shame it is, because we're supposed to be living a godly example for the world to see, according to God's Word. Let us determine and commit to living our lives with love and care for our brothers and sisters in the Lord.

> By this all will know that you are My disciples, if you have love for one another.
> —John 13:35, NKJV

According to this verse, we can't be followers of Jesus if we don't have love for our brothers and sisters in the Lord. Once again, we're faced with the importance of obeying the Word of God.

Conclusion

It's not easy for most of us to walk in the kind of love I have shared. We can give many reasons to justify our behaviour, but if our behaviour doesn't line up with the Word of God, we must do something about it. The consequences of disobeying God's Word in the area of walking in love are serious. The following two verses give us direction as to how important it is in God's eyes that we fulfill the love commandments:

> He who does not love does not know God, for God is love.
> —1 John 4:8, NKJV

> If anyone says, I love God, and hates his brother, he is a liar. For if he does not love his brother whom he has seen, how can he love God whom he has not seen?
> —1 John 4:20, MKJV

We're given very strong reasons here for living our lives with love towards others. These verses go so far as to say that if we don't love others, we cannot know God. And if we don't love our brothers and sisters, we cannot love God. This requires us to take action to make sure we're living the way God wants us to live in order to receive His blessings.

> For in Christ Jesus neither circumcision nor uncircumcision avails anything, but faith working through love.
> —Galatians 5:6, NKJV

This scripture says that neither the law nor salvation profit or benefit anything or anyone. Rather, faith produces profit or benefit when we walk in love. In short, faith works when we love others; otherwise it doesn't work.

There are several things that we can do to improve our ability to love others. The most important step is to ask God to help us. Let me share a few things we can ask God to help us with:

- Ask God to make us aware of offences when we commit them.
- Ask God to help us apologize and make things right.
- Ask God to give us tact, wisdom, and love in relating to others, including the brotherhood.

After all, the only true love that exists comes from God. When we keep our lines of communication open with God, by keeping our spirit connected to God's Spirit, we tap into His abundant love. Since faith doesn't work without love, our prayer lives will be ineffective and fruitless. Without love, we will miss out on God's abundant blessings! Let's not miss out. Let's determine to work on our love ability, with God's help, on an ongoing basis. Let's determine to stay in God's blessings!

Chapter Ten

Watch Your Mouth

Words Work

Your words will either work for you or against you. In Genesis 1, we find that everything God created in the universe He spoke into existence:

> Then God said, "Let there be light"; and there was light... Then God said, "Let the earth bring forth grass, the herb that yields seed, and the fruit tree that yields fruit according to its kind, whose seed is in itself, on the earth"; and it was so.
> —Genesis 1:3, 11, NKJV

Here we see the importance and power of God's spoken Word. Everything that exists in the universe was spoken into being by God's mouth. His Word still has the same power today.

> In the beginning was the Word, and the Word was with God, and the Word was God.
> —John 1:1, NKJV

The last four words of this verse say that the Word was God. Since God is the same yesterday, today, and forever, and He has not changed, God is still the Word today. Since God is the Word, the power of God resides in His Word. Consequently, when we speak the Word we are speaking God, who He is and what He does.

In Matthew 8 and 9, we see Jesus continuing in the same pattern that God used in Genesis 1. In verse after verse, Jesus speaks things into existence. Let's look at a few examples:

When evening came, many who were demon-possessed were brought to him, and he drove out the spirits with a word and healed all the sick.
—Matthew 8:16, NIV

But He said to them, "Why are you fearful, O you of little faith?" Then He arose and rebuked the winds and the sea, and there was a great calm.
—Matthew 8:26, NKJV

But Jesus turned around, and when He saw her He said, "Be of good cheer, daughter; your faith has made you well." And the woman was made well from that hour.
—Matthew 9:22, NKJV

He said to them, "Go!" So they came out and went into the pigs, and the whole herd rushed down the steep bank into the lake and died in the water.
—Matthew 8:32, NIV

As you've probably already noticed, in each of these scriptures, the Word coming out of Jesus' mouth produced the results of what was spoken. The words carried the anointing and the power to produce themselves. Just like God and Jesus, our words have the power to produce what we say. We have been made in the image and likeness of God, and our words are able to build up or tear down as well.

Let's take a look at a number of Bible accounts where the words of ordinary people resulted in producing exactly what they said.

Doubt and Unbelief

And when he was come into his own country, he taught them in their synagogue, insomuch that they were astonished, and said, Whence hath this man this wisdom [Where does this man get this wisdom?], and these mighty works? Is not this the carpenter's son? is not his mother called Mary? and his brethren, James, and Joses, and Simon, and Judas? And his sisters, are they not all with us? Whence then hath this man all these things? [Where does he get all these things?] And they were offended in him. But Jesus said unto them, A prophet is not without honour, save in his own country, and in his own house. [A prophet has no honor in

his own country or his own house.] And he did not many mighty works there because of their unbelief.
—Matthew 13:54–58, KJV

In these verses, we discover that the religious people of the day were questioning the credibility of Jesus to do miracles and have such great wisdom. They were actually offended with Jesus because of all the miracles He was doing. They were jealous of Jesus. They alluded to the fact that Jesus was only a lowly carpenter's son. He wasn't a religious leader in their eyes, and as such they thought He should not be doing these miracles. Matthew 13:58 says that Jesus did very few miracles there because of their unbelief. You see, the words of these religious leader's mouths (speaking unbelief) resulted in Jesus not doing many miracles there.

Let's apply the principle of sowing and reaping to this situation and ponder the results. These religious people were sowing unbelief into their minds and hearts by the words of their mouths. The words of their mouths confessed unbelief, and the results (the harvest they reaped) were very few miracles among them.

We find the next account in Numbers 13:1–2, 17–33. I won't include the whole text here, but rather a few specific verses:

> The Lord said to Moses, "Send some men to explore the land of Canaan, which I am giving to the Israelites. From each ancestral tribe send one of its leaders."
> —Numbers 13:1–2, NIV

Numbers 13 details the account of Moses sending out twelve men from the tribes of Israel to spy out the land God had promised He would give them. The spy trip resulted in two types of reactions or confessions. Upon returning from the trip, some of the spies had a positive reaction to what they saw, and the others had a negative reaction. We shouldn't forget that God had already spoken the promise of this land to the people through Moses. When Moses asked these men to spy out the land, Moses' request to them was based on God's Word to him and the Israelites. This is confirmed in the following scripture:

> And it shall be, when the Lord brings you into the land of the Canaanites and the Hittites and the Amorites and the Hivites and the Jebusites, which He swore to your fathers to give you, a land flowing with milk and honey...
> —Exodus 13:5, NKJV

When the twelve men returned from their spy trip, ten of them looked at the physical circumstances of the country and its people. They saw giants and the large number of people. They ignored God's promise and said,

> But the men who had gone up with him said, "We are not able to go up against the people, for they are stronger than we."
> —Numbers 13:31, NKJV

These ten men spoke fear, doubt, and unbelief, demonstrating a total lack of faith regarding God's promise to give them the land. We see what happened to them in the following verse:

> ...they certainly shall not see the land of which I swore to their fathers, nor shall any of those who rejected Me see it.
> —Numbers 14:23, NKJV

None of these men and their families entered into the land God had promised to give them—a land flowing with milk and honey. Why did they miss out? They missed out because they spoke words that were contrary to God's Word. Because they spoke words of doubt and unbelief, they got what they spoke.

Words of Faith

On the other hand, Caleb and Joshua, two of the twelve spies, had a different report regarding what they saw in the land:

> Then Caleb quieted the people before Moses, and said, "Let us go up at once and take possession, for we are well able to overcome it."
> —Numbers 13:30, NKJV

Caleb confessed that they should go up and possess the land right away, because he saw in faith that God had provided them the land, and that God would make sure they conquered the land. Caleb's confession was positive. His confession demonstrated faith in God, and consequently we see totally different results from it.

> But My servant Caleb, because he has a different spirit in him and has followed Me fully, I will bring into the land where he went, and his descendants shall inherit it.
> —Numbers 14:24, NKJV

The words of Caleb's mouth were positive words of faith in God, and as a result Caleb and his descendants entered the Promised Land and possessed it. These positive words yielded the fruit of victory in the lives of Caleb, Joshua, and their families.

One further note of importance, which we see in Numbers 14:24, is that Caleb had a different spirit in him than the other ten men, the naysayers—the negative ones. Caleb obviously had a spirit filled with faith because of his relationship with God. The naysayers had spirits filled with fear, undoubtedly because of their lack of a relationship with God. Speaking positive faith confessions with our mouths produces victory, and negative and fearful confessions produce defeat and death.

Confessing (speaking) the Word of God with our mouths is an act of faith, as we covered in Chapter Eight. The Bible says that faith comes by hearing, and hearing by the Word. The act of speaking the Word of God out of our mouths puts the Word into our hearts, and builds our hearts full of faith.

Planting, watering, and fertilizing a garden will produce a harvest. When the garden is mature and the fruit is ripe, the garden is ready to be harvested. Sowing the Word or speaking it with our mouths creates a garden in our hearts full of the Word of God. As we continue to plant and water the Word of God into our hearts, the time comes when the harvest is ripe, ready to be received. When an earthly garden is mature, we begin to pick the produce in order that we might eat it, to provide health and strength for our bodies. With the garden of our heart, when it is full of faith from God's Word, we are able to harvest that Word for our lives, to bring success in every area of our lives.

For example, let's say that you have just been told by your doctor that you have severe allergies, and that you will probably have a headache for the rest of your life. If the garden of your heart is full of God's Word for the healing of your body, you can call upon that Word for this situation. You can begin to speak healing over your sinuses and give God the praise for the healing. As a result, the harvest will come forth with healing, manifested by the absence of allergies and headaches. Praise God!

Our words and the confession of our mouths can be a great asset or a huge liability to us, as we shall see in the following verses:

> Offspring of vipers! How can you, being evil, speak good things? For out of the abundance of the heart the mouth speaks. A good man out of the good treasure of the heart brings out good things; and an evil man out of the evil treasure brings out evil things.
> —Matthew 12:34–35, MKJV

From these verses, we see that the things we have in our hearts are those which come out of our mouths and reveal who we truly are. It seems to me that putting the Word of God into our hearts is one of the most important things we can do as Christians. This exercise of confessing God's Word with our mouths and storing it in our minds and hearts is the right way to talk and act. After all, God is totally right and we get the right results when we speak His Word. When we fill our hearts with God's Word, we prepare ourselves for a life of success and triumph in God.

There are many examples of the power of the confession of God's Word. I suggest that you refer to the following scriptures and take a look at how the spoken Word performed in each example.

> But Peter said, "I have no silver and gold, but what I do have I give to you. In the name of Jesus Christ of Nazareth, rise up and walk!"
> —Acts 3:6, ESV

> The crowds with one accord were giving attention to what was said by Philip, as they heard and saw the signs which he was performing.
> —Acts 8:6, NASB

Blessing and Cursing

> But no one can tame the tongue; it is a restless evil and full of deadly poison. With it we bless our Lord and Father, and with it we curse men, who have been made in the likeness of God.
>
> —James 3:8–9, NASB

In James 3:8–9, we find that we have the power with our tongues (mouths) to speak blessing or cursing. We're able to speak blessing into our lives or the lives of others. Speaking blessing means that we speak positive, good things. It means that we speak words of health, happiness, and prosperity.

From what we have seen in the Word of God, it seems to me that we need to be very careful of the words we utter. I often hear Christians speak curses into their own lives, as well as the lives of others. Recently, a number of our Christian friends have been dealing with parents who have dementia. I find it very annoying to hear them make what they think are joking remarks regarding this disease. If someone happens to forget something, someone will say, "They must be getting Alzheimer's." The ones making these negative remarks don't seem to be aware that they're cursing the one to whom their words are directed. It isn't funny to infer that someone is going to get dementia.

It's important for us to speak words of blessing into the lives of others. When we do, we are obeying the second commandment Jesus gave us, which is to love our neighbour as our self. As we saw in Matthew 12:34–35, the words and thoughts we place (sow) into our hearts with our mouths are what we become and who we truly are. They will reveal our true character.

We don't have to receive curses spoken against us by anyone. If someone speaks a curse or negative word against us, we should immediately speak against the curse. We should tell the curse, not the person, that it's not true. Next we should tell the curse to leave, in the name of Jesus:

> "No weapon formed against you shall prosper, and every tongue which rises against you in judgment you shall condemn. This is the heritage of the servants of the Lord, and their righteousness is from Me," says the Lord.
>
> —Isaiah 54:17, NKJV

Conclusion

I've spent quite a bit of time sharing on the subject of watching or guarding our mouths. When it comes to speaking curses, both to us and others, and committing offences towards others, our mouths are the worst offenders. This usually happens because of ignorance of what we're doing, or when we have little or none of God's influence in our lives by His Spirit. The area of offences and curses with the tongue is undoubtedly the greatest area of downfall among Christians. It is important to keep our mouths filled with the Word of God.

I also recommend that you begin to commit Scripture to memory, and begin to confess (speak) many of the scriptures which relate to your daily circumstances. As you get your tongue more and more under the control of your spirit, and as your spirit is more and more under the influence of God's Spirit, it will make a huge difference in helping you to love your neighbour as yourself. This is what Jesus commanded us to do in Matthew 22:39. If you know and live by the scriptures, you will have a very successful, blessed Christian life.

If there's one thing I could say about our words, it would be: "You get what you say."

Chapter Eleven

The Fear of the Lord

The fear of the Lord is the beginning of wisdom; a good understanding have all those who do His commandments. His praise endures forever.
—Psalms 111:10, NKJV

In a previous chapter, we defined the term "fear of the Lord" like this: thinking of and treating the Lord with awe and reverence, mingled with respect, esteem and affection.

Let me use an example to bring this into perspective. Let's say Queen Elizabeth of England requested a visit with you. Your first reaction might be to wonder about what to wear and what you might say to her. You may be afraid that you might say the wrong thing and offend the Queen. You certainly would want to be on your very best behaviour, and dress in your best clothes in order to be accepted in her presence. This would indicate that you consider her to be worthy of high honour and respect. In comparison to the greatness of God, the Queen of England is just another human being, yet at times we would give her or other celebrities more honour and respect than we give to God.

Let's consider the following verses and see how amazingly powerful God is. Let's see who He really is. Of course, we can't even scratch the surface, but we'll still get a good idea anyway:

> Who has measured the oceans by using the palm of his hand? Who has used the width of his hand to mark off the sky? Who has measured out the dust of the earth in a basket? Who has weighed the mountains on scales? Who has weighed the hills in a balance?
> —Isaiah 40:12, NIrV

> He has made the earth by His power; He has established the world by His wisdom, and stretched out the heaven by His understanding.
> —Jeremiah 51:15, NKJV

> When I look at Your heavens, the work of Your fingers, the moon and the stars which You have established; what is man that You are mindful of him, and the son of man, that You visit him?
> —Psalms 8:3–4, MKJV

> He is before all things, and in him all things hold together.
> —Colossians 1:17, NIV

> He brightly reflects God's glory and is the exact representation of His being, and upholds the universe by His all-powerful word.
> —Hebrews 1:3, WNT

Each of the above verses describes God or His Son Jesus. God is so great and powerful; how can we as mere men, created by God from the dust of the earth, treat God with such disrespect? If He was to take away the very breath from our mouths, we would die instantly, yet people treat God like He is just another person or human being.

Everything in this universe exists because of God's hand, and it came into existence by the words of His mouth. If He was to withdraw His hand from this universe, it would fall apart immediately. God deserves far more respect and honour than anything which exists, or ever will exist, in this universe.

How We Display a Lack of Fear of God

There are many ways in which we let God know we don't respect Him. Let me share a few here:

1. We disobey God's Word. Here are a couple of examples.

    - We fail to spend much time reading God's Word.

        > So Jesus said to the Jews who had believed in him, "If you abide in my word, you are truly my disciples…
        > —John 8:31, ESV

    - We don't walk in love towards others.

> But I say to you, love your enemies, bless those who curse you, do good to those who hate you, and pray for those who spitefully use you and persecute you ...
> —Matthew 5:44, NKJV

2. We don't believe God's Word is true. "Oh yes we do," some would say! We might say we believe, but when it comes right down to living by faith, how many of God's children actually have the patience and perseverance to declare God's Word until it happens? How many of us will hang in there until we see the Word produce results in our lives?

> Now the just shall live by faith: but if any man draw back, my soul shall have no pleasure in him.
> —Hebrews 10:38, KJV

3. We fail to praise and worship God for all the things He does for us. We forget about Him until we have problems.

> ... giving thanks always for all things to God the Father in the name of our Lord Jesus Christ ...
> —Ephesians 5:20, NKJV

4. We speak evil of authorities when in fact God has placed these people in those places of authority.

> Let every soul be subject to the governing authorities. For there is no authority except from God, and the authorities that exist are appointed by God. Therefore whoever resists the authority resists the ordinance of God, and those who resist will bring judgment on themselves.
> —Romans 13:1–2, NKJV

5. We dishonour and disrespect parents and older people, whom God has placed on the earth before us to provide us with wisdom and experience.

> Never administer a sharp reprimand to a man older than yourself; but entreat him as if he were your father, and the younger men as brothers.
> —1 Timothy 5:1, WNT

6. We continue to sin over and over (repetitive sin), expecting God to overlook it by His grace, therefore taking God and His Word lightly and holding them in reproach.

> What then? Shall we sin because we are not under law but under grace? Certainly not!
> —Romans 6:15, NKJV

There are no doubt many other ways in which we display a lack of the fear or respect of God in the community of believers, but I have tried to make us aware of some of the most common ones among believers today.

Let's look at Acts 5 and the account of Ananias and Sapphira. In this passage, apparently many believers in the church were selling their possessions and bringing all the money to the church for distribution to other believers so everyone would be well provided for. Ananias and Sapphira wanted to participate in this benevolent act as well, except that they gave the impression to the church that they were giving all their money while holding back part of the money for themselves, which resulted in them lying to the Holy Spirit. Both he and his wife conspired to commit this deception (lie), and upon being confronted by the Apostle Peter both of them dropped dead immediately. Liars cannot live in the powerful presence of God (the Holy Spirit), and Peter was full of the Holy Spirit from the recent Day of Pentecost experience.

Here are some examples to bring this account of Ananias and Sapphira into relevance for today:

1. Robbing God of His ten-percent tithe from our income.

> Will a man rob God? Yet you have robbed Me! But you say, "In what way have we robbed You?" In tithes and offerings.
> —Malachi 3:8, NKJV

2. Taking communion with sin in your life.

> For he who eats and drinks in an unworthy manner eats and drinks judgment to himself, not discerning the Lord's body.
> —1 Corinthians 11:29, NKJV

3. Hating a brother, sister, or neighbour.

> By this shall all men know that [you] are my disciples, if [you] have love one to another.
> —John 13:35, KJV

4. Blaming God for everything that goes wrong. We say, "Bad weather is an act of God. A child run over by a car is God's fault. When God doesn't answer our prayers, He's to blame."

> Every good gift and every perfect gift is from above, and comes down from the Father of lights, with whom there is no variation or shadow of turning.
> —James 1:17, NKJV

5. Ignoring the fatherless children, the poor, and the widows.

> But if any one has this world's wealth and sees that his brother man is in need, and yet hardens his heart against him—how can such a one continue to love God?
> —1 John 3:17, WNT

6. Placing greater importance on the things of this world than on the Word of God.

> Do not love the world, nor the things in the world. If any one loves the world, there is no love in his heart for the Father.
> —1 John 2:15, WNT

Maybe you don't think these things are as bad as lying to the Holy Spirit, but every time we do one of these things we show our lack of respect and reverence for God. Therefore, we are just as guilty as Ananias and Sapphira.

Reverence Produces Blessings

What happened in the church when Ananias and Sapphira fell dead? This calamity created an awe, reverence, and fear of God among God's children which resulted in many signs and wonders being done among them. It also resulted in church growth exploding.

Let me share some scriptures that declare the blessings that will come upon us when we have the fear of the Lord operating in our lives:

> ...that you may fear the Lord your God, to keep all His statutes and His commandments which I command you, you and your son and your grandson, all the days of your life, and *that your days may be prolonged.*
> —Deuteronomy 6:2, NKJV (emphasis added)

> The angel of the Lord encamps all around those who fear Him, and delivers them.
> —Psalms 34:7, NKJV

> The fear of the Lord is the *beginning of wisdom*; all who follow his precepts have good understanding. To him belongs eternal praise.
> —Psalms 111:10, NIV (emphasis added)

> The fear of the Lord *leads to life, and he who has it will abide in satisfaction; he will not be visited with evil.*
> —Proverbs 19:23, NKJV (emphasis added)

> By humility and the fear of the LORD are *riches, and honor, and life.*
> —Proverbs 22:4, KJV (emphasis added)

> Then the church throughout Judea, Galilee and Samaria enjoyed a time of peace and was strengthened. Living in the fear of the Lord and encouraged by the Holy Spirit, *it increased in numbers.*
> —Acts 9:31, NIV (emphasis added)

Conclusion

We are lacking so much in the way of God's blessings in the church today because there is very little in the way of fear and reverence for the Lord among believers. Let us not forget that God is everything to us. Let us take plenty of time to get to know God and who He is, in order that we can develop a healthy respect and honour for our almighty, all-knowing, all-powerful, and everywhere-present God. Let us determine to give God His rightful place of honour and respect in our lives. As a result of this obedience to Him, we will experience more of His goodness to us. Blessed be His name!

Chapter Twelve

Banishing Strife and Discord

What does this subject have to do with God's promises, you may ask? Well, let's look at the following verse:

> For where envying and strife is, there is confusion and every evil work.
> —James 3:16, KJV

This is just one of many verses which describe what happens in our lives when we participate in strife and envy. James 3:16 says that we bring confusion and every evil work into our situation. When we do this, we push back God's hand of blessing and give Satan an opportunity to work his evil in our lives.

Let's look at some areas where we might be able to make changes to eliminate this problem of strife. As Christians, we are to live in unity and harmony in Christ, which is the opposite of strife and discord.

Unity in the Spirit

On many occasions I have been talking with other Christians when one of them presents their understanding on a particular biblical subject, resulting in disagreement in the group. Some will think one thing and others will think another. At other times, a misunderstanding will occur because of how the subject is presented. Sometimes people say the same thing, but it doesn't come out the same in their presentation. I say all that to lead up to this question: why do Christians, who are born of the same spirit, have differences in understanding when it comes to God's Word?

> Now I entreat you, brethren, in the name of our Lord Jesus Christ, to cultivate a spirit of harmony—all of you—and that there be no divisions

among you, but rather a perfect union through your having one mind and one judgement.
—1 Corinthians 1:10, WNT

In this verse, the writer indicates that we are to work towards harmony and unity to the extent that we have one mind and one understanding about God and His Word. This only happens as we get our minds united with the mind of Christ or God. We know that God, Jesus, and the Holy Spirit are all unified, one in the spirit. When we get our spirit in tune with God's spirit, we become united with God, Jesus, and the Holy Spirit. At this point, our mind is positively influenced by God's Spirit flowing through our spirit to our mind. In this state, our understanding of the Bible comes from God, not from us. This means that we must have our minds renewed on a daily basis in the things of the Lord—namely, the Word of God.

For, in fact, in one Spirit all of us—whether we are Jews or Gentiles, slaves or free men—were baptized to form but one body; and we were all nourished by that one Spirit.
—1 Corinthians 12:13, WNT

In this verse, the writer communicates that we are all to be fed by one spirit—obviously, the Holy Spirit. Now, if we are all fed by one spirit, is it possible to have a division or difference in understanding? The Holy Spirit is not divided, nor does He have ten opinions on every subject. There is only one Word, one truth, and one Spirit:

But he who is joined to the Lord is one spirit with Him.
—1 Corinthians 6:17, NKJV

We already know the six disciplines of staying connected spiritually to God. These disciplines applied and lived in our lives bring us to the place of spiritual oneness with God. This means that we can choose to think like God. If we as believers were all at the place of oneness with God, there would be no strife or divisions between us. God does not have strife with Jesus or the Holy Spirit, and this is how it should be with believers in Christ as well. The problem is not with God, Jesus, or the Holy Spirit; the problem is with us! The problem is our lack of relationship and fellowship with God.

Three Reasons for Strife

I want to share three reasons why there is division and strife among Christians and in the church today:

1. Spiritual weakness
2. Spiritual blindness
3. Lack of discernment

1. Spiritual Weakness

> And I, brethren, could not speak to you as to spiritual people but as to carnal, as to babes in Christ. I fed you with milk and not with solid food; for until now you were not able to receive it, and even now you are still not able; for you are still carnal. For where there are envy, strife, and divisions among you, are you not carnal and behaving like mere men?
> —1 Corinthians 3:1–3, NKJV

In this scripture, Paul the apostle is writing to the Church at Corinth. There appears to be a problem of spiritual babyhood in the church. He is trying to feed them from the meat of the Word, but they can't relate to it because they aren't spending enough time in relationship with God themselves. In fact, Paul says that they are acting like men of the world—unspiritual, because they spend most of their time in the things of the world (materialism, pleasure, work) and very little time in spiritual things (God's Word). Paul also says that it's because of their weak spiritual condition that jealousy and strife are prevalent among them.

2. Spiritual Blindness

Let us consider two of the causes of spiritual blindness. Spiritual blindness happens when people have been taught a certain belief or understanding about God, and they stop at that point. They fail to search for deeper understanding and revelation regarding that belief.

I keep asking that the God of our Lord Jesus Christ, the glorious Father, may give you the Spirit of wisdom and revelation, so that you may know him better.
—Ephesians 1:17, NIV

In order to get the real meaning of this verse, we need to define the words "wisdom" and "revelation." In my own paraphrase, wisdom is the right use of knowledge, and the best means to accomplish it. Revelation is the act of discovering what was before unknown to us. From this verse and these definitions, we can conclude that God wants us to have His wisdom in using the knowledge we have, and He wants us to learn and discover new things about Him and His ways. God wants to turn on His spiritual lightbulb in our minds so we can better understand Him and His ways. Wow!

For example, some religious organizations believe that God doesn't want to heal everyone from sickness. Some teach that it is His sovereign right to choose whom He heals or whom He does not heal. This teaching makes God out to be a God who chooses favourites of His people. God favours all of His children because He is no respecter of persons, as it says in Romans 2:11.

It is true that God is sovereign and that He can do as He pleases, but God is also a God of love. It is evident from scriptures such as Psalms 103:3 (*"Who forgives all your iniquities, who heals all your diseases"* [NKJV]) and many others that God wants to heal everyone. We can fail to see that God wants to heal everyone because we hang on to teachings that come from man rather than God. As a result, we limit God by our inability to open up to the truth of His Word. God's Word says that He heals all of our diseases. I believe it's only us who hinder God from healing us.

We also fail to understand the love of God, and how God desires to bless us with good and not evil. One of the keys to God's abundance is seeing God as very good, kind, loving, and wonderful, and in faith expecting good from God. When we follow beliefs that are concocted by man and set as absolutes, instead of seeking a deeper understanding, we take on a spirit of blindness which keeps us from moving forward in God and receiving His abundant blessings.

As a part of spiritual blindness, I would like to share on what I call an unteachable spirit. The word unteachable describes one who is no longer open to being taught. Unteachable people believe they have all the truth and that there is nothing more to learn. This condition usually happens because of pride, and it severely limits their spiritual growth. The following verse instructs us to grow in our experience and understanding of Jesus Christ:

> ...but grow in the grace and knowledge of our Lord and Savior Jesus Christ. To Him be the glory both now and forever. Amen.
> —2 Peter 3:18, NKJV

If there's one thing I have learned in my walk with God, it's the need for us as His children to realize that we understand so little of God. He has so much more for us than we can imagine, if we are open to receive it. If we stop at what we have, we will never grow in a deeper relationship and understanding of Him, which will result in us becoming stunted spiritually.

At times I have heard a Christian brother or sister share something from the Lord in the presence of a pastor or leader. Just because that pastor or leader didn't get the same word, the word is rejected. This tells me that some pastors think that revelation from God's Word is only for pastors and leaders in the church. No wonder the church in the free world has very little happening in the operation of the gifts of the Spirit: the people tend to be discouraged by leadership control.

All of us, including pastors and spiritual leaders, need to be teachable and open to hear what God may say through our brothers and sisters in the Lord, otherwise we become stagnant in the things of the Lord. Of course, when we hear a word from others, we must be in a place to function in the gift of discernment.

In conclusion, spiritual blindness can cause arguments and debates about the things of God. This happens because Christians have stopped seeking a greater understanding of God.

3. Lack of Discernment

Both of the first two reasons for strife and division in the church are immensely affected by the final reason: lack of discernment. Discernment is a gift of the Spirit whereby one is able to tell the difference between what does and does not come from God by being well connected to God's Spirit

It's extremely important for all Christians, especially leaders, to operate in the gift of discernment. If someone gets up in a church service and begins to give a word, it's important to know if that word is from God, from the person, or from Satan. It is only possible to determine where that word is coming from via your spirit being in tune with God's Spirit.

A lack of discernment in leadership, where the leader does not know the source of the word that's being given, can hurt a brother or sister and can create confusion in the assembly of those who hear the word. Sometimes the word should be received, and other times the word should be dealt with by leadership. When we have the gift of discernment, the Holy Spirit will guide us into truth. He will never leave us confused and wondering what is right or wrong. However, we must keep ourselves spiritually strong and connected to God in order to function in the gift of discernment.

When all Christians are able to function in the gift of discernment, they are able in unity to determine whether something is from God or not. This tends to prevent strife and discord and bring unity among believers.

Be a Peacemaker

We've looked at three reasons why there is strife and discord amongst Christians and in the church today. Now let's look at something we can do to create peace and unity in the church.

> Those who make peace should plant peace like a seed. If they do, it will produce a crop of right living.
> —James 3:18, NIrV

What a wonderful piece of advice this verse gives us. Again we are exposed to God's principal of sowing and reaping. This verse encourages us to plant seeds of peace. What are some of the seeds of peace we can plant?

- Being slow to get offended.
- Being quick to say we're sorry.
- Speaking in a calm, pleasant voice in the midst of strife.
- Allowing other people to express their opinions whether they are right or not.

What kind of harvest will seeds of peace produce? This verse says they will produce a crop of right living. People will begin to do the right thing. They will begin to desire peace as well.

My wife shared an example of this from her experience as a hospital nurse. Whenever a patient was very agitated, she would talk to them quietly and calmly. Most of the time, they would calm down and begin to listen to her.

Conclusion

I would like to tie together the three reasons for strife and discord among Christians: spiritual weakness, spiritual blindness, and lack of discernment. Strife and discord among brothers and sisters in Christ all boils down to one common cause: a lack of spiritual maturity and relationship with God. If our hearts are hungering after God, and we're taking the time to keep our spirit connected with God's Spirit, division and strife will largely disappear from the church, since Christians would be living and relating together in harmony under one spirit, the Spirit of God.

Chapter Thirteen

Victory through God's Discipline

The Question Is Why?

Why does God discipline His children? Better yet, why do we put ourselves in a place of needing discipline? Let's see if we can answer these questions.

And have you forgotten the exhortation that addresses you as sons? "My son, do not regard lightly the discipline of the Lord, nor be weary when reproved by him. For the Lord disciplines the one he loves, and chastises every son whom he receives."
—Hebrews 12:5–6, ESV

To begin with, let's define the word "reprove" from Webster's Dictionary. It means "to express blame or disapproval of; scold."[54] Next, let's look at the Tyndale Bible Dictionary to define the words "chastise" and "discipline."

- Chastise: "correction intended to produce righteousness."[55]
- Discipline: "learning that moulds character and enforces correct behaviour."[56]

Let's put Hebrews 12:5–6 into perspective by paraphrasing them using these definitions. God's children (sons) should place great importance on God's discipline, because God is revealing our faults and correcting us. We

---

54 *Webster's Canadian Dictionary & Thesaurus* (Toronto, ON: Strathearn Books, 2011), 356.
55 Walter A. Elwell and Phil W. Comfort, *Tyndale Bible Dictionary* (Wheaton, IL: Tyndale House Publishers, 2001), 263.
56 Ibid., 385.

should embrace the correction as God's love towards us—love that desires our obedience, for our good and growth, as sons of God.

Most of us can relate to raising children and teaching them to become good, responsible, law-abiding citizens. So why do we discipline our children? We discipline them because they disobey us and sometimes do bad things. Where does the disobedience and bad behaviour come from anyway? Adam, the first man created by God, was given authority over the earth, and he lived in the Garden of Eden with no sin. Then Satan came along and tempted Adam, who yielded to the temptation, disobeyed God, and committed sin. As a result of this sin, Adam gave up God's blessing and became subject to Satan's influence. Thus, sin and the curse came upon Adam and the earth. Every human being born on this earth is born with sin in them (a sin nature): this is the nature that came upon Adam when he rebelled against God. As a result of this curse, sin begins to rear its ugly head very early in a child's life.

When a child sins, we must deal with the sin and get the child off the path of sin and onto the path of right living. Sometimes a stern, firm word of warning will work to discipline a child. Other times, the child must have some of their privileges taken away. Still further, at times a child may require a little pain inflicted in the form of a spanking in order for us to see a change in the their behaviour for the better.

> Foolishness is bound in the heart of a child; but the rod of correction shall drive it far from him.
> —Proverbs 22:15, KJV

For some children, a stern word is quite painful because of their soft heart and sensitivity. For others, it takes some physical pain to get the message of correction to register with them. Does this mean we can destroy our children with our discipline of them? Does it mean we can drive over them with a car, or make them sick until they die? No! If we did these things, we would become evil, unloving, destructive parents. Instead, no matter how much we try to protect our children, they often end up failing. As a result, we instruct them regarding the things they did wrong, we encourage them in how to do things right, and sometimes we apply further consequences or discipline. The results of the discipline process must include love, character building, and success for the child.

So to answer the question—why?—it's us who initiates the need for correction, because of the things we say and do. God wants our actions and words to line up with His Word, and when they don't God must apply corrective action to our lives.

How Does God Discipline Us?

God disciplines His children in a similar way to how we discipline our children. First of all, when we disobey God we are subject to the consequences of our actions and words. We live in a world where the principle of cause and effect, or sowing and reaping, exists. For example, if we destroy someone's house by fire, we could go to jail. If we don't give God the tithe from our earnings, Satan is permitted to destroy our finances.

God doesn't do bad things to us to teach us His ways. It's our sin and disobedience that causes our trials and heartaches. So if it's sin and not God that causes our heartaches and trials, where does God come into the picture?

First of all, when trials happen it's usually because we haven't been the listening to God in some area of our lives. It might be unbelief, disobedience, or any number of things we're doing or saying contrary to God's Word. When we keep ignoring God, after a while God's first step is to let us do things ourselves. This is when things go wrong and trials happen.

> All Scripture is inspired by God and profitable for teaching, for reproof, for correction, for training in righteousness; so that the man of God may be adequate, equipped for every good work.
> —2 Timothy 3:16–17, NASB

When things go wrong, God doesn't leave us high and dry if we turn to Him for help. He uses Scripture to teach, reprove, correct, and train us in the right way. That's why it is important for us to be reading and meditating in His Word daily.

It is God's will that we always come out of our trials with triumph and victory in our lives. He makes a way with His Word for us to come out victorious. If we're not applying His Word to our lives, however, we may never come out of the trial successfully, as promised in His Word. Let's consider the following verse:

> Now thanks be to God, who always causes us to triumph in Christ...
> —2 Corinthians 2:14, MKJV

A number of years ago, I came down with chronic fatigue syndrome. I had come through a period of problems with my extended family which seemingly couldn't be resolved. In addition, my wife and I were experiencing a rocky road financially at the time. As well, we had some problems with two of our four children. As a result, my body couldn't take the stress.

At the time, I was selling real estate as a career. Real estate is a very demanding business and requires sometimes long hours of work. When the fatigue happened, I only had enough energy to work for an hour or two at a time. Then I would have to lie down and sleep for several hours. I knew I couldn't sell real estate sleeping on the sofa for most of the day.

As I was lying on the sofa, I was overwhelmed with fear that I wouldn't be able to provide for my family. During this time, I talked to God and told Him that I was finished unless He came to my rescue. I told Him that I was depending totally on Him to help me. By the way, at the time I didn't understand faith and healing the way I do today. However, I did know some scriptures relating to God's financial provision for me. I brought those scriptures to mind and clung to them.

The long and short of this event is that God began to send real estate clients to me. He did it in a way that I could handle the business in the limited time I had, between periods of rest. God provided a miracle of supply way beyond our need. I ended up having the best year ever financially to that point, and sometime later in the year I was healed and delivered from the fatigue. Praise God!

Because I totally trusted God to help me through this trial, I experienced the triumph as promised in 2 Corinthians 2:14. God didn't put the fatigue on me. It came on me because I left God out in some areas of my life. However, God was there when I turned to him. He was there to offer triumph in our finances and in my healing. Praise God! I knew from His Word that He wanted to deliver me. I knew from God's Word that He would never leave me or forsake me.

To recap how God disciplines, first of all, it is through God letting us fail when we ignore Him. Secondly, as we turn to God in the trial, He corrects and teaches us with His Word. The result is that we get the promised victory from God. This is how God gets involved in our trials to bring victory.

Looking at Ourselves

What does the following verse say about looking at ourselves?

> For if we would judge ourselves, we should not be judged. But when we are judged, we are chastened of the Lord, that we should not be condemned with the world.
> —1 Corinthians 11:31–32, KJV

It says that if we were to examine ourselves, or look at our lives critically on a regular basis, we would not require God's correction. It's important to ask God to reveal our sins and shortcomings on a regular basis, but it's equally as important for us to repent and correct our ways. Then we will continue to live in God's blessings. When we follow this path, we require less of God's discipline. If we're doing the things God wants us to do, as He has revealed in His Word, we can stay in His blessing and protection. So we need to look at and judge ourselves often in order that we not be condemned with the world, and in order that we not be subject to God's discipline.

The Victory Is Ours

Even when the devil comes to try and oppress or afflict us, as we keep our focus on God and His Word we will always rise up out of the oppression into a place of victory, that place which God provides for us every time. The pain which results from trials and difficulties isn't something we like to call "good." Nobody wants to call pain and suffering good. The hardship of financial lack or health issues don't feel very good; in fact, they can be very painful. However, the good we celebrate is the success we achieve as we rise above the trial into a place of obedience to God and into a place of victory, which God so much desires for us, as seen in the following verse:

> But thanks be to God, who gives us the victory through our Lord Jesus Christ.
> —1 Corinthians 15:57, ESV

Although discipline and correction aren't pleasant, they are necessary to help us mature and grow stronger in our Christian lives.

> All discipline for the moment seems not to be joyful, but sorrowful; yet to those who have been trained by it, afterwards it yields the peaceful fruit of righteousness.
> —Hebrews 12:11, NASB

Let's look at the words *"trained by it"* for a moment. When an athlete is training to win, he must take instructions and correction from his coach. In the same way, the Bible and the Holy Spirit are our coaches to instruct and correct us in our Christian lives. As well, if we have allowed ourselves to come under God's discipline, we will need to follow the coach's instructions and correction. It's important that we cooperate with God in the correction, and that we receive and learn from the discipline in humility. It's also important to thank God that He cares enough to correct us and keep us on the right path. Correction is for our benefit to draw us into a closer relationship with Him.

Hebrews 12:11 also brings us to a key point with respect to God's correction and discipline of us. If we miss the point in this verse, we have really missed the whole understanding of God's love and discipline of us. The point is that if we don't embrace the correction and discipline of God by allowing it to change our lives for the better, we will not benefit and grow in our walk with God. This is what God wants to achieve in our lives.

Summary

Discipline usually happens when we get off the path God has for our lives. It also happens when we remove ourselves from following God's Word in the way we live. God wants us to live and walk in His ways in order that we might keep from hurting ourselves. So be diligent to examine yourself on a regular basis in the light of God's Word.

When you find things in your life that need changing in order to line up with God's Word, change them. Repent of any sin and choose to make changes in your life which will enable you to live under God's abundant blessings. If you're faithful to do these things, you'll find that you are less likely to be the subject of God's discipline. And if you do end up under His discipline, you will come out of it victorious. This is God's desire and plan for you and me.

Chapter Fourteen

Flex Your Muscles

By this chapter's title, I'm not referring to flexing your physical muscles, but rather your spiritual muscles. In this chapter, I'm going to share on the subject of the authority of the believer. Notice that I said "believer," which means "a believer in Jesus Christ who has a close relationship with God and His Son, Jesus."

We have already covered the process by which we as believers can achieve the victory of living Christ-like, Spirit-led lives. God has so much for us and we don't want to miss out on any part of God's promises. There is another important aspect of His abundance which is available for us, which is: the believer's spiritual authority.

What is spiritual authority? First of all, let's look at the definition of "authority" as found in Strong's Hebrew and Greek Dictionary. Strong's defines the Greek word *exousia* (authority), as found in Matthew 21:24, as "delegated influence... authority, jurisdiction, liberty, power, right, strength."[57] In Webster's Dictionary, the word "power", as found in Matthew 22:29, is defined as "possession of control, authority, or influence over others."[58] To expand on these definitions, it would follow that authority is a legal right to exercise control in completing an action. If we were to expand this into the realm of godly spiritual authority, the definition would go something like this: a right given to us by God to exercise His power in completing an action. From this definition, we can see further that one who has spiritual authority has received a license (right) to use God's power to accomplish a task. However, the task will always be within the boundaries of God's Word.

---

57 James Strong. *Strong's Dictionaries of the Hebrew and Greek Words*, "Exousia" (Nashville, TN: Abingdon Press, 1890).
58 *Webster's Canadian Dictionary & Thesaurus* (Toronto, ON: Strathearn Books, 2011), 327.

Created to Rule

Why did I bring up ruling and reigning? Well, it requires authority to rule and reign. As well, authority is useless unless it is exercised or used. When authority is exercised, it always involves controlling or ruling. In order to see where it all started, let's look at Genesis 1:26:

> And God said, Let us make man in our image, after our likeness: and let them have dominion over the fish of the sea, and over the fowl of the air, and over the cattle, and over all the earth, and over every creeping thing that [creeps] upon the earth. (KJV)

I would like to focus on two portions of this verse—*"and let them have dominion"* and *"over all the earth."* By putting these two passages together, we can see that it was God's plan for man to rule over the earth. We were made to reign and have dominion over the earth, but Satan spoiled that plan when he deceived Adam in the Garden of Eden. Adam disobeyed God by eating from the forbidden tree and giving his authority to Satan; thus, Satan became the ruler over all the earth, as noted in the following verse:

> And he led Him up and showed Him all the kingdoms of the world in a moment of time. And the devil said to Him, "I will give You all this domain and its glory; for it has been handed over to me, and I give it to whomever I wish.
>
> —Luke 4:5–6, NASB

As a result, mankind became subject to Satan and his evil influence in the world. Was it possible for mankind to get out from under Satan's authority in this world? Yes, both under the Old and New Testaments.

In the New Testament, everything changed: Jesus came on the scene as the Son of God.

> Whoever makes a practice of sinning is of the devil, for the devil has been sinning from the beginning. The reason the Son of God appeared was to destroy the works of the devil.
>
> —1 John 3:8, ESV

People who keep on living a life of sin belong to the devil, but believers who have accepted Jesus, the Son of God, can experience a godly life in a world where the devil and his works have been destroyed. Jesus destroyed the devil and his authority over this world. He defeated Satan on the cross. Everything Satan had before the work of the cross has been stripped away from him. The question is, who's in charge of this world now?

We will now look at quite a number of scriptures with regard to this subject.

> You made human beings the rulers over all that your hands have created. You put everything under their control.
> —Psalms 8:6, NIrV

This verse clearly says that God has given the earth to His children to rule over it. If we go back a few paragraphs, we are reminded of God's mandate to us in Genesis 1:26 to have dominion over all the earth. This makes it pretty clear that God intended, and still intends today, for His children to rule over the earth.

Some might say that it says in Psalms 24:1 that the earth is the Lord's. Yes, it is His, but He has ordained His children to rule over it. The most important factor in our authority is that we have to take charge, or else Satan will take over. Let's see how things develop as we proceed.

> ...that they all may be one, as You, Father, are in Me, and I in You, that they also may be one in Us, so that the world may believe that You have sent Me.
> —John 17:21, MKJV

We are one with God and with Jesus, because our spirits are joined with their spirits when we become believers in Christ. As children of God, we belong to God and we are His and He is ours.

> ...seeing that His divine power has granted to us everything pertaining to life and godliness, through the true knowledge of Him who called us by His own glory and excellence. For by these He has granted to us His precious and magnificent promises, so that by them you may become partakers of the divine nature...
> —2 Peter 1:3–4, NASB

Let's digest these verses a little bit. By His power, God has given us everything we need and desire to live our natural and spiritual lives. Furthermore, God has given us His precious and magnificent promises because we know Him and are recipients of them by His divine power. The latter part of 2 Peter 1:4 indicates that we can actually participate in the nature of God because He has given us this gift as a part of His promises to us. The nature of God is His character and who He is. This means we should be able to think like God, speak like God, and do what God does. The ability to do these things is only available if we are totally and completely led by God's Spirit to do them. We can think like God when we renew our minds in His Word, we can speak like God when we speak His Word, and we can do like God when we heal the sick, in Jesus' name. Wow!

> By this, love is perfected with us, so that we may have confidence in the day of judgment; because as He is, so also are we in this world.
> —1 John 4:17, NASB

This verse confirms that we cannot only act and be like God but also act and be like Jesus here in this world. We know that Jesus only did what His Father did and said what His father gave Him to say. We are to imitate God and Jesus in the things we do and say.

So I ask the question again, who is in charge of this world? First of all, we discovered that God has ordained from the beginning that His children are to rule over the earth. Secondly, we see in the above three scriptures that we are in God and in His Son, by our spirits being connected to their Spirits. We also see that we are to imitate God and Jesus in the way we live on this earth. So if God and Jesus are the ultimate authorities on the earth, and if we are to imitate and live like them, then believers have the authority on this earth. Don't forget that Satan is defeated.

Let's delve into our authority by first looking at Jesus' authority.

Jesus Christ's Authority

Let's look at the following scriptures to see who this Jesus is.

> And being found in human form, he humbled himself by becoming obedient to the point of death, even death on a cross. Therefore God has

highly exalted him and bestowed on him the name that is above every name, so that at the name of Jesus every knee should bow, in heaven and on earth and under the earth, and every tongue confess that Jesus Christ is Lord, to the glory of God the Father.
—Philippians 2:8–11, ESV

Because Jesus died on the cross and made the ultimate sacrifice for us, God has placed Jesus and His name above every person or thing that exists in the whole universe, in both the natural and spiritual realms. Everything in the whole universe has a name, and the name of Jesus has authority over those names. This means that the name of Jesus has authority over every person, creature, and object in the universe. God has highly elevated the name of Jesus, and nothing even comes close to matching Christ's place and authority in the universe.

...which He worked in Christ when He raised Him from the dead and seated Him at His right hand in the heavenly places, far above all principality and power and might and dominion, and every name that is named, not only in this age but also in that which is to come. And He put all things under His feet, and gave Him to be head over all things to the church, which is His body, the fullness of Him who fills all in all.
—Ephesians 1:20–23, NKJV

In this passage, we see that Jesus has been given a seat in God's throne room. A throne room is a place of authority, but this is God's throne room. There is no authority above this throne room authority. Ephesians 1:21 says that every name of anything in heaven and on earth, and every spiritual power that will ever exist, comes under Jesus' authority.

Let's expand further on the name of Jesus and His authority:

And Jesus came and spoke to them, saying, "All authority has been given to Me in heaven and on earth."
—Matthew 28:18, NKJV

This verse further confirms that God has given Jesus all authority in heaven and on earth. All authority means that there is no greater authority then Jesus' authority. Jesus has authority over everything, so what He says goes.

Our Authority

Next, let's look at what God has done for us:

> But God, who is rich in mercy, because of His great love with which He loved us, even when we were dead in trespasses, made us alive together with Christ (by grace you have been saved), and raised us up together, and made us sit together in the heavenly places in Christ Jesus, that in the ages to come He might show the exceeding riches of His grace in His kindness toward us in Christ Jesus.
> —Ephesians 2:4–7, NKJV

Ephesians 2:5 describes what happens when we receive the gift of salvation: our spirit is made alive as we connect with Christ's Spirit. In 2:6, we find that as believers in Christ we have been elevated to the same place as Christ, in the throne room of God. In 2:7, the writer indicates that we have been raised up for the years to come on this earth so that we might be recipients of God's blessings. As believers, as long as we stay in Christ, we have the privilege of being in God's throne room. In God's throne room, we have the same authority placed upon us as the authority which was placed upon Jesus. Praise God!

Now that we occupy the same place of authority as Jesus does, we also have the right to exercise that throne room authority and power. We can exercise authority over principalities, powers, and every name that is named in heaven and earth. We have authority over every name or thing that exists in the universe because they come under the authority of the name of Jesus. We even have authority over nonbelievers, because their father is the devil. We do not have authority over other believers unless they are being used by the devil. You might say, "You mean we have this right and power available to us when we become believers?" Yes, absolutely! We have authority to rule and reign over this earth! All we need to do is get in Christ, and stay in Him, to operate in His authority. We can say with confidence that we, God's children, have the authority to rule and reign over this earth.

> And whatever you do in word or deed, do all in the name of the Lord Jesus, giving thanks to God the Father through Him.
> —Colossians 3:17, NKJV

This verse confirms that we are to use the name of Jesus in everything we do and say. Of course, when we use His name we have His power and authority in what we do and say.

> Truly, truly, I say to you, whoever believes in me will also do the works that I do; and greater works than these will he do, because I am going to the Father.
> —John 14:12, ESV

Finally, in this verse we discover that we will perform the same kind of works Jesus did. What were they? He healed the sick, fed the hungry, raised the dead, and set free those who were in bondage, those who were bound by addictions, sickness, and Satan. However, Jesus went one step further by indicating that we, God's children, would be doing even greater works than those which He did.

Our Spiritual Condition Matters

I could share so many real life stories regarding walking and living in the believer's authority. However, if there's one thing I would like to emphasize it would be that we must have a good and constant spiritual relationship with God in order to operate in the believer's authority. If we attempt to use the name of Jesus when we aren't spiritually connected to God the way we should be, we may find that we have no authority. Remember, the key is having a spiritual relationship with God. To further emphasize the spiritual condition required to operate in His authority, let's look at this scripture:

> Finally, my brethren, be strong in the Lord, and in the power of his might. Put on the whole armour of God, that [you] may be able to stand against the wiles of the devil. For we wrestle not against flesh and blood, but against principalities, against powers, against the rulers of the darkness of this world, against spiritual wickedness in high places. Wherefore take unto you the whole armour of God, that [you] may be able to withstand in the evil day, and having done all, to stand. Stand therefore, having your loins girt about with *truth*, and having on the *breastplate of righteousness*; and your feet shod with the preparation of the *gospel*

of peace; above all, taking the *shield of faith*, wherewith [you] shall be able to quench all the fiery darts of the wicked. And take the *helmet of salvation*, and the *sword of the Spirit*, which is the word of God: *praying always* with all prayer and supplication in the Spirit, and *watching* thereunto with all perseverance and supplication for all saints.
—Ephesians 6:10–18, KJV (emphasis added)

In the above scripture, we are told to put on the whole armour of God. The word "armour," according to Webster's Dictionary, means "a covering (as of metal) to protect the body in battle."[59] In Ephesians 6:14–18, we are given eight pieces of armour to put up on or in us to protect us in the daily spiritual battles we face. I have emphasized each of the pieces of armour with italics so they can readily be seen.

To begin with, let's look at each of the different pieces of armour and define them so we can relate to them a little better. This will enable us to apply the armour and wear it in our lives. First of all, we have truth, and further down we have the sword of the Spirit. These are very similar in that they relate to the Word of God. It means that we need to put God's Word into our minds and hearts. Next, we have the breastplate of righteousness, and we apply this to our lives by regularly declaring our righteousness. Then there's the gospel of peace, which encourages us to use our feet to take us out to share the gospel. The shield of faith means that we are to live our lives by faith in God. The helmet of salvation is the first one we should put on in our lives; it is the piece of armour that initiated our relationship with God and His Son Jesus. Praying is the piece of armour that encourages us to talk to God regularly throughout each day. Finally, the piece of armour called "watch" encourages us to be wary of Satan's tricks; we need to be a step ahead of him all the time.

The process of putting on the armour is one whereby we actually take each of the eight pieces of armour (tools) and use them in our lives. They give us the resources we need to beat the forces of darkness and win. These tools are there to help us live the Christian life successfully. If you want to be successful in living the Christian life, use all of the above armour daily.

---

59 *Webster's Canadian Dictionary & Thesaurus* (Toronto, ON: Strathearn Books, 2011), 21.

The Believer's Authority Established

Since we have looked at a lot of scripture, I would like to summarize what we've discovered so far regarding the believer's authority in the following seven points:

1. We, God's children, were created to rule over the earth.
2. We, as believers, are one with the Father and Son, and we are to imitate them in our lives.
3. We have established that the name of Jesus is exalted above every name or thing in the whole universe.
4. We have discovered that Jesus occupies the throne room of God, and that He has God's throne room authority and power.
5. We have found that we have also been given a place with Jesus in the throne room of God.
6. We've learned that we have God's throne room authority and power available to us.
7. In order to exercise our authority in Christ, we must keep ourselves in a close relationship with Him, God, and the Holy Spirit.

I ask the question again, "Who is in charge in this world?" I think by now we can conclude that Christians are to be in charge if they take their rightful place of authority, and if they accept their responsibility in this area.

In God's Spirit realm (kingdom), all authority comes from Him, and the license to use that authority comes from Him through our place in His throne room in heaven. In the rest of this chapter, we will look at how to function in the believer's authority.

Operating in Authority

We have gone in several different directions up to this point. We have covered dominion, who is in charge, Jesus' authority, our authority, and the importance of our spiritual condition. In order to bring this all together so we can begin to exercise and use our authority, I'm going to try simplifying the process by clearly defining the different actions we need to take when operating in the believer's authority.

1. Believe

The first step which we must take in the believer's authority is to believe. Believe in what? We must believe that:

- We are seated with Jesus, in the authority centre of the universe, God's throne room (see Ephesians 2:6).
- We have throne room authority over the evil spirit realm (see Ephesians 1:19).
- We have the name of Jesus to use, and it is above every name in existence (see Philippians 2:9–10).
- We have the word of God to use, and He is ready to perform it (see Jeremiah 1:12).

As I have shared before, we must also have faith. The act of believing is part of faith. Romans 1:17 says, *"The just shall live by faith"* (MKJV). The faith act of believing means that we know we possess what we have asked for, even though we don't see it yet. This principle is outlined in Romans 4:17.

2. Our Seat

Ephesians 2:6 says that we, as believers, have been raised up with Christ and seated in God's throne room. This happened when Jesus went to heaven. It's not something which will take place during the rapture; it has already been done. We have a seat prepared for us in God's throne room right now.

So how do we take our seat? There's only one way to do this, and it is by faith. By faith, we speak that we take our seat. By faith, we visualize and see ourselves seated next to Jesus in the throne room of God. Wow! What a blessing! What a provision!

3. Confession

The words we speak activate our belief and faith. We must speak words and scriptures which line up with what we believe.

For assuredly, I say to you, whoever says to this mountain, "Be removed and be cast into the sea," and does not doubt in his heart, but believes that those things he says will be done, he will have whatever he says.
—Mark 11:23, NKJV

In the last part of this verse, we're told that we will get what we say. This means that if we say we have throne room authority, because of our seat in God's throne room, we will have what we say. We get what we say. The act of speaking what we believe in order to get the results we're looking for is also supported in 2 Corinthians 4:13.

4. Direction

So why does God want us in His throne room? Well, first of all, because God loves us. Secondly, God wants us to get our directions from Him directly. He wants us to do and say what He desires. Thirdly, He wants us to partake of His glory in order to complete our part of His plan on earth. In this way, our ministry becomes a heavenly ministry. We operate the same way heaven and God operate.

Blessed be the God and Father of our Lord Jesus Christ, who has blessed us with every spiritual blessing in the heavenly places in Christ...
—Ephesians 1:3, NKJV

5. Speaking with Authority

When someone is operating in authority, they must speak or communicate in order to exercise that authority. If you want your employee to cut the grass, you have to tell them to cut the grass. So it is with spiritual authority; we must speak words to exercise authority.

There are two ways in which we can use our words to exercise this authority. These are commands, and binding and loosing.

Commands

A command is an order which has power or authority backing it, and the best examples of this can be found in the Bible.

> I say to you, Arise, and take up your cot, and go to your house. And immediately he arose and took up his cot and went out before all. So that all were amazed and glorified God, saying, We never saw it this way.
> —Mark 2:11–12, MKJV

These two verses come at the tail end of the account of a man who was sick with palsy. This man was carried on a stretcher to where Jesus was ministering. The place was so packed out that the man's handlers couldn't get him into the building, so they decided to make a hole in the roof above where Jesus was standing. Next, they lowered the sick man down in front of Jesus. Jesus asked a few questions, and then decided to heal the sick man.

Mark 2:11–12 gives us the command which Jesus spoke to exercise authority over the sickness—*"Arise, and take up your cot, and go to your house."* Jesus told the man to get up, take his bed, and return home. The man obeyed Jesus and he was healed. This is just an example of many accounts in which Jesus commanded or spoke with authority to complete a task. In other words, Jesus took control and spoke to the problems. The results always turned out good and positive.

> Then Jesus said to him, Go, Satan! For it is written, "You shall worship the Lord your God, and Him only you shall serve." Then the Devil left him. And behold, angels came and ministered to Him.
> —Matthew 4:10–11, MKJV

Here we see that the devil had been harassing Jesus, trying to get Him to sin. The devil wanted Jesus to come under his authority. Instead, on the devil's third try, Jesus let him have it. Jesus commanded the devil to get away from Him, and of course the devil left. The devil had no choice because he must obey Jesus' authority.

We are to follow Jesus' example of authority. When we come across sickness, poverty, demons, or any other evil, we are to exercise authority over them. We do that by direct orders or commands using the name of Jesus. Sometimes we may want to quote Scripture, just like Jesus did to the devil in Mark 4:3 –11. Finally, we can also speak (declare) the blood of Jesus over a situation. This declaration applies the blood of Jesus to the situation, and His blood protects us and delivers us from sickness, poverty, sin, and any kind of evil.

Binding and Loosing

The second way in which we can speak with spiritual authority is called binding and loosing,

> And I will give the keys of the kingdom of Heaven to you. And whatever you may bind on earth shall occur, having been bound in Heaven, and whatever you may loose on earth shall occur, having been loosed in Heaven.
> —Matthew 16:19, MKJV

This is a very interesting verse. To begin with, we are given the keys to the Kingdom of Heaven, but we are not told what they are. As a result, I've had to look at my experience as a believer and determine that there are two keys: the name of Jesus and the Word of God. The Scripture references I have used for these keys are Luke 10:19 and Isaiah 55:11.

Next, we notice that we are given the authority to bind, prohibit, or stop things on earth, and heaven will stop them in agreement with us. What kind of things can we stop? We can stop any kind of evil, sickness, poverty, and harm—anything Satan and the curse would try to bring against us or others. Praise God!

In addition, we can loose, liberate, set free, release, and break off things on earth, and heaven will come into agreement with us. What kind of things can we loose, release, or break off? We can release the blessings of God into our life and others. We can release blessings of health, finances, revelation, and the fruit of the spirit, just to name a few. What kind of things can we break? We can break any kind of evil and its hold on people. Praise God!

These spiritual tools of binding and loosing are used with the name of Jesus and the Word of God. Again, we use our mouth (words) to activate binding and loosing; we speak to each situation what we want to see happen. Binding and loosing are administered in the form of a command as well. Some examples of ways in which we can use the tools of binding and loosing are:

- "I bind or stop you, Satan, from stealing our finances, in the name of Jesus!"

- "The Word of God says that by Jesus' stripes we are healed; therefore, based on the Word of God, I loose or break off cancer from Johnnie's stomach!"

Let me give you an example of operating in authority, from my own experience. In the summer of 2013, it seemed like almost every week we had major summer storms with damaging hail, high winds, and floods. Many millions worth of dollars of damage was done to homes and vehicles in our city as a result of these storms. However, I decided prior to the storm season that I wasn't going to put up with storm damage to our property. So every time a thunderstorm came in our direction, I would speak to it and tell it not to drop any damaging hail or produce strong winds that would harm our property. Only once did the clouds try to drop larger hail, and only for a matter of a few seconds; however, I spoke to the clouds and told them in no uncertain terms that they were not to drop hail on our property. To God be the glory, we didn't have any damage to our property, in spite of the fact that many all around us suffered from the wrath of these storms.

I could use many scriptures as the basis for my authority against the storms, but the following verses fit very well:

> He said to them, "Where is your faith?" And they were afraid, and they marveled, saying to one another, "Who then is this, that he commands even winds and water, and they obey him?"
> —Luke 8:25, ESV

> Truly, truly, I say to you, He who believes on Me, the works that I do he shall do also, and greater works than these he shall do, because I go to My Father.
> —John 14:12, MKJV

You see, Jesus commanded the wind and the water, and they obeyed him. In John 14:12, Jesus told us that we shall be able to do the same things He did. In fact, He said that we would do greater things than He did. Thus we are able to command even the wind and water, and they must obey us.

The above testimony is just one of many examples I could share of how God wants to bless us in the area of the believer's authority.

The Battle Is Not Ours

Our warfare as Christians is often not against other people; it comes from the evil spirit realm, as we can see in Ephesians 6:12:

> For we wrestle not against flesh and blood, but against principalities, against powers, against the rulers of the darkness of this world, against spiritual wickedness in high places. (KJV)

Even when we're being attacked by another Christian operating in the soul realm, the devil is often behind the attack. As Christians, if we have a weak relationship with God we can be used by the devil to do and say things for the devil. As a note of clarification, if a Christian is used by the devil it doesn't mean they are demon-possessed; real Christians cannot be possessed by Satan.

When we come under attack in the spiritual realm and we are wearing the armour of God, we can take the name of Jesus and the Word of God, which is part of our armour, and speak in authority against the spiritual evil; it must obey us.

In Ephesians 6:12, we are told the names of our enemies. The enemy's names are principalities, powers, rulers of the darkness of this world, and spiritual wickedness in high places. We have authority in the spirit realm over all these powers in the name of Jesus.

> [You] are of God, little children, and have overcome them: because greater is he that is in you, than he that is in the world.
> —1 John 4:4, KJV

The word "them" in 1 John 4:4 refers to the forces of this world which are against Christ. Let me paraphrase this verse to give it a more relevant meaning for today: "If we keep a healthy, fresh, spiritual connection with God daily, we can defeat the forces of darkness in this world with great success because we have the power of God within us."

Let me give you another example of spiritual authority from real life. Several years ago, one of my children was experiencing fear in her bedroom. She came out of her bedroom one evening filled with fear. She had been hearing voices in her room. I knew immediately there had to be an evil presence in her room. I asked her to come back into the room with me, and then I asked, "Are the voices still here?" She replied, "Yes." In fact, I could also sense the evil presence as I stood in her room. I proceeded to speak with my mouth in the name of Jesus, telling this evil presence to leave her alone at once and get out of her room. Immediately, my daughter exclaimed, "They're gone!" I then shared with her that we needed to praise God for getting rid of the evil presence for us! We have tremendous authority over Satan's evil realm, and we need to use it at every opportunity. We are encouraged to do this in the following verse:

> Submit yourselves therefore to God. Resist the devil, and he will flee from you.
>
> —James 4:7, KJV

Conclusion

Let me recap what we have shared in this chapter:

- We have discovered that, in Christ, we are in the throne room of God, and that we have the same authority in the spiritual realm as that which Christ possesses.
- We have also learned according to the scriptures that we have the authority and power to speak with wisdom in the name of Jesus.
- We are to believe and expect, in faith, that what we speak will happen.
- We have also discovered that we can speak to the evil spirit realm and stop its influence in our lives.
- We can speak to things (names), such as animals, the weather, objects, evil actions, and others. We have discovered that the words of our mouth, in the name of Jesus, will stop evil and influence the weather.
- Finally, we have learned that in order to operate in the believer's authority, we must have our spirit connected to and fellowshipping with God's Spirit daily.

Let me encourage you to begin to exercise, with the wisdom of God, the authority you have in Christ as opportunities present themselves. You will be pleasantly surprised at the victories you experience as you exercise the authority God has given you in Christ Jesus.

Chapter Fifteen

God's Gold Medals

We have spent considerable time sharing about God's promises and how we can go about receiving God's abundance on a continual basis if we are obedient to do what God wants us to do. Although receiving from God does take effort and discipline, we don't receive because of our merit or works. God's abundance comes from our obedience to Him and His Word, and His abundance flows out of His giving heart of love and mercy toward us. Our part in this relationship is to receive God's promises, and we do that with the words of our mouths.

There is another aspect of God's blessings I would like to share with you, and it is God's gold medals or rewards. What are God's gold medals? The International Standard Bible Encyclopedia defines "rewards" as "something given in recognition of a good act."[60] There are rewards here on this earth given by men and or God, there are rewards in heaven which come from God, and there are even negative rewards of hell given for those who continue in bad deeds. This reward of hell is actually not a reward but a punishment, and it is meted out to those who refuse to accept Jesus as their Saviour and make Him Lord of their lives.

Rewards are different from gifts. God gives gifts such as salvation which do not require any work on our part except to receive them. Salvation is one of God's gifts, which we receive by believing in our heart and confessing with our mouths that Jesus is Lord of our lives. God gives many gifts, such as the Holy Spirit, ministry gifts, and God's Word, to mention a few.

On the other hand, rewards are given by God for our efforts and obedience. Our efforts and obedience entail such things as reading God's Word, worshiping God, and dealing with sin. Our efforts and obedience also encompass such things as living according to His Word and loving God and our

---

60 *International Standard Bible Encyclopedia*, "Rewards" (Grand Rapids, MI: Wm. B. Eerdmans Publishing Co., 1979).

neighbours. Can you see the difference? Gifts are unmerited (undeserved) presents from God, and rewards are earned presents from God because of how we use the gifts. The gifts are not the rewards, and the rewards come because of how we use His gifts.

Most of us are aware of the Olympic Games, which are held regularly in different places around the world. At these games, athletes compete in all kinds of sports and competitions for the purpose of winning gold medals. Winning a gold medal—first place in the competition—is the main goal of each of these athletes. They prepare themselves in every possible way to succeed in bringing home a medal, even if it's not the gold medal. There are those who win silver medals for second-place finishes, and bronze medals for third-place finishes. There are also those who go home without winning a medal.

In the same way that athletes compete and win medals at the Olympic Games, God's desire is to give His children rewards, both here on earth and also in heaven, for our efforts and obedience toward Him. There will be those who receive no reward, some who receive a little reward, and those who receive great rewards. We find an indication of what happens to those who get no rewards in the following verse:

> ...the true character of each individual's work will become manifest. For the day of Christ will disclose it, because that day is soon to come upon us clothed in fire, and as for the quality of every one's work—the fire is the thing which will test it. If any one's work—the building which he has erected—stands the test, he will be rewarded. If any one's work is burnt up, he will suffer the loss of it; yet he will himself be rescued, but only, as it were, by passing through the fire.
> —1 Corinthians 3:13–15, WNT

Here, the writer indicates that if the things we have done for God in our lifetime cannot stand the test of God's Word, our efforts or works will be burnt up or destroyed. As a result, we will receive no reward; however, we will still get into heaven. The portion of this verse which says "stands the test" means that we are obedient to do what God wants us to do, according to His Word; and thus, our work is acceptable to God.

If God didn't tell you to do the work, don't do it. Furthermore, don't try to figure out what to do on your own, then pray over it and ask God to bless it. It won't work. If God isn't in what you're doing, it doesn't matter how good it might look to you; it will not bear fruit for God's kingdom, and you certainly will not be rewarded by God for your work. Find out what God wants you to do first, then do it with God's help and God will bless you for it and in it.

> Now he who plants and he who waters are one, and each one will receive his own reward according to his own labor.
> —1 Corinthians 3:8, NKJV

We see here that there are rewards for our work on earth. For example, if we lead one of our loved ones to Christ, we receive the reward of great joy and happiness here on earth. As well, we receive the reward of knowing that our loved one will be with us in eternity.

> Rejoice and be glad, because great is your reward in heaven, for in the same way they persecuted the prophets who were before you.
> —Matthew 5:12, NIV

We understand from this verse that those who suffer persecution for Christ's sake will receive great rewards in heaven.

With respect to persecution, let me tell you a true story about a brother and sister. The sister had been married for many years before she found out that her husband had been unfaithful to her. He had been seeing other women for many of those years. She had come from a very dysfunctional family. Their dad had been involved in molesting and abusing her and her sister. She felt that this had caused her to end up in a bad marriage, resulting in divorce.

For many years, every time she got together with her brother, she would relive the past and agonize over it. Eventually, it began to take a toll on their relationship, because the brother didn't want to continue reliving the past. Every time the brother tried to encourage her to forgive and move on, she would get angry.

Finally, the brother decided to write a letter and explain to his sister that she was hurting herself by continuing to live in the past. Most importantly, she was living with unforgiveness, which is very damaging to one's emotional and physical well-being. He had the letter proofed by a trusted, mature woman who gave her stamp of approval. In fact, when the sister received the letter, instead of letting it encourage her, she took it as criticism. The letter was meant for good but instead it drove her and her brother further apart. She blamed him for not being supportive towards her.

The long and short of this story is that the brother ended up being persecuted, even though he wanted the best for his sister. All in all, I don't think the brother was looking for a reward in heaven when he wrote the letter: he was just trying to help his sister get victory in her life.

Conclusion

Finally, with respect to God's rewards, we must be willing to use the gifts God has given us. If we don't use them, we certainly won't get any rewards for them. God wants us to use our gifts.

As well, God rewards those who use the faith He has given them. All believers have been given a plentiful measure of faith to live by. God wants us to build that into big faith in our lives, faith to believe Him for big things and see the results. What is the highest reward in building faith? It is seeing the success, seeing what we've believed for come to pass in the physical realm before our very eyes. That's the gold medal for using our faith. Maybe we should consider the victories of our Christian lives here on earth as bronze and silver medals, since the ultimate goal for all of us is eternal life in heaven with Christ—the real gold medal!

> ... with my eyes fixed on the goal I push on to secure the prize of God's heavenward call in Christ Jesus.
> —Philippians 3:14, WNT

Chapter Sixteen

Are There Any Loose Ends?

There certainly could be loose ends, considering the many aspects we have covered regarding living a life in God's abundance. I have tried to cover this subject in a manner that is balanced and detailed enough to enable you to put the message I've shared into practice in your life. I have not, and could never have, covered each subject totally, because with God there is no end to learning and new revelation. There's much more I could have written, but I didn't want the book to become lengthy and cumbersome to read.

I've shared on a lot of different topics relating to how to live the Christian life, and how to receive God's promises. I have tried to cover every aspect of the Christian life to provide balance in Christian living. In order to tie up any loose ends and add weight to the message contained in this book, I would like to share one of the victories that has happened in my own life. During the past thirty-five years, I have lived with a headache almost one hundred percent of the time. These headaches made my head feel thick and dull, something like having a big watermelon on top of my head. The headaches had a tendency to slow me down and make me tired.

Over these thirty-five years, I have been to medical doctors many times in an effort to find out what was wrong with me. Finally, I was told that I had extreme allergies to certain things, including deciduous tree leaves. I was given numerous kinds of medication to try and alleviate the headaches. I've been to medical doctors, chiropractors, physiotherapists, allergy specialists, and homeopathic doctors. None of these were able to provide a solution and successfully treat these headaches. In fact, the allergy specialist indicated that I would probably suffer with this condition for the rest of my life, because the allergies were very severe.

I have been prayed for many times for healing, by many people over the years. I have prayed for myself for healing from these headaches many times, but nothing changed. In fact, in recent years, the headaches were beginning to affect my memory quite drastically. I had come to the place where I accepted the headaches as my lot in life. Well, you already know from reading this book that I changed my mind. The Lord showed me how to receive healing—that which has already been provided for me at the cross of Calvary.

It has been more than ten years now that the Lord revealed to me how to take hold of my healing, and I began to actively practice what I've written in this book. Praise God! Well, I have a great report to give! After persevering in faith and in the Word, I received my healing. Praise God! It seems so strange for me not to have a headache after thirty-five years of the same. What a release it has been!

I have to encourage you who are reading this testimony to begin to put into action what you've learned in this book. You can also receive your healing; it is available for all of God's children.

I would like to emphasize that this testimony is just one example of what God has done for me. God's promises are available for our finances, protection, health, love, joy, wisdom, direction, emotions, and indeed every area of our lives. It doesn't matter what the circumstances or situations are; God has a blessing for every circumstance and every situation.

I would like to say, in concluding, that you can read this book over and over, but unless you put it into action in your life it will not be of much benefit to you. I strongly suggest that you begin immediately to put it into action, because once you experience God's abundance you will be looking for more, and you won't ever want to turn back! May God receive all the glory and praise!

About the Author

I was born in a small town in Saskatchewan, Canada. I was born again as a Christian when I was eight years old and baptized in the Holy Spirit, with an anointing, at thirteen years of age. During my teen years, my parents decided to stop attending church services, and as a result I never got back into regularly attending church services until after I left home. I never turned my back on God at any time, even though I rarely attended church for almost nine years. I still prayed to God most days and read my Bible occasionally. However, I lived my life contrary to biblical teachings, in many areas, and that means I did many things that wouldn't have pleased God.

After I got married, I got back into attending church services again—that good female influence. A few years later, I was involved in the beginnings of a new Christian assembly, and I've stayed with that assembly and its affiliates for forty years. I have been involved in church leadership for twenty years, having served as a deacon and an elder for many years. I've also led and taught many small groups and Bible studies. In addition, I have served in almost every other position or function except for pastor. I've considered it very important not just to attend services but to be a part of the church by giving of myself in service to it.

For many years, I lived what I would call a very noncommittal Christian life, much the same as what many other Christians were doing. I don't say that to condemn anyone, but rather to indicate how we fall into patterns of life and become comfortable with our lives and the influence of the world around us. My Christian lifestyle consisted of reading the Bible for maybe five to ten minutes some days, and spending maybe five to ten minutes praying almost every day. I relied a lot for my Christian teaching on attending church services two or more times a week. I'm a family man, so I spent plenty of time with my wife and children when I wasn't working. I became a workaholic by working long hours and chasing the dollar. I immersed myself in pleasure and fun and didn't have a close relationship with God.

I ran my own business for most of my adult life. In the late 70s, I went into a business partnership with another Christian man, and during this time I decided to make some changes in my life. My partner was a man who had a close relationship with God, and I noticed how he would get his direction from God, how God would speak to him, and how the blessing of God was upon him in many areas of his life. I began to get a hunger and desire to see those things in my life.

I grew up in a very dysfunctional home, and as a result I needed to make a lot of changes in my life in order to get to the place where I wanted to be in my relationship with God. I had a lot of emotional scars and wounds from my childhood and teen years which I needed to deal with. However, I didn't have any idea just how drastic the changes would have to be. I spent a year taking a twelve-step recovery program, which was invaluable in helping me to make many wonderful changes. I'm also thankful to a mature Christian man in our church who the Lord brought into my life to help me successfully live the Christian life. I certainly don't consider myself to have arrived at perfection, by any means, but I now live a victorious Christian life, for which I am very thankful to God.

Over the many years of my life, I have been taught by many fine men and women of God. During the last twenty years, I have learned to be taught by the Holy Spirit, which has been absolutely wonderful! In more recent years, the Holy Spirit has been opening my understanding to the vastness of God and how much God wants to share that abundance with His children—that's us. As a result, my God-given desire is to share with others the understanding of how to tap into the astounding, bountiful promises God has for His children.

Richard Gill Ministries
Edmonton, Alberta, Canada
www.rgministries.ca

About the Author

Books Available:

Winning with God's Promises!

This book was compiled to help us speak God's Word for our life situations, and put it into our hearts until we no longer doubt it. Instead, we believe and expect that everything God's Word says will indeed happen in our lives. As a result, we will experience God's promises in our lives daily! We can truly live successful, prosperous lives with God's Word.

This book has well over twelve hundred scriptures in twenty-three different categories. The categories relate to our daily life situations, enabling us to take hold of God's promises for our lives. The categories include healing, finances, direction, peace, protection, among others. Many have found this book to be a tremendous asset in their lives, enabling them to experience much more of God's promises.

> # Tap into God's Promises
>
> *Release health, prosperity, protection, peace, joy, and love with Bible Scriptures for every situation in life*
>
> **Richard L. Gill**

Tap into God's Promises

The main reason we miss out on God's blessings is because of what comes out of our mouths. The prime purpose of this booklet is to get us to speak God's will and Word for our lives. This will release God's promises to bring us success. The booklet contains over three hundred Bible verses, all categorized for life situations. It will help you to be a winner. You can't afford to be without it. It fits into a shirt pocket or purse.

To order these books, please go to the website
www.rgministries.ca

www.ingramcontent.com/pod-product-compliance
Lightning Source LLC
Chambersburg PA
CBHW032106090426
42743CB00007B/255